SELF-MANAGEMENT STRATEGIES

SELF-MANAGEMENT STRATEGIES

Theory, Curriculum, and Teaching Procedures

MICHAEL B. MEDLAND

PRAEGER

New York
Westport, Connecticut
London

Library of Congress Cataloging-in-Publication Data

Medland, Michael.
    Self-management strategies : theory, curriculum, and teaching
procedures / by Michael B. Medland.
        p.   cm.
    Includes bibliographical references.
    ISBN 0-275-93519-1 (alk. paper)
    1. Classroom management.   2. Self-management (Psychology) for
teenagers.   I. Title.
    LB3013.M395   1989
    371.1'024 — dc20   90-31211

Library of Congress Catalog Card Number: 90-31211
ISBN: 0-275-93519-1

First published in 1990

Praeger Publishers, One Madison Avenue, New York, NY 10010
An imprint of Greenwood Publishing Group, Inc.

Printed in the United States of America

The paper used in this book complies with the
Permanent Paper Standard issued by the National
Information Standards Organization (Z39.48–1984).

10 9 8 7 6 5 4 3 2 1

To a world of students and teachers

CONTENTS

FIGURES AND TABLES

FIGURES

TABLES

PREFACE

Our larger educational goal is to teach students to control their future so that they and later generations can live responsible, productive, and happy lives. *Self-Management Strategies* presents a plan to achieve part of that goal. It illustrates how to teach students to manage themselves individually and in groups. Although the plan increases the immediate demands placed on educators, it reduces them in the long term. When students can manage themselves many of the managerial tasks performed by educators are eliminated. As students take on a larger responsibility for their learning the focus becomes one of instructing students in the other skills necessary to achieving our larger educational goal.

The plan for teaching self-management skills consists of three components. The first is theoretical: A language is needed to unambiguously reference behavior and its evolution. Beginning with the foundations provided by the analysis of behavior, this text unites behavioral and instructional theory. The second is curricular: Self-management behavior needs to be clearly defined. The curriculum presented is a technical repertoire that allows students to control themselves and to influence their environment. It provides students with the greatest degree of adaptability within a cooperative framework. The third is technological: Teaching procedures are needed to ensure that all regular classroom students will gain self-management competence. Seven procedures are presented. By combining them as illustrated teachers can evolve complex student self-management behavior.

To help with the task of teaching self-management skills this text is organized into four parts. Part 1 introduces a language for discussing the classroom and then applies it to analyze that environment, including the self-management strategies curriculum. A preliminary glimpse is given of strategies to plan, organize, supervise, learn, intervene, help, and share. Part 2 presents the skills and procedures to teach self-management. The skills of using statements, questions, example sets, and postings are combined into a series of procedures that makes self-management teaching effective. Part 3 focuses on teaching self-management strategies. It provides an analysis of each strategy and how it can be taught and transferred to the everyday realms of home, work, and leisure. Part 4 presents educators with the planning procedures required to build a tailored self-management curriculum and implement it successfully.

As an outcome of learning to teach self-management skills, educators gain a highly technical repertoire that allows them to design instruction, solve instructional problems, and communicate with other professionals. With the development of a district-wide program, teachers and administrators can provide all students with self-management skills. With them, students will be better able to manage the world when it is theirs.

ACKNOWLEDGMENTS

A number of people took part in the making of this work. Mark Hubbard edited every version of every chapter over its seven years of development. His help was critically important. Tom Stachnik and James Henning listened, encouraged, and supported me during times of need. The tables and figures were given final form by Ward Barnett Computer Services in Minneapolis. The people at Praeger believed in the work and gave it final form. My thanks goes to all of them.

1

INTRODUCTION TO
SELF-MANAGEMENT STRATEGIES

Our educational goal is to teach students so they can, individually and in groups, solve the problems that confront them when we are not around. Extensive knowledge is required to accomplish this goal. This text provides a critical piece of that knowlege—teaching students self-management skills. To do this, the text provides the answers to three questions: What is self-management (SM)? How is it taught? And, what knowledge base supports its teaching?

The objective of this chapter is to overview the text by presenting an initial picture of SM, the reasons for teaching it, the underlying assumptions, and a first glimpse at the theoretical and technological knowledge necessary to build the required teaching procedures.

A FIRST LOOK AT SELF-MANAGEMENT

Self-management is not inherently difficult to identify or define. It is a set of behaviors, or skills, that facilitate the individual or group to begin, continue, and end the performance of a task. Thus, SM behavior is behavior that helps other behavior—the task behavior. For example, if Zelda's task is to read within a group, she must minimally gather her book, find a place in the group, follow along, answer questions, and take her turn. None of these has anything to do with reading, but they all facilitate its performance. The same is true if Jose has to perform a chemistry experiment. He would have to retrieve the materials, put on the safety equipment, insure that others are out of danger, follow the directions in the manuals and turn in the results to the teacher. For both Zelda and Jose, all the listed behaviors facilitate the beginning, continuing, and ending of the task behaviors of reading and of performing an experiment.

For those simple tasks performed day in and day out, we execute SM behaviors automatically, without awareness. But in the context of a complex task in a new situation, much more has to be done to insure the performance of the task behavior. Here, SM becomes a highly technical repertoire, a system of strategies, involving behaviors that we traditionally call decision making and problem solving. This text covers strategies for planning, organizing, supervising, learning, intervening, helping, and sharing. By using these SM strategies when the need arises, students increase their chances of beginning, continuing, and finishing their tasks.

Moreover, if tasks take place in the classroom, where the students often work in groups, the SM behaviors used must be harmonious with those of others. Performing a task harmoniously with others implies that the SM repertoire is also a social repertoire. Working in groups requires SM behaviors that an individual working alone may not need. Educators have often called such behavior prosocial or cooperative.

It is easy to imagine a classroom in which students obtain the materials needed, immediately undertake their task, work steadily, and finish on time. These are the students everyone calls well managed. They seem diligent, motivated, energetic. They are also the ones we call independent learners. Such students make teaching a rewarding profession. There can be many more of them, but first we must move from imagination to practice.

REASONS FOR TEACHING SELF-MANAGEMENT

Three valuable reasons can be identified for teaching SM skills:

First, academic learning depends in part on the level of SM skills that students possess. They must participate in instruction as Zelda and Jose did in the previous example. Moreover, as their knowledge expands, students have to take on a larger responsibility for their learning. This means that they have to supervise themselves and learn independently in many situations. Such skills are part of the SM curriculum.

Second, education does more than impart academic skills. It socializes the student by establishing relationships with others. The extensiveness of school truancy, dropout rates, crime, discipline problems, and teenage suicide attests to the fact that often such socialization is not taking place. Today, educators across the country have realized this and have called for solutions at the classroom and school levels. The SM curriculum and teaching procedures facilitate appropriate socialization.

Third, when today's students become tomorrow's citizens, they inherit a set of global problems from crime to drugs to political terrorism to the threat of nuclear holocaust. If we acknowledge our responsibility, we must give them the skills to survive. We must help them to become citizens who can work individually and with each other to solve the problems that we hand them.

ASSUMPTIONS OF THE CURRICULUM AND TEACHING PROCEDURES

Every curriculum is based on certain assumptions which it will help the reader to know.

Self-Management Is of Social Origin

Students acquire SM skills primarily by imitating others. The consequences that follow strengthen or weaken their use. Being of social origin means that SM skills are publicly observable and that language plays a major role in their transmission. Within the classroom, the teacher can demonstrate (model) the behavior, point out its critical elements, observe students' behavior (imitation), and provide consequences relative to its occurrence. Language plays a part in three of these steps: it points out elements, it enables observation, and it provides and indicates consequences.

Teachers Are Teaching Self-Management

Given the definition of SM skills and their social origin, the assumption that teachers are teaching these skills cannot be avoided. The problems facing our students and culture clearly suggest that SM teaching needs improvement. Moreover, if teachers are to be charged with the task, the skills that reliably and effectively produce success should be provided. The present goal is to help them meet this charge by presenting the necessary curriculum and teaching procedures. When they are learned, there will be one less implicit curriculum within the classroom.

Self-Management Must be Continuously Taught and Reinforced

This assumption impacts the content and use of the SM curriculum teaching procedures. Several observations support continuous teaching and reinforcement. First, student behavior constantly changes and becomes more complex; second, the classroom conditions are also always changing and becoming more complex; and third, the transfer of skills across different subject domains and settings has been shown to be limited. Therefore, the week, quarter, or semester course used to teach SM simply does not work. Students cannot learn the range of skills needed within such a short time. To be successfully learned, SM skills must be continuously taught and reinforced.

Effective Self-Management Skills Can Only be Achieved in a Consistently Positive Environment

This fourth assumption concerns the outcomes of teaching SM. If the classroom environment punishes students for their efforts or presents few if any rewards for success, the students may direct SM skills toward an escape from learning academic skills. If the classroom environment is positive, students' SM skills will promote learning. With parents and teachers voicing the need for positive and motivated students, an affirmative environment is an excellent starting point. The following curriculum and teaching procedures have a positive focus.

FOUNDATIONS FOR TEACHING SELF-MANAGEMENT

To teach SM successfully, it is necessary to understand the teaching process. Because SM is assumed to be of social origin, that understanding involves an analysis of the teaching environment. The major questions of interest are: Which elements describe the teaching process? How do these elements interact? Which outcomes result from these interactions? The answers to these three questions give a cause and effect picture—we know that within a specific setting (the classroom), a specific set of elements (what the teacher does) produces a specific set of outcomes (what the student learns).

The answers to the previous questions come from theory and research and involve a language for discussing the teaching process.[1] The vocabulary is highly practical: it guides the development of effective teaching procedures, decision making, and problem solving. This section introduces the foundations of that language and identifies the related chapters of the text.

The Elements of the Teaching Process

The teaching process has four primary elements. Three elements refer to teacher-implemented causes—settings, conditions, and consequences—and one element references effects or changes in students—the desired or performed behaviors. Each is described.

Setting. The classroom setting represents an environment in which instruction takes place. The physical background of tables, chairs, desks, and their arrangement comprise the setting. Each of these setting elements contribute to achieving desired student behaviors. The procedures a teacher uses for academic instruction must fit or operate within this setting. The SM behaviors required by students to perform academic tasks are also determined by this arrangement. For example, when students are grouped together as opposed to separated, the SM behaviors required for success differ.

Conditions. Conditions refer to the environmental elements that set the occasion for student behavior. How teachers prepare, initiate, and prompt students for learning form the major components of classroom conditions. Under effective conditions students are more likely to perform the desired behavior. The two most powerful conditions within classrooms include the structuring of classroom activities and the teacher's verbal statements which reference desired student behavior. The structure of activities provides a background of consistency or pattern in which students behave. The teacher's statements and questions provide details that alter and reinforce the patterns of student behavior within the classroom structure. The analysis of classroom activities begins in Chapter 4, and the analysis of statements and questions begins in Chapter 6.

Behaviors. Behavior includes all that the student says and does, including thinking and feeling. There are two major behavioral repertoires of interest: SM and academic behavior. The focus of this text is on the analysis and teaching of SM behavior, and its relationship to academic behavior. Chapters 2 and 12 analyze behavior in general terms, and Chapters 3, 4, and 13 through 18, analyze SM behavior.

Consequences. Consequences are all the events that follow students' behavior. There are two important types of consequences: reinforcements and punishments. Your verbal statements are among the most powerful consequences readily available in the classroom. If used correctly, they can radically increase or decrease student performance. This text advocates the use of reinforcing consequences along with special forms of consequences called corrections. Technically, a correction includes reinforcing and punishing consequences, and more: it stops inappropriate behavior, sends the student in the correct direction, and follows up new appropriate behavior with reinforcement. Chapter 5 analyzes consequences, Chapter 6 begins the analysis of reinforcing statements, and Chapter 11 covers correction procedures.

The Teaching Process Interactions

The teaching process elements interact, or enter into certain relationships with each other. When the teacher arranges the setting, conditions, and consequences that surround student behavior, contingencies are established. It is the appropriateness and consistency in carrying out these contingencies that determines the success of SM teaching. Therefore, Chapters 20, 21, and 22 present procedures to build, implement, evaluate, and improve the teaching contingencies within a SM program.

Two critical relationships—condition-behavior and behavior-consequence—make up the teacher-established classroom contingencies.

Condition-Behavior Relationship. Two forms of the condition-behavior relationship are important. The *condition-behavior match* refers to events in which student behavior conforms or is appropriate to the established conditions.[2] If a student is asked to read (conditions), then reading (behavior) would be matching or appropriate.

The *condition-behavior nonmatch* refers to events in which student behavior does not conform or is inappropriate to the conditions. If a student is asked to read, then doing anything that is not reading (e.g., daydreaming, writing notes to friends) would be nonmatching or inappropriate. For both the matching and nonmatching relationships, the conditions precede student behavior.

From the teaching perspective, it is your responsibility to establish conditions that are consistent or predictable so that the chance of appropriate behavior is substantial. An inconsistent set of conditions focuses the student on trying to figure out what is going on, rather than on learning the material. Almost every chapter in this text shows how to set up consistent, as well as instructively effective, conditions.

Behavior-Consequence Relationship. The behavior-consequence relationship refers to the interaction of behavior and consequence elements. Student behavior is followed by consequences. There are two major categories of consequences (reinforcements and punishments), and two major categories of behaviors (matching and nonmatching).

Because we neither want to reinforce nonmatching behavior nor punish matching behavior, it is necessary to attend carefully to the types of consequences applied to each behavior. Our first goal is to build appropriate behavior, so a reinforcing consequence is presented contingent on the occurrence of a condition-behavior match. Our second goal is to stop inappropriate behavior, so a correcting consequence is presented contingent on a condition-behavior nonmatch.

The Principles of Behavior and Technology

Specific types of contingencies established by the teacher produce different changes (effects or outcomes) in student behavior. When described as general rules, the different interactions are called *principles of behavior*. The teaching procedures presented in this text are based on these principles of behavior.

1. Conditions set the occasion for the behavior they precede.
2. Reinforcements increase the future probability of the behavior they follow.
3. Reinforcements increase the future probability that conditions will set the occasion for behavior.
4. Punishments decrease the future probability of the behavior they follow.
5. Punishments decrease the future probability that conditions will set the occasion for behavior.

Principle one indicates that conditions precede behavior and set the occasion for it to varying degrees. For example, the conditions that make up the post office, bank, classroom, or library engender a variety of different behaviors. Principles two and four point out that reinforcements and punishments follow behavior, with reinforcements increasing and punishments decreasing the repetition of the behavior they follow. Principles three and five point out that conditions come to set the occasion for behavior or not through their association with consequences. Said another way, reinforcing consequences cement conditions and behaviors together, and punishing consequences break them apart.[3]

These five principles are not enough. Behaviors are not to be randomly reinforced or punished. So an overall sense of direction is provided by following additional *principles of technology*. They state three relationships which should exist among conditions, behaviors, and the types of consequences:

6. Conditions are structured to set the occasion for desired behavior.
7. Reinforcements follow condition-matching behavior.
8. Punishments follow nonmatching behavior.

Principle six mandates that the elements of the conditions must be congruent with and set the occasion for desired behavior. This represents the rights of students and the responsibility of teachers. In other words, students have the right to effective instruction and teachers have the responsibility to provide it. Principles seven and eight mandate that reinforcements and punishments must follow matching and nonmatching be-

Figure 1.1
Contingency and Principles Relationship

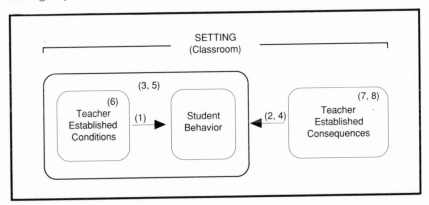

havior respectively. Notice that there is no principle of technology for setting the occasion for inappropriate (nonmatching) behavior, or for correcting appropriate behavior. This lack of symmetry points out the direction in which our culture wants to build behavior; that is, toward condition-matching. These three principles form the foundation for the ethics of our curriculum and teaching procedures, and thus, the profession.

Figure 1.1 illustrates a three-term contingency and its relationship to the principles of behavior and technology. The setting provides the ongoing context in which teacher-established conditions precede student behavior and are followed by teacher-established reward or correction consequences. The arrows, pointing toward student behavior, indicate that the teacher-established condition and consequence events influence or cause student behavior. The numbers in parentheses correlate to the numbered principles. Viewing the classroom in contingencies and the principles provides an initial foundation of knowledge for understanding and integrating the contents of this text.

I

Analyzing the Environment

The instructional environment includes the conditions in which teaching occurs, the behaviors to be taught, and the consequences that follow. Part 1 begins by providing a language to talk unambiguously about behavior (Chapter 2), and then uses that language to talk about the SM curriculum (Chapter 3). The remaining chapters—4, 5, and 6—provide the language and procedures to analyze your classroom's activities, activity SM behaviors, and reinforcing consequences. Knowledge of these environmental components is prerequisite to building and using the teaching skills and procedures presented in Part 2.

2

REFERENCING AND RELATING
BEHAVIOR

We set out to educate students, to teach them skills that increase their chances of surviving and having happy lives. To be successful, our talk about behavior must be technical; talk that is technical supports the rest of our technologies. If we are to evolve adaptive human behavior as successfully as engineers build bridges or physicians repair bodies, our talk about human behavior also has to be technical.

Mastering this language is challenging because it requires a change in the way we talk about and view human behavior. Once learned, this language facilitates the building of curriculum, the design of instruction, the observation of behavior, the implementation of teaching procedures, and the solving of recurrent instructional problems.

This chapter continues the technical language begun in Chapter 1. It provides a way to talk about the elements of behavior and their relationships. Chapter 12 presents the language required to talk about the evolution of behavior.

REFERENCING BEHAVIOR

The first step in talking unambiguously about behavior is to clearly reference, or classify, what we see. This section examines how we reference behavior and how to insure that the referencing is accurate and rigorous.

Instances of Behavior

We refer to, or talk about behavior in two ways: First, we talk about single occurrences of a behavior by an individual or group. These single occurrences are *instances of behavior* because each is bound to a particular time and place. Consider the following examples with the behavior in CAPITALS.

1. Zelda HELPED during reading today.
2. The Electric Reader Group will ORGANIZE their questions prior to the special presentation.
3. Sidney IDENTIFIED the necessary art supplies.

Each of these examples talks about one occurrence of behavior. Examples one and three talk about past behavior, example two about future behavior. These instances are fleeting, ephemeral things that make behavior a difficult subject matter.

Classes of Behavior

We also talk about behavior in a second way, this time as if it were a permanent thing; something we can grasp, expect, or consider a permanent part of the individual or group talked about. When behavior is referenced in this way, the talk is about *classes of behavior*. Consider the following talk about behavior that parallels the previous examples of instances.

1. Zelda is a HELPFUL individual.
2. The Electric Reader Group is very ORGANIZED.
3. Sidney IDENTIFIES the tasks assigned him.

Zelda is a helper, the group is organized, and Sidney is an identifier. All are spoken of as real parts of the person or group. Thus, referencing classes of behavior, with their element of historical permanence, radically departs from talking about the momentary instances of behavior.

The Relationship of Instances and Classes of Behavior

Both ways of referencing behavior are closely tied because our knowledge of the instances of behavior controls our referencing of any class of behavior. Zelda has been helpful every day for three months without fail. The members of the Electric Reader Group have organized resources all but one day in the first semester. Sidney has never failed to identify the task assigned.

The dependence on the observation of multiple instances in the referencing of a class is even more apparent when the class undergoes change. The preceding examples have again been modified.

1. Zelda used to be HELPFUL, but now she is an UNCOOPERATIVE student.
2. The Electric Readers were DISORGANIZED, but now they are ORGANIZED.
3. Sidney has always IDENTIFIED the critical components of his task.

Examples one and two concern a change in the class of behavior which describes the individual or group. But example three concerns the consistency, or maintenance, of behavior over time. To make these *class statements* about individual or group behavior, the speaker must have observed a number of instances over an extended time period. Because observation occurs over an extended period and instances are fleeting, our talk about behavior is often ambiguous or inaccurate. Therefore, to insure reliable and accurate observation of instances of behavior, classes of behavior require clear definition and examples.[1]

Class Names and Class Definitions

The previous examples reference the classes of helping, organizing, and identifying. These terms denote *class names*, and they are our verbal referents, or words, used in our talk about behavior. They are not the *class definitions*. Class names may refer to observable things, but they are not fine-grained enough for reliable and accurate observation, talking, and teaching. A class name usually has multiple definitions, as any dictionary points out. To achieve relatively unambiguous status, class definitions are composed, for the most part, of observable terms that focus on the critical attributes observed in past instances.[2]

Any term can be used as part of a class name or a definition if this leads to reliable and accurate observation and referencing of behavior. There are some terms it is best to avoid using. For a number of reasons they add confusion to the problem of developing rigorous definitions. One major reason is that they have so many referents. Terms such as *know, understand, grasp, internalize,* and *believe* are just a few.[3]

If these problem terms are used as class names in talk about behavior, ask for clarification. If they are used in a definition, realize that the person is talking ambiguously, which some call failing to communicate. The terms that promote agreement between observers are *observable terms*. They have been so well defined that the population of interest (educators, in our case) all agree on what they refer to, or mean. There is both interobserver and intraobserver reliability.

The identification of behavior is often problematic because much of the behavior is private to the individual. For example, Tony does addition and all we see is the answer. The same is true for many SM behaviors. Such behaviors have to be *overtized*, or made overt, for successful teaching to take place.[4] This is one task of the SM curriculum.

In isolation, the definition of a class always has some ambiguity. Therefore, defining closely related classes is extremely important to eliminate ambiguity. In defining related classes, each definition helps define the boundary or limits of the other classes. You see this in Chapter 3 and again in Chapter 9, which illustrates defining behavior through sets of examples.

RELATING CLASSES OF BEHAVIOR

The specification of class relationships, the second step toward reliably and accurately observing and talking about behavior, makes it possible to describe and eventually construct complex behavior.[5]

Two categories of relationships are covered: hierarchical and historical. The examples that follow are not fully defined classes. The idea at this point is to see relationships without focusing simultaneously on the problem of building accurate and reliable definitions through statements or examples. A general idea of what the classes entail suffices for the present.

Hierarchical Behavior Relationships

Hierarchical relationships denote whether a class is or is not a member of another class. Such relationships are analogous to set-subset descriptions. Two hierarchical class relationships are important: inclusive and mutually exclusive.

Inclusive Classes. An inclusive class has a number of member subclasses. The subclasses help define the contents of the more inclusive class by further clarifying what constitutes the class. The SM classes of behavior can be represented inclusively. Figure 2.1, a tree diagram, provides an example. Sharing and taking turns are less inclusive subclasses of SM, which facilitates the starting, continuing, and ending of task behavior. Sharing is a subclass that represents one of the ways task behavior can be

Figure 2.1
Inclusive Class of Self-Management with Subclasses

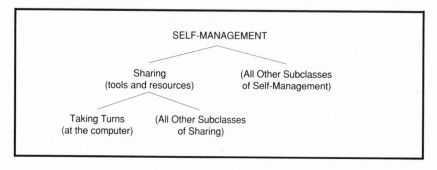

facilitated; it may require individuals to use tools and resources with others. Where could that sharing take place? In classrooms with computers, taking turns on the machines could be a possible subclass of sharing. Sharing art supplies is another.

When our definitions reach the level of detail allowing for reliable observation, we have defined *activity-level classes*. Activity-level classes represent the least inclusive classes of interest. They are guides or templates for classifying the instances of behavior to be observed. By looking at the tree diagram from the top down, we get a vertical picture of SM behavior and see the levels of inclusiveness.

Mutually Exclusive Classes. Mutually exclusive classes have no instances or members in common. Mutual exclusiveness is represented horizontally on a tree diagram, as presented in Figure 2.2. Planning, organizing, supervising, learning, intervening, helping, and sharing are mutually exclusive to each other, and the most inclusive subclasses of SM. Now we have a horizontal picture of self-management. These inclusive subclasses define the universe of SM behavior. All of these inclusive subclasses have less inclusive and mutually exclusive subclasses. For example, Figure 2.3 illustrates that organizing has four less inclusive and mutually exclusive (although related) subclasses. The classes and subclasses of SM show it to be very complex behavior. Together they define the universe of SM behavior. To illustrate how each class differs from the others is one task of a curriculum. Chapter 3 presents a complete tree diagram of the SM curriculum classes.

Historical Behavior Relationships

Often the learning or performance of one class of behavior is dependent on another. Saying that classes are dependent indicates that they have a time-based relationship. Thus, they are *historical relationships*. Without knowledge of historical relationships, it would be impossible to sequence

Figure 2.2
Mutually Exclusive Subclasses of Self-Management

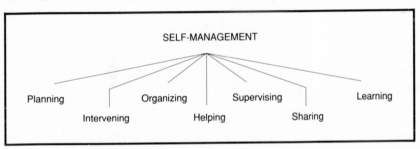

Figure 2.3
Mutually Exclusive Subclasses of Organizing

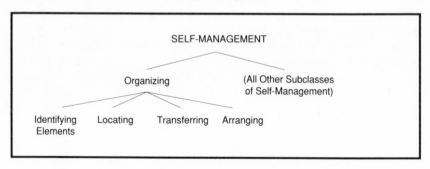

instruction or accurately reference the change in student behavior. For the SM curriculum, two historical relationships are important.

Performance Dependent Classes. When one class of behavior is dependent on the prior learning of other behaviors, it is a *performance dependent* class of behavior. For example, the relationship between SM and academic skills is performance dependent. If students do not have sufficient SM skills, academic behavior is less efficiently learned or performed, if learned or performed at all. Students simply cannot perform academic tasks without performing at least some SM behaviors.

Knowledge of performance dependent relationships not only helps sequence instruction and teach a skill but it also has great import relative to the way in which teachers interact with students. Consider the following teacher statement: "Quincina, by ORGANIZING your materials before you started on the assignment, you were able to complete it much faster than usual. Now you have time to work on your favorite project."

Finishing faster and having time for a favorite project are dependent on (or the consequences of) Quincina's organizing. Only if teachers have knowledge of such dependencies can they use them to change student behavior. Chapter 6 covers the content of teacher statements.

Procedurally Dependent Classes. When a number of subclasses must be performed to reference a more inclusive class, a *procedurally dependent relationship* exists. Often, the subclasses are performed in at least a rough sequence. All inclusive SM classes are procedurally dependent. For example, the class of organizing can only be referenced if four subclasses have been performed. Figure 2.4 is a diagram similar to the tree diagram that appeared in the hierarchical relationship section. This figure emphasizes the dependent, sequential relationship between the subclasses of organize. If Jeffery cannot identify the materials required and then locate, transfer, and arrange them to facilitate task performance, can we refer to him as organized? It would seem not. Within the classroom much of the organizing required of students goes unnoticed. Teachers, similar to other

Figure 2.4
Historical Subclass Relationships of Organizing

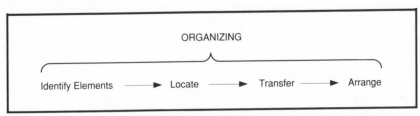

adults, simply expect it. But for Jeffery and other students it is new behavior, with no real permanence as yet. The automatic behavior of an organized, self-managed adult can be achieved more reliably and in a shorter period of time if step-by-step practice is provided across a range of classroom activities.

Another SM skill identified in the hierarchical relationship section was planning. Figure 2.5 illustrates its four inclusive subclasses that form a procedurally dependent relationship. In planning, Clare begins with some type of problem, designs one or more solutions to solve it, makes a final determination about its adequacy or selects from among several solutions designed, and following implementation evaluates the outcome to see if it did indeed solve the problem. If any one of these subclasses is absent, planning breaks down and becomes ineffectual. Moreover, the planning process more or less follows this sequence indicated. It would, for example, be difficult to design a solution without first identifying the problem it was to solve.

THE TYPES OF BEHAVIOR

Chapter 1 defined behavior as all that the student does, including thinking and feeling. We can classify this behavior from a number of directions. For one, we can classify it in SM and academic behavior, two inclusive

Figure 2.5
Historical Subclass Relationships of Planning

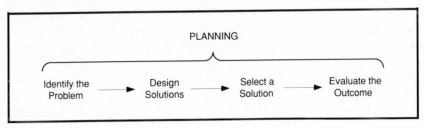

subclasses. Relative to the analysis of curriculum and the design of teaching procedures, a more useful classification is in the contingencies of reinforcement. From this perspective, behavior has two inclusive subclasses, discriminations and operations, and their combination into procedures.

Discriminations and Operations

When students are required to tell the difference in various classes of conditions, to sort or classify or identify the array of things, actions, features, relationships, events, or states that exist in the world, the focus is on teaching *discrimination behavior*. Learning to discriminate a conflict from events that are not conflicts is one example. Another is learning to identify when help is needed. Yet another is learning to identify a problem so planning can begin.

Operations are small performances, like saying a sound or word, circling or crossing out an object on paper, or walking. There is no need to reduce them any further for most teaching; they can be modeled with short sets of examples and nonexamples. For SM, students learn operations like offering help, accepting or rejecting help, pointing out consequences, stopping conflicts, and monitoring conflict resolutions. By operating on the world, instead of classifying it, changes or consequences are produced. The world is simply a different place.

There are no pure discriminations or operations. All discriminations require some form of behavior as evidence. There must be a performance. This performance is an operation, a manipulation of the environment, whether by speaking, marking, pointing, or any of numerous other ways. When the focus is on teaching discriminations, the operation chosen is one the student can already perform. When the teacher is more interested in how the behavior is performed, the focus is on learning operations. In this case, discriminations such as when to perform are initially isolated from the situation. These two forms of behavior are related to contingency elements in Figure 2.6. Contingencies are being taught and, depending on the focus, we can talk about teaching discriminations or operations or both.

Procedures

Procedures are complex behaviors composed of a set of related discriminations and operations. Examples include all the inclusive subclasses of SM behavior such as the planning, organizing, and learning strategies. Each of these procedures is a mix of discriminations and operations. There are discriminations of when to start performing the procedure and when to change from one step, or element, of the procedure to another.

Here procedures differ from the usual view where they are seen as a

Figure 2.6
Contingencies, Discriminations, and Operations

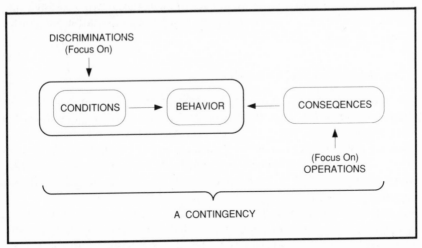

fixed set of steps. They represent an inclusive class comprised of four subclasses. The defining property of these subclasses is the probability of success when applying the procedure. Figure 2.7 identifies these procedures as trial and error, heuristic, strategic, and algorithmic. A trial and error procedure represents guessing how to perform the task and, thus, its probability of success is low. A heuristic procedure is a set of simple guidelines for performing a task. Because it gives some places to start and go, its probability of success increases over that for trial and error. A strategic procedure sets out the major steps for performing a task. The probability of success is greatly increased over a heuristic procedure. Finally, an algorithmic procedure provides a detailed analysis of virtually all

Figure 2.7
The Four Subclasses of Procedures

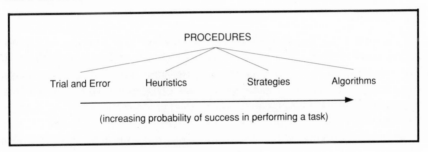

the discriminations and operations, and their relationships required in performing a task. The probability of success is 100 percent if the algorithm is followed exactly. The procedures for adding, subtracting, multiplication, and division are algorithmic procedures. The arrow line below the subclasses in Figure 2.7 indicates the direction of increasing the probability of success in task performance.

Each of the seven inclusive classes of SM behavior is best classified as a strategy, as are their teaching procedures. Additionally, each of these inclusive SM classes has several subclasses of procedures called *steps*. Thus, there are procedures within procedures. Only with this careful analysis of behavior into hierarchical and historical relationships is it possible to teach such complex behavior to young students.

To avoid confusion, the term *procedure* is used to reference the procedures for teaching SM. The term *strategy* is used to reference the SM procedures students are to learn. The major goal of this text is to overtize, or make clear, the behavioral elements involved in both the SM strategies and the teaching procedures required for instruction. Additionally, the terms *skill*, *repertoire*, and *knowledge* are used. They are used essentially as synonyms for the term *behavior*. They refer to inclusive sets of behaviors.

OBSERVING BEHAVIOR IN THE CLASSROOM

Given unambiguous analysis and definition of behavior by classes, subclasses, and their relationships, the observation of classroom behavior, in isolation, is reliable and accurate. But observing classroom behavior does not happen in isolation; it occurs in the context of management and instructional tasks. Therefore, these tasks need to be well learned. If they are not, there is little chance to observe the details of student behavior. Once these skills are fully mastered, there is fast, appropriate action relative to your observations.

Observing during instruction is not the only way to learn observation skills. During the preparation of instruction, the teacher remembers, thinks about, and defines what the student has done and what he or she wants the student to do. All of these contribute to accurate, consistent observation.

SUMMARY

Talk about behavior takes two forms: the instance and the class. The behavioral element is the instance. It is what we see; it is also ephemeral and fleeting, although it may take a long time to perform as does an instance of sitting during a lecture. A set of related instances is a class. Behavior is defined by classes, from the detailed activity-level class, as an example of what we want to see, to the large, inclusive classes such as planning, organizing, supervising, and learning. The ideal is to define a class so that class membership, across levels of inclusiveness, can be accurately, reliably, and quickly determined. If this can occur, the class of behavior is unambiguously defined through statements and/or examples.

An unambiguous class definition can only be rigorous in the context of other definitions. Drawing hierarchical and historical relationships helps define the limits of a class and, therefore, facilitates unambiguous definitions and observation. The classes of SM behavior can be represented by procedures called strategies. By overtizing these SM classes, they can be unambiguously taught and observed.

A major consequence of defining and analyzing behavior is that very little else is required in learning to see it take place in the classroom. Once the delivery of instruction skills has been firmly learned, nothing interferes with the observation and teaching of SM behavior.

3

THE SELF-MANAGEMENT
CURRICULUM

This chapter defines SM behavior and its less inclusive classes, and illustrates their relationships.[1] To insure clarity, three related classes of behavior are examined: cooperation, adaptation, and management.

THE DEFINITION OF SELF-MANAGEMENT

At the most inclusive level, *SM behavior* is any behavior by an individual or group that facilitates the beginning, continuing, or ending of their task behavior within some task environment. Similar to any inclusive definition, this one only makes sense if its terms are clarified.

A *task* is any work assigned or undertaken by an individual or a group in a *task environment*, which is often called an activity in the classroom. The task is often something such as doing a worksheet in math, listening to a lecture, or reading in a group. *Task behavior* is the specific behavior required to perform the assigned task. For most classroom tasks, it is also called academic behavior. If the task is to work the problems on a math worksheet, the task behavior is adding, subtracting, and so forth. Yet performing task behaviors requires much more. It requires facilitation by SM behavior. In this context, *facilitate* means to increase the probability of the task behavior. Together, SM and task behaviors represent the universe of behaviors required to perform a task within some task environment, or activity.

The *any behavior* element of the SM definition divides into two inclusive classes. The first, *activity SM behaviors*, are intended to facilitate task behavior only within a specific or limited set of activities. For example, during a math worksheet activity, Wilber will have to gather the materials needed, work quietly so others can also do the task and turn in the work-sheet to consider the assignment finished. None of these are part of the task behavior and all are more or less specific to a particular activity design.

The second class of SM behaviors is a *system of strategies* that can be applied to almost any task to increase the chance of task performance, even those entered for the first time. For example, Wilber and Patty could use the planning strategy to design an activity to perform some task behavior, and then use a supervision strategy to keep the implementation of their plan moving forward. The components of the planning and supervision strategies would be essentially the same across all activities. During the activity, we see activity SM behaviors because those are what the plan identified and what the supervision strategy helped them perform. In other words, the SM system strategies are, in part, SM behavior that designs, helps carry out, or embellishes activity SM behaviors performed during an activity.

SELF-MANAGEMENT AS A SYSTEM OF STRATEGIES

Chapter 2 pointed out that a strategy is a procedure composed of discriminations and operations that changes the environment in some way. By performing the system strategies, students control, manipulate, or modify the environment so that all their task behavior can be performed. Each strategy contributes to controlling the task environment, or activity, in specific ways.

Seven strategies form the SM strategy system: planning, organizing, learning, supervising, intervening, helping, and sharing. Figure 3.1 illustrates how these seven strategies form a system to control the task environment so task behavior can be performed.

Within an activity, such as individual reading or a group writing project, students may or may not have to plan what to do and how to do it, learning something if they see the task cannot be performed with what they know, organize the materials and other resources necessary, supervise themselves throughout the task, intervene to stop problems that arise among themselves, help each other to keep the task moving, and share resources when they are scarce.

Planning is the key SM system strategy because it can be used to modify the activity SM behaviors, all the system strategies (including itself), and the task behaviors. Planning is the mechanism of evolution, making behavior adaptive to the changing environment.[2]

THE COMPONENT SELF-MANAGEMENT SYSTEM STRATEGIES

Just how do SM strategies function to facilitate task performance? The answer comes in defining each system strategy as a set of steps, or less

Figure 3.1
The Self-Management Strategy System

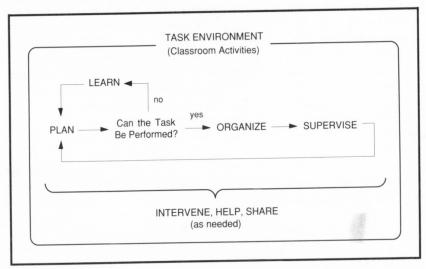

inclusive classes, each composed of discriminations and operations (Chapter 2).[3] Chapters 13 through 18 expand on the following initial pictures of the SM system strategies.

Planning

Planning, by a student or group, determines which elements and element relationships are required to start, continue, and finish a task. Elements involve the who, what, when, where, why, and how of any activity. Their relationships concern the ways in which they come together and interact. In this context, planning is seen as problem solving. It has four inclusive steps.

Identifying the Problem. Identifying the problem has two parts. First, the student or group must discriminate that a problem exists, and second, discriminate what the problem is. For example, Ethel says that the get help procedure used during math is not working and others agree (problem existence identified). Next, others say they usually have to wait a long time for help (problem identified).

For many tasks, identifying the problem is as far as planning goes. A way to take care of the problem exists. For example, Jennifer sees that a math problem needs an answer and automatically performs the needed behavior.

Designing Solutions. Designing solutions is rarely done in a void; planners work from an old behavior or strategy that has been identified as defective. By redesigning the old behavior, one or more solutions are found. To design a solution, they identify the behavior or strategy steps causing the problem, design replacement steps, and modify the remaining steps accordingly. How to satisfy these design elements needs to be taught. For the getting help procedure, Ricky sees that the teacher alone cannot get around fast enough to give everyone help (problem causing step). So the students decide to supplement getting help with student monitors (replacement solution step). Next, they decide that the monitors themselves may need to get help occasionally (added solution step).

Selecting a Solution. Selecting the solution for implementation determines the acceptability of the design. To make the selection, planners must consider how the solution could fail, whether it fits the resources, and if everyone agrees to try it. For example, the class members predict that the new getting help strategy will work because no one should have to wait for help, a number of students could act as monitors, and everyone is willing to try the new strategy. The actual implementation of the selected solution is part of activity behavior, not part of planning.

Evaluating the Outcome. After a solution has been implemented, it must be evaluated. The evaluation step involves assessing the agreement between the planned solution and its implementation, whether there were still problems, and if further changes are needed. For example, the class compared the new getting help procedure with what was actually performed (assessment of performance) and then agreed that no one was waiting (assessment of solution).

To work effectively, all four planning strategy steps must be used. But if we had to go through all the planning steps for each day's activities, we would soon be exhausted. Fortunately, many tasks are preplanned; that is, previous plans are used again.

Organizing

Organizing, by a student or group, brings together the elements (students, materials, tools) required to begin, continue, or end a task. The organizing strategy has four steps.

Identifying the Elements to be Organized. The organizers begin by looking to the plan to identify the elements required and when they are needed. If there is no plan, the organizers become planners, often making predictions from past requirements in similar situations.

Locating. Once identified, the elements must be located at an appropriate time before the task. Again, if no plan exists for locating, planning is undertaken.

Transferring. Once located, the organizer must move the elements required for the task from one person or place to another. In the classroom, the terms *passing, conveying, communicating,* and *accompanying* are used to refer to transferring.

Arranging. Those who arrange, set out in sequence or order the task elements needed for performing a task. They must know when and how to arrange the elements. The plan is the first place to look, and experience is the second. The organizers do not govern how elements are used during task performance; that is part of the supervision strategy.

These four steps can occur in many ways within the classroom. For example, Zelda could perform all four steps, or a group could divide up the organizing. Sidney could identify and pinpoint the location of all the elements that Tina's plan indicated. Next, Jose could transfer the elements to where the project was to be performed. Finally, Cindy could arrange the elements so that the four of them can perform the project efficiently. Together, the group has performed all the elements of organizing for the group project as planned by Tina.

Supervising

Supervising, by a student or group, initiates, maintains, and ends the performance of their task behavior steps. Supervising interacts with and usually occurs throughout the duration of the task behavior to facilitate its performance. Supervisors are only concerned with facilitating the performance of previously learned behavior. When there is a performance problem, the learning or planning strategy is required. The supervising strategy consists of these six steps:

Identify the Need for Supervision. Not all tasks need supervision. Some are automatically performed. Others require the use of the supervision strategy.

Informing of the Plan. Some of those being supervised need knowledge about the task. Supervisors may need to specify the task, the resources required, who will do what, or when to perform the task. Just how this is done depends on the background of the supervisor and those supervised.

Setting Task Goals. Setting task goals often focuses on task criteria. Supervisors may need to inform those supervised about how performance and product should look. Moreover, the goals must be obtainable.

Directing Task Flow. Once those supervised know the task and the goals, the supervisor may need to maintain their performance. If those being supervised are proficient at performing the steps of an activity, the supervisor would direct these students differently than others who are new at the activity. Making this discrimination can be difficult for supervisors.

· Looking for Success. Looking for success is one part of maintaining performance at criterion levels. The key to this assessment is the match between what has been done (performance) and what should be done (plan). The closer the two, the greater the degree of success. Supervisors make this assessment often during an activity.

Pointing Out Consequences. Many things happen because a task has or has not been performed to criterion. Given a level of success, the supervisor must identify who needs to know about success and, then, point out the consequences of their behavior. Chapters 5 and 11 illustrate the range of consequences available to students or teachers.

The six supervision steps are interactive. They often occur in a spiral fashion throughout task performance when the performer is new at the task. For the experienced performer, supervision occurs in a more sequential fashion. Thus, to be effective, the supervisor must make adjustments dependent on the experience of those being supervised.

Learning

Learning, by a student or group, is acquiring the knowledge necessary to perform a task or some element of it. Those who use the learning strategy set out to change themselves so they can reenter the task environment with an increased chance of success. Learning is not to be confused with supervision, which manages the use of known behavior. The acquisition of the learning strategy fosters the continuing-to-be-educated adult. It has four steps.

Identifying the Learning Problem. Not all tasks require the use of the learning strategy. But it is critical that students discriminate when it is needed. If learning is required, students must further identify the learning problem before they proceed with the strategy.

Organizing the Knowledge Sources. Given a learning problem, the next step is to identify which sources can help, and then locate, transfer, and arrange those sources. At times only one source is needed to solve the problem. But for complex tasks, such as writing a review paper, multiple sources like bibliographies must be used. Thus, students need skills in discriminating the applicability of many knowledge sources.

Unpacking the Knowledge Sources. Once sources have been organized, learners must interact with them to obtain the knowledge related to the problem. The task of using the knowledge sources is as varied as the sources. The common denominator for all unpacking is the use of specific language tools that help students see the elements and relationships that are packed into the knowledge sources.

There are three inclusive classes of knowledge sources: textual, observational, and experimental. Their use must be taught to students. This text is limited to learning from written sources.

Packing the Knowledge Found. After knowledge is unpacked, it must be repacked. The guide is the learning problem. The packing often requires fitting knowledge together from multiple sources. If it is presented from different perspectives, it may even be conflicting. The learner must sort out and integrate that material into a unit or whole. Often much of what is found is not applicable to the present problem and for the present must be discarded. But if the material has been integrated first with other knowledge, it has a higher probability of being remembered during other problem situations, thus supporting future learning or planning.

Intervening

Intervening, by a student or group, stops, halts, or settles a quarrel, disagreement, or conflict between two or more parties, when it is keeping their task from beginning, continuing, or ending. An intervention strategy allows students to short-circuit present conflicts, eliminate future ones, and return to their task as quickly as possible. It has four steps.

Identify the Need for Intervention. Many interactions occur within the classroom. The potential intervener must appropriately decide which are conflicts.

Stopping the Conflict. Once identified, interveners must stop the conflict. Stopping refers to the immediate, short-term cessation of the conflict. If an intervention strategy is to be used, appropriate operations for stopping the conflict must be taught.

Finding Better Ways. To insure that conflicts do not continue, this text advocates finding better ways, or behavioral options to inappropriate conflict behavior. These better ways are not only identified by students but also practiced. Interveners must be able to determine what is a better behavioral replacement and where and when it can be practiced.

Settling the Conflict. Not only must better ways be found, but conflicts must also be permanently settled. Without permanent resolution, the parties can continue to have the same conflicts in the future. Such a settlement operation requires identifying the available settlement options. The settlement operation needs to be designed and taught to fit more than a single classroom. If it is not, settlements are inconsistent and conflicting across the larger school or district environment.

Documenting the Conflict. An intervention strategy fits within the larger legal systems of school and state; therefore, conflicts must be documented. If the documentation system is to be practical and successful, students need to be taught which elements to record and how. When documenting the settlement, for example, students must be taught two behaviors: monitoring the settlement implementation and documenting its outcome.

Intervention strategies fall into three subclasses. When the settlement is directed by a third party, who decides the final settlement, an *arbitration* occurs. When a third party prompts the parties in conflict into reaching a solution, it is *mediation*. When the two parties direct themselves in settling the conflict, it is *negotiation*.

Helping

Helping by a student or group involves working with others so the others can begin, continue, or end their task or task element. Over the long run, helping others facilitates the helper's task behavior. Because it involves working with others, helping is separated from other SM strategies. With an intervention strategy, students can stop inappropriate behavior; but with a helping strategy, students can increase the chance of appropriate behavior. The helping strategy has two steps.

Identifying the Need for Helping. Out of all the tasks occurring, only a small percent require help. Potential helpers must be able to identify these.

Providing the Help Needed. Given the need for help, supplying it follows. Because help can be given in various ways—many of which are inappropriate—it is necessary to teach a range of appropriate helping.

There are three subclasses of helping behavior. *Aiding* denotes that the helper is stronger or a necessary element to continue the performance of the task. If Zelda fails to find the spelling of sophisticated and Sidney says "s-o-p-h," Sidney would be aiding Zelda. *Assisting* denotes a subordinate role on the part of the helper—the task is simply made easier. If Sidney is shelving library books and Zelda starts to shelve them with him, she would be assisting because Sidney could have completed the task by himself. *Supporting* denotes an even weaker form of help than assist, more in the sense of "cheering one on," "being in one's corner," or "not getting in one's way" while a task is being performed. If Sidney had finished his math problems and is reading quietly at the desk next to Zelda, who is working on her math problems, Sidney would be supporting Zelda's math task. This example represents the lower limit of what could be considered working with another on her task. When support becomes reciprocal, the classroom becomes a very positive place.

Sharing

Sharing, by a student or group, grants and provides to another individual or group the use of an object or tool required to perform a task. The sharer may grant temporary, long-term, or permanent use. The sharing strategy has two steps:

Identifying the Need for Sharing. Of the many tasks occurring, only some require sharing. The potential sharer must be able to identify them.

Providing the Sharing Needed. Given the need to share, providing it follows. Similar to helping, sharing can be done in many ways, some of which are inappropriate. We would not, for example, like Sidney and Jose to share answers during a test. Therefore, it is necessary to teach a range of appropriate sharing behavior.

The definition of sharing just given encompasses the traditional classes of *reciprocating, lending,* and *giving.* Within the classroom, the lending usually involves a pencil or book, giving usually involves a sheet of paper or knowledge, and reciprocating involves the mutual use of materials given by someone such as the teacher.

PERSPECTIVES ON SELF-MANAGEMENT BEHAVIOR

Self-management is an inclusive class name for a set of less inclusive classes of behavior that facilitate the performance of task behavior. By clearly defining these less inclusive classes, as done above for the system strategies, a great deal of ambiguity in our talk about SM is eliminated. But a level of confusion remains until other classes, related to and equally as inclusive as SM, are also clearly defined. Three such classes are of interest: cooperation, adaptation, and management. The key is to see that any instance of SM behavior can simultaneously belong to one or more of these classes.

Cooperation

The term *cooperation* denotes reciprocal interactive behaviors.[4] When all individuals involved in an activity perform their assigned or undertaken task element in that activity, cooperation exists. Cooperation can occur when SM behaviors, SM and task behaviors, or task behaviors interact. In the first case, Anna and Innis may each perform different components of the SM behavior that facilitate their individual task assignments. In the second case, Paul may do all of the SM behavior as he and Willie build a science project. In the last case, Latrina and Vince each write different parts of a report for history. If all of the members of a group do their part, perform their self-management and/or task behavior elements, cooperation is occurring.

Cooperation is one end of a continuum. The other end, behavior which is interactive but not reciprocal, is competition. Relative to the analysis of behavior (Chapter 1), cooperation denotes a situation in which mutual condition-behavior matches exist. For example, Zelda hands Jose a pencil and Jose accepts it and says, "Thanks." In turn, she says, "You're welcome." They are both matching the conditions established by the other. When individuals or groups respond with mutual nonmatching behavior, competition exists. One of the main goals of SM teaching is to promote cooperation—we desire students to operate with others.

Participating, collaborating, and synergizing are a family of descriptive terms related to cooperation. By *participating*, the student or group does its part and achieves a specifiable result, related to some standard of performance. When we reference interactive behavior as *collaboration*, everyone is cooperating, usually closely, on a task. But we can only reference behavior as *synergistic* when reciprocal interaction exists and the level of effectiveness reached is higher than an individual could have achieved. We might consider the group behavior exceptional, creative, unique, or one that "goes beyond what is expected."

Adaptation

The environment in which students live is constantly evolving. When behavior changes so that a condition-behavior match is reestablished between the students and some new environmental conditions, *adaptation* has occurred.[5] Instances of SM or task behavior can change to match these new conditions. If the behavior does not change with the environment and is no longer related to performing the activity task, it would be reclassified as maladaptive, or inappropriate. Several descriptive terms are related to talking about behavior as it enters the adaptive process. They represent when and how the behavior adapts.

Agreeing. A student or group *agrees* when they come to terms or settle matters concerning the performance of an activity. Agree is often the first step in adapting to changing conditions. Two classes of behavior are related to agreeing. *Concurring* denotes agreeing with what others have proposed. *Consenting,* often done by those being managed, denotes agreeing to what others have proposed. One consents to do a task or to take on a responsibility.

Following. A student or group follows when they perform as requested by those who manage. When students do what is asked by the teacher or student manager, they are adapting in the sense of following directions, written or verbal. Following often comes after agreeing.

Following has three related subclasses: obeying, complying, and executing. The differences among the three focus on the conditions under which the following is performed. *Obeying* focuses on the following of rules, *complying* on following oral directions, and *executing* on following preset and often complex procedures. These small distinctions are not hard and fast.

Adjusting. A student or group adjusts when they change their behavior under conditions involving some sudden or exigent occurrences that arise during an activity. Without the adjustment, task behavior could be stopped or impeded. The term *adjust* is reserved for conditions in which an individual or group is supervising itself. Adjusting occurs, for example, when one seeks clarification on a task, or when the planned materials are not available and the group modifies what is available to continue.

Three classroom relevant class terms are related to adjusting. *Accommodating* denotes adjusting to a sudden, unexpected change in the person with whom one is working. *Conforming* denotes adjusting according to prevailing standards or customs or rules. *Reconciling* denotes adjusting by changing how one sees the new conditions. Often, the individual and group reconcile themselves to the change by coming to see that their behavior is still rewarded and the punishments feared are not present. Accommodating, conforming, and reconciling can be seen as elements of the same adjustment. For example, the handshake and mutual, positive verbal expression of "looking forward to working with you" is an example of adjustment that has elements of accommodating, conforming, and reconciling.

Receiving. A student or group who receives, adapts to elements transferred to them. The element received can be an object, person, or a statement. Two relevant subclasses are related to receiving: *Accepting* denotes receiving that which is offered with favor, consent, or approval. *Admitting* denotes receiving after a period of time in which a refusal, denial, investigation, or deliberation about the object, person, or statement occurred.

The four inclusive classes of adapting—agreeing, following, adjusting, and receiving—are neither meant to represent the universe of subclasses related to adapting, nor to be strict, mutually exclusive subclasses. Yet they help in referencing SM behavior from the adaptive perspective; you will be better able to show students another side of their SM behavior, increase the chance that SM behavior occurs under appropriate conditions, and add variety to your talk with students.

Management

The component classes of SM behavior are what most would view as management skills. That perception is correct but incomplete. When we speak of someone as a manager, whether a planner or supervisor, the focus is on the activity task behavior to be performed, not on the behaviors required to begin, continue, or end that task behavior.

When one of the system strategies becomes the task behavior, it is no longer SM behavior. It is behavior to be facilitated. For example, Zelda, Sidney, and Jose may be assigned the task of planning a class play. To facilitate this planning assignment, they have to at least plan a time to meet, organize the materials needed, and supervise themselves as they perform the planning task.

Thus, the difference between SM and management skills is simply a difference in focus on what is the task behavior. In the end, to teach SM is to teach management. As the students move into the working world, task focus will change and the skills used to self-manage will be those used to manage. Yet they will still have to self-manage their management task behavior.

SUMMARY

Self-management behavior facilitates task behavior. In teaching SM skills, we can proceed in two ways: The first is to teach activity-specific behaviors that facilitate task behavior. The second is to teach a system of strategies that supports task behavior performance under a wide variety of conditions. The system of strategies presented includes planning, organizing, supervising, learning, intervening, helping, and sharing. Each one contributes support to task behaviors. Together, they maximize the probability of task performance. Figure 3.2 outlines the steps of each system strategy.

Cooperation, adaptation, and management are inclusive classes of behavior related to SM. When SM behaviors are interactive and reciprocal,

Figure 3.2

Components of the Self-Management Strategy System

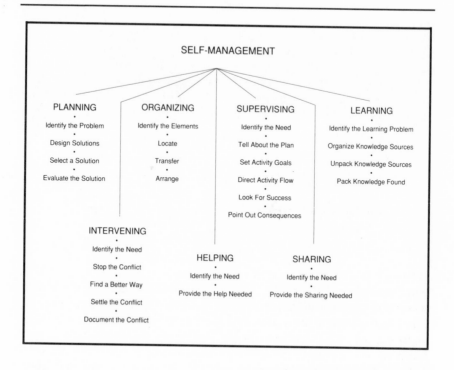

the term *cooperation* applies. When SM behavior changes with the evolving environment, it can be referenced as adaptive. When the system strategies are the task behavior, these behaviors are referred to as management. Cooperation, adaptation, and management are different descriptions of SM behavior from different points of reference.

By defining SM in terms of its subclasses and related classes, an unambiguous picture of the SM curriculum begins to arise. Later chapters continue to clarify this picture. But for students to learn them, these skills must be rigorously taught and used across a wide range of contexts.

4

PLANNING ACTIVITY
SELF-MANAGEMENT BEHAVIOR

Before students are taught the SM system strategies, they must be able to behave appropriately within an existing set of classroom activities. The SM behaviors required of these activities need to be carefully planned so they can be quickly taught and reinforced. This chapter illustrates how to plan classroom activities and their activity SM behaviors. Within these activities students first apply the SM system strategies and later plan and implement activities to solve their own or curriculum-related problems.

ANALYSIS OF A CLASSROOM PLAN

Activity SM behaviors are part of a classroom plan. A *classroom plan* outlines the identification, organization, and functioning of activities.[1]

The Identification of Classroom Activities

Activities are those classroom events in which students participate and which contribute to their instruction. For example, Figure 4.1 presents a list of activities for a typical first-grade classroom. Each activity involves students and contributes in some way to their instruction. Figure 4.1 identifies the activities and their overall organization. It does not indicate the organization of individual activities or how they function.

There are two types of classroom activities. *Regular activities*, like those in Figure 4.1, are events that the classroom regularly cycles through. *Special activities* are those events that occur when there is a sudden or uncommon change in conditions. Besides events such as fire drills, assemblies,

Figure 4.1
First-Grade Activities

1. Opening Activity	10. Penmanship
2. Teacher Reading Presentation	11. Spelling
3. Independent Reading Worksheet	12. Recess
4. Teacher Language Presentation	13. Art
5. Independent Language Worksheet	14. Music
6. Teacher Math Presentation	15. Lunch
7. Independent Math Worksheet	16. Media
8. Science/Social Studies	17. Computers
9. Physical Education	18. Closing Activity

and field trips, there are four critical special events required in all classrooms: getting help, getting a resource, projects for those who finish early, and stopping conflicts. These activities insure that students always have access to appropriate behavior. They are like an overlay to the regular activities, engaged in only when conditions arise. It is necessary to plan both types of activities to determine the full range of activity SM behaviors required for each.

The Organization of Activities

The organization of activities occurs on two levels. The organization, or arrangement, within an activity includes the available space, the arrangement of tables and desks, the grouping of students, and the materials needed to perform the task. Usually, students are grouped to work alone, in pairs, in triads, in small groups (four to six students), or in a large classroom group. This organization sets the boundaries of how students can function in a SM and an academic sense.[2]

Activities are also organized relative to one another. The arrangement of a day's regular activities and their time frames represents a *classroom procedure*. Because activities in art, music, media, computers, and physical education are not performed every day, there can be a number of different classroom procedures. The time frame for an activity is called the *activity duration*. The students must be able to perform the task and SM behaviors within this time frame.[3]

The Functioning of Activities

The *functioning of activities* refers to how students need to interact to complete an activity task. The interactions identified by the classroom plan are called activity SM behaviors. Determining activity organization (student grouping or physical arrangement) is the first step in planning activity SM behaviors. To plan activity SM behaviors so they can be quickly taught and reinforced requires a detailed procedure based on two different views of activity interactions. Both identify important activity SM behaviors.

The first view is time independent. It asks, at any moment how must the members of an activity interact? This includes the interactions involving the teacher and students, students and students, and individuals with themselves. The answer gives some very basic interaction requirements. For example, students need to listen to the teacher and each other, and to keep hands and feet to themselves in most cases; individuals may need to attend to their own work and keep working. Often we think of such SM behaviors as the rules of the classroom.

The second view is time dependent. As an activity unfolds, what must students do to begin, continue, or end an activity task? This view shows the jobs and/or procedures performed to complete a task. This view becomes very important when individuals and groups are working alone to complete a task. It is necessary to define what the individuals do. For example, in a group one student may be the supervisor, one may be the recorder of group input, one may be the data taker in a group experiment, or one may be the group materials gatherer. All of these jobs could be part of the step-by-step procedure required to complete an activity task.[4]

PROCEDURE TO PLAN ACTIVITY SELF-MANAGEMENT BEHAVIORS

Given the identification of activities and their organization, the procedure to determine activity SM behaviors requires four steps. Each one helps to further explicate what is required of students to perform successfully within an activity.[5]

Step 1: Determine the Major Activity Self-Management Behaviors

For each regular and special activity, simply walk through it, taking the role of the student, identifying each behavior that students need to perform. The aim is to give each behavior as descriptive a class name as possible. While walking through an activity ask the following questions:

1. How must members behave at any moment to maintain the organization of the activity?
2. How must each member behave to start, continue, or end an activity task?

These questions relate to the preceding analysis of activity functioning and the answers should state what students need to do to be successful.

Figure 4.2 presents the major activity SM behaviors for six activities. Some of these are from the activities of Figure 4.1 and others are more or less common to many elementary and secondary classrooms.

The teacher presentation activity is organized in the form of a standard teacher lecture with a large or small group of students at individual desks. Students must sit, look, and listen throughout the activity. The activity task behavior is a private event called learning. Except for putting work away, these SM behaviors could occur at any time during the activity. They are not part of a step-by-step procedure. The teacher would unfold what little procedure there is to this activity.

For the seatwork check activity in Figure 4.2, students could be seated at individual desks or at large tables. The teacher would be supervising the check. Eventually, a student could do it. Behavior three represents the

Figure 4.2
Examples of Activity Self-Management Behaviors

TEACHER PRESENTATION
1. Putting work away
2. Sitting in seat
3. Looking at teacher
4. Listening to others' answers
5. Accepting mistakes made by others
6. Accepting one's own mistakes
7. Raising hand to ask a question
8. Answering questions when asked

SEATWORK CHECK
1. Having checking pencil ready
2. Exchanging papers
3. Checking answers +
4. Returning work
5. Checking grade
6. Changing grade
7. Commenting positively about grades

FIRST-GRADE OPENING
1. Coming when asked
2. Making room for others
3. Sitting quietly
4. Acquiring knowledge
5. Listening to teacher and others
6. Answering questions when asked
7. Asking questions when needed
8. Accepting the teacher's comments
9. Returning to seat when asked

FIRST-GRADE LUNCH
1. Lining up
2. Walking in line
3. Waiting in line
4. Requesting food
5. Watching others' movements
6. Eating lunch
7. Handing food to others
8. Acknowledging requests
9. Disposing of lunch items
10. Exiting lunchroom

GAME
1. Gathering equipment +/–
2. Getting on the field
3. Deciding on positions +/–
4. Deciding on turns +/–
5. Playing the game
6. Accepting the mistakes of others
7. Accepting one's own mistakes
8. Cheering others on
9. Stopping when asked
10. Returning equipment +/–

GROUP COMPOSITION
1. Arranging themselves
2. Deciding on content +/–
3. Deciding on project tasks +/–
4. Performing individual tasks +/–
5. Organizing task products +/–
6. Editing project +/–
7. Deciding when project is finished +/–
8. Deciding how to present project +/–
9. Practicing presentation +
10. Presenting project +

activity task behavior. The six behaviors form a definite multistep procedure.

A first-grade classroom's opening activity could be organized in many
ways. In this case, students go to a carpeted area and are supervised by the
teacher, with the objective of identifying or predicting the day's classroom
plan, and practicing important SM behaviors. It is an excellent place to
teach SM skills. The behaviors form a simple procedure with three
through eight occurring at any time during the activity.

The physical education class game activity and the group composition
are highly interactive. The composition activity could be done in a small
group. The teacher may or may not perform many of the activity SM
behaviors. Playing the game is the task behavior for the physical education
activity and building a composition is the task behavior for the group
composition activity. The building of a composition occurs as a result of
behaviors two through eight.

Step 2: Determine the Need for Further Analysis

Following step one, many of the identified SM behaviors are still ambiguous. To identify these behaviors, walk through the activity, asking three
questions about each SM behavior.

1. Is it possible to represent the behavior by a simple set of examples and
   nonexamples?

If an instance of the class of behavior can be pointed out and performed in
a few seconds, even though it can occur over a long period of time, it is
simple. If this is the case, the answer to the question is yes and further
analysis is *not* required.

2. Can the SM behavior be performed in numerous ways?

This question focuses on those behaviors whose appropriateness depends
on the conventions of the classroom. If the behavior identified is one that
can be performed in many ways, further analysis is needed.

3. Is the SM behavior a complex, interactive event?

A complex, interactive event involves two or more students interacting on
a task. Each student must perform a set of behaviors that match other
students' behaviors. When only one person in a group performs a part of
the interactive event, such as organizing materials for a group, it is called a
job. These sets of behaviors or jobs must be analyzed into their behavioral
components (subclasses). If the answer to question three is yes, further
analysis is required.

Those activity SM behaviors in Figure 4.2 that may require further analysis have a " + " sign after them. A " + / − " sign means that the teacher could perform the behaviors and, thus, simplify the activity SM behaviors required of students.

All of the behaviors of the teacher presentation can be described through a simple set of examples and nonexamples. Therefore, no further analysis is required.

For the seatwork check activity, exchanging papers, checking answers, and changing grades are interactive events that could be performed in multiple ways. A convention, as procedure, must be established for each; therefore, further analysis is required.

The first-grade activity behavior, make room for others, is interactive, but the behavior does not require further analysis because it can be easily demonstrated through examples and nonexamples, and the possible variations are limited. There are not many ways to ask another to move over and not many ways to do it. Additionally, there is no need to strictly define what is appropriate asking and moving.

The first-grade lunch activity has a number of interactive behaviors and behaviors that can be performed in various ways. Because all can be demonstrated with simple examples and nonexamples, no further analysis is required.

For the game activity, the complex interaction SM behaviors could include one, three, four, and nine. Teachers can reduce the level of complexity by performing them or assuming a strong supervisory role. They could, for example, perform some of the more difficult behaviors such as making decisions about positions (3) and directing the taking of turns on the field (4). But if one desires to promote a life-style incorporating physical activity, these are the SM behaviors that need to be a part of the students' repertoires. The teacher needs to execute these behaviors only when students are starting to perform in these skill areas. Given that students do perform behaviors three, four, and nine, a further analysis is needed. Just how they are performed needs to be determined; they require conventions.

The group composition, as part of an upper elementary or secondary activity, contains many complex interactive behaviors. The teacher could perform these, but if students do, further analysis is required.

Step 3: Design the Behaviors Identified for Further Analysis

Once it is determined that further analysis is needed, walk through each identified *behavior*. During the walk, try to satisfy two requirements.

1. Each component behavior can be represented by a simple set of examples and nonexamples.
2. When all components are followed, the task would be completed.

Analyzing interactive SM behaviors requires multiple walks through the event. The behaviors of each group member must be determined. The goal is to design the behaviors that are congruent, or cooperative, with one another. There are two real difficulties here. First, many of the interactive SM behaviors intertwine with the task behavior. They become almost inseparable, with the task behavior becoming the content that the SM behaviors try to bring out. When planning is involved, with its decision-making and problem-solving components, this is always the case. Second, many of the SM behaviors have private components. They are thinking steps. These covert, or unseen, behavioral events should not be dealt with now. They are part of the domain of the SM system strategies. The goal at this point is to design SM behaviors for activities that can be taught through relatively simple examples and nonexamples. The design step is applied to two of the previous examples identified for further analysis.

Example: Checking Papers. Checking papers has to be performed in the same manner by all students. If it is not, students have a difficult time determining their success and the teacher is not able to check for problems nearly as fast. In this situation, the teacher reads off the answers. The SM question is, which behaviors are the students performing to check the worksheet? Here is a possible list of things that need to be performed.

1. X the wrong items to the right of the answer.
2. Leave the correct items alone.
3. Raise your hand if you fall behind.
4. Give items missed when called on.
5. When finished, count up the number wrong.
6. Mark the total wrong on the first page, top left.
7. Give number wrong when called on.

All of these behaviors can be demonstrated to students through simple verbal description and demonstration, thus meeting the first criterion of design. Additionally, following the list would lead to the desired result.

Many variations of steps one through seven are possible. For example, the way items are marked could be changed: items could be circled, or all items marked (the correct ones marked with a "C"). For another, totaling the number wrong might be done by the teacher. To insure success in moving through the activity SM behaviors, the teacher has to employ the SM supervision strategy.

Example: Deciding on Project Content. One of the behaviors composition students have to perform to effectively complete a group presentation is deciding on project content. Imagine the teacher restricting the decision to a topic concerning the history of technology, having already lectured on it and given the students several related articles to read. How are students to conduct themselves to arrive efficiently at a consensus that interests all group members? Given that the behavior is to be performed interactively, the following eight steps represent one possible design.

1. The students select a supervisor and secretary.
2. The supervisor directs the presentation.
3. The group gives suggestions without evaluation.
4. The secretary outlines group input.
5. The group evaluates suggestions without advocacy.
6. The supervisor summarizes the suggestions and evaluations with group members.
7. A decision vote is taken about content.
8. If no consensus is reached, the group meets later.

There are, again, many alternatives to these steps. For example, the teacher may select the supervisor and secretary for the group, and suggestions and evaluations may occur interactively. A more radical alternative would be to have students independently offer suggestions on paper with one of the members elected to summarize them. All are workable conventions. At this point, further analysis is not needed; each behavior can be described and demonstrated to students very simply. What is needed is a decision about which convention is to be used.

Step 4: Design for Commonality and Flexibility

From the start of planning, design your classroom so that there is some commonality across activities and flexibility within them. Activities have *commonality* when their SM behaviors are similar. It assists students in predicting what is required of them (Chapter 8). Activities have *flexibility* when students are given a clear, appropriate way to behave for any need that arises. Together, commonality and flexibility allow you and the students to focus on the content of instruction. As you review the SM behaviors again, it is helpful to ask:

1. Is there a common base of SM behaviors across all activities?
2. Is there a fair level of flexibility within all the regular activities?

Much of the flexibility in a set of regular classroom activities comes via the special activities that allow students to continue appropriate behavior. Because special activities are complex SM behaviors used across activities, it is especially important to design them for commonality. But commonality can also be a property of regular activities. For example, all teacher presentations and worksheet activities can have the same basic operation. If both commonality and flexibility are present, students can attend to the content of instruction and not the process of instruction.

In attempting to achieve commonality, the terms used as class names (Chapter 2) often cause a problem. Try for consistency in the use of SM class names across activities. Often, the array of SM behaviors initially found during steps 1 through 3 of the planning procedure can be greatly reduced (gain in commonality) if edited with a focus on using consistent class names.

Two examples are presented. The first concentrates on designing for commonality and the second for both commonality and flexibility.

Example: Organizing Project Task Products. Again, imagine composition students working on a group project. This time the group behavior is organizing project task products. They have individually or in small groups built the pieces of the project. The design question is, how do the students work together to organize them? Because organizing a task product can function similar to an interactive planning event, it can duplicate the deciding on project content format:

1. The students select a supervisor and a secretary.
2. The supervisor directs the presentation.
3. The group gives suggestions without evaluation.
4. The secretary outlines group input.
5. The group evaluates suggestions without advocacy.
6. The supervisor summarizes suggestions and evaluations with group members.
7. A decision vote is taken.
8. If no consensus is reached, the group meets later.

The SM behaviors are the same as those for deciding on project content. Only the academic content, the suggestions and the evaluation criteria, would be different. Additionally, the student supervisor can implement the supervising strategy. The SM behaviors (as procedure, process, or strategy) required to bring them out or have them applied would be essentially the same. This commonality of SM behavior makes it possible for the teacher to focus on the content and not on the procedure to arrive at the content. Once learned, the students are free to attend to the content. With the addition of SM system strategies such as planning, learning, and supervising, students further increase the probability of carrying out such tasks.

Example: Getting Help, Getting a Resource, and Finishing Early. These are three of the four special activities mentioned earlier that are important to every classroom. They occur within almost every regular activity. Their design is important because they make the environment flexible enough to accommodate the range of needs students have at any moment. Might they have a common design as well?

Imagine a classroom where every desk and table has a short pole, about 14 inches high and 2 inches in diameter, made of plastic or cardboard, that inserts into a flange taped to the desk. One end of the pole is green and the other is red. When a student or group has a need they turn up the red end of the pole and when they are moving along without a problem, the green end is up. Given this common background, the SM behaviors for the three special activities could look like Figure 4.3. With each activity, students begin and end by interacting with the pole. The only difference is the task behavior. The SM behaviors are almost identical. Moreover, the students are not acting impulsively. They have something to do and think about before they start to behave in ways that could disturb others.

By looking for commonality, the array of activity SM behaviors to teach and learn has been reduced. By insuring flexibility, students can operate as needed on their tasks. At this point you have been the designer, but once students learn the planning strategy presented in Chapter 16, they can undertake the design of activities. Your activities represent the models students use to begin planning. If your designs have commonality and flexibility, student designs will have them also.

RELATING INCLUSIVE AND ACTIVITY SELF-MANAGEMENT BEHAVIORS

By performing the four planning steps, a clear and very complete picture of your activity SM behaviors can be gained. But the picture does not relate to the SM strategy curriculum as outlined in Chapter 3. What do they have to do with the more inclusive SM system strategies? Although the students are not using the system strategies, they are at times clearly planning, organizing, supervising, and learning. To determine just which strategy classes the activity SM behaviors are members of, ask the following questions:

1. Are the students solving problems or making decisions about which element and element relationships are required to perform a task?

If the answer is yes, the SM behaviors can be described as planning.

Figure 4.3
Possible Self-Management Behaviors

Getting Help	Getting a Resource	Finishing Early
1. Turn up red pole	1. Turn up red pole	1. Take down pole
2. Work on other problems until help arrives	2. Get resource	2. Go to finished work area
3. Work with helper	3. Turn up green pole	3. Select an activity
4. Turn up green pole		4. Stop when directed
		5. Turn up green pole

2. Are the students moving or arranging themselves or objects needed to perform a task?

If the answer is yes, the SM behaviors can be described as organizing.

3. Are the students using texts to find an answer or make a decision?

If the answer is yes, the SM behaviors can be described as learning.

4. Are the students maintaining themselves on the task?

If the answer is yes, their SM behavior can be described as supervising. The difficulty with supervision is that there can be an element of it in all of the other strategy-related behaviors. Here are two descriptions that separate the confusion:

> Vetabeth, the way you kept the group giving and evaluating suggestions was effective supervision. It facilitated the planning of the project.
>
> Blue Group, the quickness with which you organized the materials indicates to me that you are really learning how to supervise yourselves.

In the first, the supervising refers to an element of how one member of the group supervised (kept up the giving of suggestions and their evaluation) in relation to the more inclusive set of SM behaviors of the group (planning project content). This supervising is not part of the activity level SM behavior; it is the explicit use of parts of the SM strategy. In the second example, group supervising is inferred, and the speed of the organizing by members was the evidence for it.

There are many cases where no element of planning or organizing is present. For example, most of the SM behaviors of the teacher presentation (except one) should be classified as supervisory. The same is true for the seatwork check, the first-grade opening activity, and lunch. These, as presented in Chapter 6, can be described as supervision.

> Raising your hands to ask questions is a great example of how you supervise yourselves so that you can complete your task.

In this instance, raising the hand has been classified as an examination of supervision behavior.

SUMMARY: PLANNING ACTIVITY SELF-MANAGEMENT BEHAVIORS

The procedures for determining activity SM behaviors and their relationship to the inclusive SM strategies are summarized to help with planning.

1. Determine the regular and special activities of the classroom.
2. Determine the major activity SM behaviors. Walk through each activity asking:
   a. How must students behave at any moment during the activity?
   b. How must students begin, continue, and finish their tasks?
3. Determine the need for further analysis. Ask three questions:
   a. Is it possible to represent the behavior by a simple set of examples and nonexamples?
   b. Can the SM behavior be performed in numerous ways?
   c. Is the SM behavior a complex, interactive event between students?

If the answer to the first is no or the answer to either of the last two is yes, further analysis is required.

4. Design the behaviors identified for further analysis. The design is sufficient if:
   a. Each component SM behavior can be represented by a simple set of examples and nonexamples.
   b. When all components were followed, the task would be completed.
5. Design the SM behaviors for commonality and flexibility. Consider:
   a. Is there a sameness of behaviors across activities? (Commonality)
   b. Can all student needs be met in all activities? (Flexibility)
6. Relate the activity SM behaviors with inclusive SM classes. Ask:
   a. Are the students solving problems or making decisions about what element and element relationships are required to perform a task? If yes, classify the behaviors as planning.
   b. Are the students moving or arranging themselves or objects needed to perform a task? If yes, classify the behaviors as organizing.
   c. Are the students using text sources to make a decision or solve a problem? If yes, classify the behaviors as learning.
   d. Are the students maintaining themselves on the task? If yes, classify the behaviors as supervising.

By following this procedure you can arrive at a clear picture of the activity SM behaviors required of your students.

5

PLANNING CLASSROOM REWARD CONSEQUENCES

Consequences select behavior—they increase or decrease its probability. If we are to reliably and consistently build strong classes of SM and academic behavior, it is necessary to have extensive knowledge of consequences. This chapter takes a first step in that direction by providing both a language with which to talk about consequences and procedures to plan and evolve reinforcing consequences within the classroom. When these procedures are put to use, you will see an immediate increase in the performance and positiveness of students and yourself.

THE ANALYSIS OF CONSEQUENCES

Consequences are changes, or effects, that follow behavior. The focus is on changes produced by students and teachers, not those changes that accidentally follow. This chapter examines reinforcing consequences. As stated in Chapter 1, such consequences function to increase the probability of a class of behavior they follow, and they should follow appropriate behavior. Chapter 11, Corrections, looks at consequences that correct or decrease the probability of inappropriate behavior.

To control the consequences that take place, it is necessary to look at consequences from eight different perspectives: relativity, range, reciprocity, direction, compatibility, evolution, placement, and schedule.[1] Each helps insure that the planned consequences influence behavior as desired.

The Relativity of Consequences

A consequence works differently on different people. For some it is reinforcing, for some it does nothing, and for some it is punishing. In other words, the probability of a consequence increasing or decreasing a class of behavior is relative to the individual it impacts.

In the classroom, the implications of relativity surface: do not expect the same reinforcers to work on everyone. For example, Verbina is reinforced by statements from Mrs. Gladden, her teacher. She positively glows. At the same time, Ronny pays no attention to them. But he will do anything for a chance to feed and care for the insect colony, of which Verbina wants no part.

The Range of Consequences

Reinforcing consequences are not limited to passing out M & Ms for correct responses and saying "Great work, Johnny." In fact, there is a whole array of changes that can impact the probability of behavior. We can conveniently, if not rigorously, group the range of consequences into these three categories:

Emotional consequences include the "wow" of doing a somersault or hitting a home run, the exhilaration of playing tennis or solving a problem, and the relaxation of reading a good novel or playing a board game with a group of friends. Because of such consequences, we tend to repeat the class of behavior. Emotional changes are usually short-lived.

Restructuring consequences alter or rearrange the environment. Such consequences take place because the environment is manipulated in some way. Varying the elements of a problem brings about a solution; going to and working at school are followed by a diploma; completing an assignment precedes the teacher's positive comment; and exercise produces bigger, stronger muscles. With the exception of exercise, nutritional, and surgical behavior, restructuring occurs outside the individual. Thus, the skin usually defines the boundary between emotional and restructuring consequences or changes.

Access consequences are events or activities that can be participated in because of our behavior. Such changes occur whenever students finish one task that allows them to start another. Hitting a home run allows a student to run around the bases and be congratulated by peers and spectators. Writing a poem allows one to read it and have it read by teachers and parents. Finishing the requirements for school allows one to attend graduation and possibly have access to different employment.

Emotional, restructuring, and access reinforcing consequences often occur close together, with each contributing to increasing the probability of behavior. For example, if Barney's teacher, Mr. Findley, pats him on the back and says, "You got number 6 correct. Why don't you show the class how you did it," a good case could be made for all three working in combination and occurring almost simultaneously.

The Reciprocity of Consequences

When people interact they can reinforce each other, and when they do so a *reciprocal reinforcing relationship* is established — the behavior of each party acts as a reinforcing consequence for the other parties. For example, when Cathy writes a poem, it reinforces her teacher, Mrs. Esparza, who has encouraged writing. The teacher's behavior changes and this change, which takes the form of more encouragement, reinforces Cathy's writing. The poem writing will increase, as will the encouragement. Notice that this positive interaction supports both behaviors into the future.

The reciprocity of consequences is not always reinforcing. Suppose that Mrs. Esparza sees the poem as not good enough. Her behavior still changes, but now it goes from encouragement to degrading remarks. The effect is a decrease in poem writing as well as encouragement. Notice that this negative (punishing) relationship can effectively stop both the poem writing and the encouragement. The culprit is the error of high standards for new, fledgling student behavior. Realistic standards of performance are required of teachers, peers, and parents.

The Direction of Consequences

Reciprocity implies that consequences have direction. A student's behavior can cause changes that affect the probability of the behavior of others. The poem writing affects the behavior of the teacher, the parents, and others. For the parents, the parenting behavior was reinforced. For the teacher, some teaching behaviors were reinforced. The major directions within the classroom are the student, peers, teachers, and parents.

The Compatibility of Consequences

Consequences are compatible when they contribute to changing behavior in the same direction. Compatible reinforcing consequences interact to increase the probability of the desired behavior. Imagine what would happen if Zelda, Gilda, Ronny, Jimmy, and Ms. Nguyen, their teacher, all reinforced working on assignments. All the different reinforcements would interact, or summate, to insure the performance of behavior. If reinforcing consequences are not compatible, the effectiveness of instruction is greatly diminished. The goal is to have everyone increase or decrease the same classes of SM and academic behavior.

The Evolution of Consequences

Over time, consequences become more or less reinforcing — they evolve. For example, Lena found access to reading first-grade books in the first grade reinforcing, and it increased the probability of her other behavior. But in the fifth grade she finds reading them a punishment. They are "boring" and "too easy." Similar to all of us, Lena's biological and social development not only means an evolution of behavior but also an evolution in the consequences which determine the probability of the behavior.

The Placement of Consequences

Consequence occurs at some point in time following behavior. Consequences placed or delivered fairly close in time with the behavior are called *immediate consequences*. For example, if Martha and Sidney help each other on their individual tasks, they can more quickly have access to their special projects. Those consequences that occur later are called *delayed consequences*. For example, Martha and Sidney may have to get 95 percent or better on Tuesday's spelling test to access extra project time on Friday. Because there are only so many chances to reinforce behavior in the classroom, the rule is to immediately reinforce new behaviors and delay reinforcers for firm behaviors.

The Schedule of Consequences

Consequences usually do not occur after every instance of behavior. Many instances are often required for a reinforcing event. For example, Sidney and Martha may have to finish all their assignments for the week to access Friday's extra project time. Many delayed consequences require the performance of multiple instances before the consequence occurs. Additionally, the schedule of consequences may be probabilistic; there may simply be a chance that the consequence follows the behavior at some point in time. In social situations, many examples are competitive, such as winning a game or joining a team.

PROCEDURE TO DETERMINE CONSEQUENCES

The procedure to determine the consequences of SM behavior (or academic behavior) follows from the preceding analysis. Its steps are interdependent. The modification of one step leads to changes in another. Six questions represent the procedure.

1. What is the self-management behavior of interest?

Simply start with an activity and select a SM behavior. You have to do this for all activities and their associated SM behaviors. The situation is manageable because there is a lot of redundancy. If you are going to supplement consequences, you should first decide on the contingent SM behavior.

2. Who are the possible recipients of changes brought about by this SM behavior?

As stated, the direction of student consequences includes not only the student but also peers, siblings, teacher, parents, and community. The latter are not present but they can easily be referenced in your descriptive statements to students (Chapter 6).

3. Which changes could be brought about for each recipient because of the SM behavior?

They can be emotional, restructuring, or access to events. Remember, all types are woven together to provide the strength needed to change behavior. Find something related to all types.

4. Which reciprocal changes could be brought about because of the SM behavior?

From the answers to question three, there are changes in the recipients of the SM behavior. They may smile, thank the student, or be able to continue their work. Additionally, the supplemental consequences discussed below are considered at this point.

5. Are the changes brought about reinforcing to the various recipients?

This will be a guess about the relativity of consequences. If a positive guess cannot be made, change the consequence. The immediate consequences of SM behavior are usually positive because the SM behavior facilitates other behavior. Assessing additional consequences becomes more difficult. The supplemental procedures help you control relativity.

6. When will these consequences take place?

Will they be immediate or delayed? As stated, the general rule is to provide immediate consequences for new behavior and delayed consequences for firm behavior.

When these six questions are repeatedly asked and answered, a list of consequences emerge for all parties involved. Table 5.1 illustrates a range of immediate consequences for the student, peers, and teacher for three activity SM behaviors analyzed in Chapter 4.

For raising the hand to ask a question during a teacher presentation, the student has better access to getting an answer (1) and increases the probability of continuing to gain knowledge from the presentation (2). Blurting out the question may get it asked faster, but there is no guarantee of an answer, especially if the teacher is managing effectively. If the student

Table 5.1
Immediate Consequences for Three Activity Self-Management Behaviors

DIRECTION OF CONSEQUENCE	BEHAVIORS		
	RAISING THE HAND (Teacher Presentation)	EXCHANGING PAPERS (Seatwork Check)	SELECTING SUPERVISOR (Group Project)
THE STUDENT	1. Getting the answer [A] 2. Gaining knowledge [R] 3. Interacting with others [A] 4. Enjoying the presentation [E] 5. Starting the next activity [A]	1. Getting one's paper corrected [R] 2. Beginning the checking [A] 3. Giving the grade to the teacher [A] 4. Getting the corrected paper [A] 5. Finding out the score [R] 6. Enjoying the score [E] 7. Interacting positively with others [A] 8. Starting the next activity [A]	1. Organizing the group [R] 2. Gaining knowledge [R] 3. Enjoying the structure and knowledge created [E] 4. Starting the next element of the project [A]
OTHER STUDENTS	6. Continuing the presentation [A] 7. Gaining knowledge [R] 8. Enjoying the presentation [E] 9. Starting the next activity [A]	9. Getting a paper to correct [A] 10. Getting one's paper corrected [R] 11. Beginning the checking [A] 12. Giving the grade to the teacher [A] 13. Getting the corrected paper [A] 14. Finding out the score [R] 15. Enjoying the score [E] 16. Interacting positively with others [A] 17. Starting the next activity [A]	5. Receiving knowledge [A] 6. Gaining knowledge [R] 7. Enjoying the presentation [E] 8. Enjoying knowledge [E] 9. Starting the next element of the project [A]
THE TEACHER	10. Managing students [A] 11. Continuing the instruction [A] 12. Changing student knowledge [R] 13. Enjoying the instruction [E] 14. Starting the next activity [A]	18. Managing the activity [A] 19. Continuing the instruction [A] 20. Changing student knowledge [R] 21. Enjoying the instruction [E] 22. Starting the next activity [A]	10. Managing the activity [A] 11. Continuing the instruction [A] 12. Changing student knowledge [R] 13. Enjoying student change [E] 14. Enjoying the instruction [E] 15. Starting the next activity [A]

[A] = Access Consequence   [R] = Restructuring Consequence   [E] = Emotional Consequence

consistently followed the procedure to ask a question, there would be a greater chance of acceptance by other students (3). This access consequence is reciprocal. The emotional outcome (4) is most likely to be positive. Starting of the next activity is the most distant immediate consequence (5).

Raising the hand to ask a question has an effect on others. The effects for other students are not so different from that for the student. Additionally, there is significant impact on the teacher when a student manages appropriately. The teacher has two tasks: the management and teaching of students. Both of these are facilitated in the sense of being made easier; there is just less to do—less correcting of inappropriate management behavior and more time for delivering instruction.

The second SM behavior in Table 5.1, exchanging papers during the seatwork check, has a number of immediate consequences. For the student, exchanging papers results in a series of immediate access consequences that involve other behaviors of the seatwork check (2–4). The others are restructuring, emotional, and access consequences similar to those for raising the hand to ask a question. For other students and the teacher, the immediate consequences run parallel to those of raising the hand to ask questions according to procedure.

The third SM behavior, selecting a group supervisor, has the same immediate consequences for each group member. The other students section refers to consequences for different groups within the classroom. If the students selecting a supervisor proceed appropriately, the teacher can attend to the other groups in the classroom. Thus, the other groups are able to receive their share of instruction (5), gain knowledge (6), and enjoy instruction and knowledge (7, 8). The immediate consequences are the same for the teacher as for the other SM behaviors.

SUPPLEMENTING IMMEDIATE CONSEQUENCES

You want to insure that classroom consequences are positive to all and strong enough to insure the performance of SM and academic behavior. But just knowing your immediate consequences is not enough. To evolve consequences, to control the diversity of relativity, to make them compatible and positive, you must supplement. *Supplementing* reinforcing consequences involves publicizing, expanding, and linking them.

Publicize

Most teachers admit that they did not see the extent or range of consequences before performing the preceding analysis on their classrooms. Therefore, students cannot be expected to see them either. They, like all of us, need some guidance. In other words, teachers need to *publicize* consequences, make them known in some way.

Reinforcing consequences are made public by using statement and question procedures as discussed in Chapters 6 through 8. By combining these with recognition reinforcers, the store of available consequences increases. The letter to parents, the certificate, the button, the ribbon, the mark on a chart, or the note from the principal are all forms of recognition. When you put a little ceremony around it, a recognition activity exists that publicizes. All of these are presented contingent on the consistent performance of SM or academic behavior.

Expand

Recognition reinforcers are also a first step in expanding the reinforcers available in the classroom. Additional expansion can be given by providing access to reinforcing activities contingent on behavior. These include individual and group activities like classroom messenger, feeding classroom animals, working on a special project, or games. Classroom management texts present numerous lists of reinforcing activities.[2] This text advocates access to classroom management activities relative to the SM curriculum. Chapter 16 shows how students can plan such reinforcing activities. Chapter 19 illustrates classroom and school level planning and management activities.

Link

Linking procedures help insure that the consequences are compatible, control relativity, and build new reinforcers. Within the SM curriculum and teaching procedures, there are two basic forms of linking.[3] The first, *verbal linking,* involves pointing out or asking the students to point out the range or relationship of consequences within and across activities. The central goal of verbal linking is to evolve students so the task and self-management behaviors are immediately reinforcing in and of themselves, or intrinsically reinforcing as some would say.[4] Chapters 6, 7, and 8 illustrate how to construct statements and questions within activities. Chapter 19 illustrates how to do it across activities.

The second procedure, *student-based planning,* has students participate in the design, decision making, and problem solving that take place within the classroom. They have a say, for example, in the form and content of activities, and the consequences that result. Because all students have participated in the planning and committed themselves to it, the problem of the teacher managing the evolution, reciprocity, and relativity of consequences is reduced. Chapter 16 illustrates how to teach and carry out student-based planning. Chapter 15 provides support by showing how to teach students to supervise the planning.

SUMMARY: PLANNING CLASSROOM REWARD CONSEQUENCES

This section outlines a planning procedure to help you determine the reinforcing consequences for your classroom. It refers you to many other chapters. When the procedures of these chapters are known, you will be able to complete your plan.

1. Determine immediate classroom consequences. Ask the following questions.
   a. What is the SM or task behavior of interest?
   b. Who are the possible recipients of changes brought about by the SM or task behavior?
   c. What changes could be brought about for each recipient because of the SM or task behavior?
   d. What reciprocal changes could be brought about by SM or task behavior?
   e. Are the changes brought about reinforcing to the various recipients?
   f. When will the consequences occur?

2. Design how reinforcing consequences will be supplemented. Consider:
   a. Publicizing all available reinforcers. Make immediate and all other consequences known (see Chapters 6, 7, and 8).
   b. Expand the available consequences. Consider:
      1. Adding extra activities that are reinforcing.
      2. Adding student-based planning of consequences (see Chapters 16 and 19).
   c. Link the consequences occurring in the classroom. Consider:
      1. Using verbal linking procedures.
      2. Adding student-based planning of all activities (see Chapters 16 and 19).
   d. Evaluate your design. Ask:
      1. Are these reinforcers for the students?
      2. Are the reinforcers adequate to evolve SM behavior?

3. Design your implementation according to the procedures in Chapters 6 through 11, 16, and 19.

4. Check reinforcing consequence procedures to see that they are compatible with correction consequence procedures in Chapters 11 and 18.

Remember, you will evolve your consequences when you move from teacher-based to student-based planning and management.

II

Self-Management Teaching Procedures

Teaching SM behaviors, activity and strategy alike, involves the use of five basic teaching skills: statements, questions, example sets, postings, and correcting mistakes. Each of these contributes to teaching the discriminations, operations, and strategies of the SM curriculum. Chapters 6 through 11 analyze and give examples of each of the skills. To bring them into perspective, Chapter 12 presents a language to talk about the evolution of behavior and the procedures of teaching based on the five skills. This language is another skill—one for communicating with other professionals during the building and diagnosis of instruction.

6

STATEMENTS

Your statements help students begin, continue, and end the tasks that confront them. Yet, statements have been left largely unanalyzed. This chapter provides that analysis. It details statement function, types, components, and a procedure to design them for classroom use. Once designed, statements can be implemented using the skills presented in Chapter 8. During implementation, an appreciation of this chapter's work develops — a positive, warm climate pervades the classroom because students know where they have been, where they are, and where they are going. Your talk is second nature and all it needs is a little polish, some clear direction.

THE TYPES AND FUNCTIONS OF STATEMENTS

Statements perform a number of vital functions, each of which is related to the principles of behavior and technology presented in Chapter 1. The three types of statements are condition, reward, and combination.[1] Table 6.1 illustrates the relationship between the statements and five principles of behavior and technology. By combining the principles related to each type of statement, their functional definitions emerge.

Condition statements precede and set the occasion for the desired behavior. Reward statements follow condition-matching behavior and increase the probability of the behavior occurring during matching conditions. Combination statements function as both condition and reward statements. The function of each type of statement includes both principles of behavior and technology.

But the picture is not complete. Statements operate over time to perform these functions, and thus form contingent relationships with the behavior. They interact with the ongoing stream of student behavior to

Table 6.1
The Functions of Descriptive Statements

	TYPES OF STATEMENTS		
PRINCIPLES	CONDITION	REWARD	COMBINATION
1. Conditions set the occasion for the desired behavior. (Technology)	Yes	No	Yes
2. Conditions set the occasion for the behavior they precede. (Behavior)	Yes	No	Yes
3. Rewards follow condition matching behavior. (Technology)	No	Yes	Yes
4. Rewards increase the future probability of the behavior they follow. (Behavior)	No	Yes	Yes
5. Rewards increase the future probability that conditions will set the occasion for behavior. (Behavior)	No	Yes	Yes

insure that it remains adaptive or adapts to a change in the conditions of the classroom. The examples in this chapter and Chapter 8 illustrate this interaction.

THE COMPONENTS OF DESCRIPTIVE STATEMENTS

To function as they do, condition, reward, and combination statements are composed of one or more of four components.[2]

The Description of Behavior Component

Almost all teacher statements describe student behavior—what someone has done (past), is doing (present), or is about to do (future). This talk about behavior can reference instances, classes, or their relationships. When talking about instances and classes, the description can be about single or multiple behaviors. When relationships are described, multiple behaviors are always referenced.

Describing Single Behaviors. The following examples illustrate describing a single behavior. The behavior is in CAPITALS.

Hober, please TAKE YOUR TURN TO READ when I ask.

Vernice, SHARING YOUR ART SUPPLIES has helped others finish their projects.

Lamont, I am going to have to call you an ERRORLESS READER. Not one error this week!

Volum, thank you for SUPERVISING THE GROUP.

The first example is about a future instance of behavior. The others are about past behavior. The description of Lamont as an errorless reader, although a little unnatural to our adult ears, has clear referents, and would bring a beam-wide smile to Lamont. The last example is descriptive only if the student has learned on previous occasions what supervision entails (See the subsequent section and Chapter 8).

The following statements DO NOT describe behavior; they are nonexamples:

Mandel, you are a TREMENDOUS WORKER.

Fire Engines, that was a GREAT READING SESSION.

Technically, "tremendous worker" could be a clearly defined class name. But if it is not defined over time, as is usually the case, the description is really an expression of teacher approval, as is the second nonexample. Words such as tremendous, great, good, excellent, fantastic, wonderful, and so forth are not descriptions of behavior.

Describing Multiple Behaviors. The description of multiple behaviors brings out the relationships among behaviors. Chapter 2 outlined two types of relationships important to describing multiple behaviors: hierarchical and historical.

1. *Hierarchical descriptions.* Statements containing hierarchical descriptions of behavior describe inclusive and mutually exclusive relationships.

Star, by KEEPING AT YOUR TASK you have shown me a fine example of SUPERVISING yourself.

Essie, I appreciate that you SHARE YOUR ART SUPPLIES and HELP OTHERS ON THEIR PROJECTS.

In the first example, "keeping at a task" is an instance of the inclusive class of supervising. The second example describes instances of two mutually exclusive classes: sharing and helping. The elements of "art supplies" and "on their projects" help to make the descriptions clear.

2. *Historical descriptions.* Chapter 2 outlined two types of historical descriptions: performance and procedural. Examples of each are given.

Marvel, PLANNING THE DETAILS OF YOUR PROJECT assisted you in FINISHING IT BEFORE THE DEADLINE.

Woody, your CORRECT PREDICTION ABOUT THE TOOLS NEEDED has made it possible for you to WORK WITHOUT INTERRUPTION.

These two examples illustrate performance relationships. The first points out the dependence between self-management behavior (planning) and academic/technical behavior (Marvel's project). The term *assisted* denotes the strength of the relationship between the behaviors. The second example does the same thing but focuses on "predicting" and "working without interruption," with the first "making it possible" for the second.

The procedural dependency establishes a link between classes of behavior. The SM system strategies are good examples, as are many academic behaviors.

> Tina, remember to IDENTIFY, DESIGN, and SELECT before you begin, and EVALUATE when you are finished.

> Tina, remember to PLAN by IDENTIFYING, DESIGNING, and SELECTING before you begin, and EVALUATE when finished.

The procedural steps (in capitals) are component behaviors to the planning SM strategy. The statement to Tina arranges them in their order of occurrence to each other and the task (implied from prior interaction). If the teacher references planning, the statement would be a mix of performance and procedural description, as is the second example. These two examples assume that prior instruction on planning has occurred. Later, the teacher may only have to remind Tina and others to plan. Statements get shorter after inclusive classes of behaviors have been taught.

Hierarchical and historical descriptions give students a broad picture of their behavior. Inclusive hierarchical descriptions provide a vertical picture—students see how their behavior is a part of a larger class. Mutually exclusive hierarchical descriptions give a horizontal picture—students see the parts of behavior required to perform a task. Historical descriptions present students with a sequential picture—students see how their behaviors are linked over time.

The Description of Behavior-Change-Over-Time Component

All behavior evolves. It is important to show students how they are evolving. The change-over-time component provides students with a close-up picture of this evolution, or change. Most behavior-changes-over-time can be categorized into one of two forms: (1) How often it has been performed and (2) where it has been performed. The first references the rate at which instances of a class have occurred. The second focuses on changes in the location where behavior has been performed. Usually, we want behavior to transfer from the classroom to everyday life situations.

How Often Behavior Has Been Performed. Usually, the reference to how often the behavior has been performed focuses on: (1) the first time, (2) the

Xth time, (3) the Xth time in a row, or (4) the continued (maintained) performance. Each of these denotes the occurrence of instances. The next four examples respectively illustrate such referencing. The change-over-time is denoted in CAPITALS.

> Marlowe, that is the FIRST TIME you have helped Sharon without my asking you. Thank you.
>
> Marlowe, I appreciate your CONTINUING to help Sharon without being asked.
>
> Stacy, you have successfully completed your experiments FOUR OUT OF FIVE TIMES this grading period.
>
> Thank you, everyone. You have assisted me EVERY DAY THIS WEEK.

The first example referenced Marlowe's first instance of helping without being asked. The second example shows what form a future statement may take if the behavior maintained itself. The third and fourth examples are simply other possible variations.

These forms of behavior-change-over-time can be mixed together to provide greater description in referencing change.

> Thank you everyone. You have cooperated EVERY DAY THIS WEEK and this is the FIRST WEEK that has happened. Enjoy your weekend.

The Xth time in a row and the first time have been combined to accurately reference changes in behavior. The other forms could also be mixed.

Where Behavior Has Been Performed. SM behaviors are performed in a number of locations. The following are examples of statements describing changes in location.

> Betrice, you can now successfully supervise YOURSELF AND A GROUP. That is the kind of big change I like.
>
> Willie, thanks for doing your homework. YOU HAVE ALWAYS COMPLETED THE WORK IN CLASS AND NOW YOU ARE DOING IT AT HOME AS WELL.

Many students can manage themselves on individual tasks but in a group they do not do as well, or vice versa. Betrice has made the advance from individual to group supervision. The second example describes a location apart from school.

The Description of Consequences Component

This component references the consequences of student behavior. The three types of consequences (emotional, restructuring, and access) and their direction (individual and others) play an important part in the construction of this component. By exposing these consequences, you increase the probability of the student behavior that brought them about.

Consequences for the Individual. The following three examples illustrate the description of consequences aimed at the student who produced them. The consequences are in CAPITALS.

Ronda, this plan has clear steps. You should FEEL GOOD about it.

A good feeling could be the emotional consequence that follows seeing a clearly laid out plan. If it is not for Ronda, the teacher's attention, via the statement, should bring about the feeling. By associating the good feeling with the plan, planning behavior eventually produces the same feelings. Some would say that planning becomes intrinsically reinforcing.

Stacy, successfully completing your last experiment gives you that GRADE OF A you have been working for.

The "grade of A," a restructuring consequence, was not completely gained by the single experiment but it was a necessary element in the causal sequence leading to it.

This group has organized so quickly that I know you will have time to WORK ON YOUR SPECIAL PROJECTS.

Working on a special project is an access consequence for each individual in the group. The relationship between the two behaviors, organizing and working on a special project, is historical. It was examined in the section on the description of behaviors. Thus, when you reference a historical relationship between behaviors, one of those behaviors functions as a consequence for the other.

Consequences for Others. The impact of behavior goes beyond the individual performing it. Others are affected, also. Statements by teachers can describe these consequences. Again, the consequence is in CAPITALS.

Marlowe, helping Sharon made it possible for her to FINISH HER ASSIGNMENT on time.

Marlowe, your helping Sharon has ALLOWED ME TO WORK WITH OTHER STUDENTS on their math assignments.

Marlowe, your helping Sharon has allowed HER TO FINISH and gave ME TIME TO WORK WITH OTHERS. I ENJOY such work, as you should.

The first statement points out how Marlowe's helping with the assignment made it possible for Sharon to finish on time. The second statement focuses on a consequence for the teacher. And the third statement describes multiple directions and uses the tactic of associating attention by the teacher with the emotional consequence such helping should produce. These statements only suggest the variety that is possible. By planning consequences as outlined in Chapter 5, you can widen the array described in your statements.

The Setting Component

The fourth and final component sets the occasion for appropriate behavior, and thus, it is called the setting component. Much of instruction focuses on setting the occasion for behavior. Chapters 9 and 10 deal with the instructional side of setting the occasion. For the present, the concern is for setting the occasion in the sense of pushing the behavior off the starting block. In the classroom, it takes the form of a bell, a particular time or place, or what the teacher says. Sometimes it is as simple as saying, "Please start." More effective and descriptive ways to get behavior moving involve (1) establishing a commitment to the desired task, and/or (2) giving support for what they are about to do. The following examples illustrate two methods of establishing commitment and giving support: open and modeled challenges.

Open Challenges. For the open challenge, the teacher asks students if they can perform the task assigned. If the students agree that they can, they have committed themselves to trying. The following examples illustrate the open challenge with and without overt teacher support. The setting component is in CAPITALS. The symbols (SR) stand for student replies or students reply, whichever is appropriate.

Sharing materials during such a difficult task is not easy, but WHO CAN DO IT? (SR)

Sharing materials is not always easy. But WHO THINKS THEY CAN DO IT? (SR) I SUPPORT YOUR TRYING AND WILL HELP WHERE I CAN.

Zilon, by organizing the task you can do it very fast. I THINK YOU CAN DO THE ORGANIZING. WILL YOU GIVE IT A TRY? (SR)

The first example is unembellished. The second adds teacher support. The third example first supports the student's behavior and then asks for a commitment. Following Zilon's reply, the teacher could simply nod an acknowledgment or give Zilon a pat on the back. In any case, the student is ready to work and has knowledge of one consequence for doing so.

Modeled Challenges. Modeled challenges indicate what has been done and ask students if they can do the same thing. Such challenges are designed to indicate appropriate behavior, not to promote competition. The following examples illustrate:

Everyone, THE FIRST CLASS followed the rules for the whole period. CAN YOU DO IT TOO? (SR) GREAT! GO TO IT.

Harry, YOU completed your problems yesterday. WILL YOU DO IT TO-DAY? (SR) I KNOW YOU WILL.

The first statement uses another class as a model and the second uses the student's past behavior as the model. In both examples, the description of behavior is embedded in the modeled component of the challenge.

THE DESIGN OF STATEMENTS

With the four components, you can compose all three types of statements. Table 6.2 outlines statement composition. The following examples illustrate complete and partial statements. For each example the statement components are emphasized as follows: the descriptions of behavior, CAPITALS; the consequences, **bold**; the setting, *italics*; and the changes over time, ***bold italics***.

Complete Descriptive Statements

The following examples illustrate three types of complete statements:
Condition Statements. Condition statements precede behavior. Thus, they describe desired behavior and possible consequences, along with a setting component.

Rushan, *can you* ASSIST NAHSUR IN PAINTING THE SCENERY FOR THE PLAY? (SR) That will **help make it possible for us to be on time.**

Table 6.2
The Composition of Statements

COMPONENTS	TYPES OF STATEMENTS		
	CONDITION	REWARD	COMBINATION
DESCRIPTION OF BEHAVIOR	Desired Behavior	Performed Behavior	Performed & Desired Behavior
DESCRIPTION OF CHANGE OVER TIME	No	Yes	Yes
DESCRIPTION OF CONSEQUENCES	Possible Consequences	Possible & Gained Consequences	Possible & Gained Consequences
SETTING COMPONENT	Yes	No	Yes

The first sentence combines a setting component in the form of a commitment request and a description of a SM behavior, assisting. Notice that the described behavior is only one of numerous behaviors required to achieve the consequence.

I would like each group to SHARE THE DISSECTING KITS. *Will you do it? (SR) I know you can,* and **I will be very delighted to see it.**

The students commit to "sharing the dissecting kits" and the consequence is an expected emotional change.

Reward Statements. Reward statements follow an instance of behavior and thus describe past behavior, along with a description of consequences and change over time.

Ford, **thank you** for SHOWING THE NEW STUDENT AROUND THE CLASSROOM. Your *continued* HELP **makes it possible for me to finish my tasks.**

"Showing the new student around" describes an instance of behavior that is a member of the helping SM behavior class. Therefore, a hierarchical relationship has been referenced. There are two consequences, and "continued" indicates that the student has maintained the behavior over time, an example (instance) of which is showing a new student around.

Everyone, you should **feel terrific** because each of you has **completed your assignment on time.** Using your new GROUP PLANNING STRATEGY made it possible *for the first time.*

Performing a group planning strategy brought about two consequences. The change-over-time points out that it was the first time the behavior was performed by all the group.

Kamond, *from your first day,* you have FOLLOWED THE CLASSROOM RULES. That should be something **your parents would be happy to hear.**

This time the statement begins with a change-over-time component. The clarity of the behavioral description depends on the history related to defining the rules.

Combination Statements. The combination statement follows a behavior and then asks for it again. While asking to have it done again, the teacher can request some change in behavior. In doing this, all four elements of descriptive statements often come together. When they do, it is a complete combination statement.

Everyone, *yesterday was the first time* that the DISSECTING KITS WERE SHARED BY EVERYONE. *Can you do it again today?* (SR) *That is the spirit.* It will **help you finish early like yesterday.**

The start of the statement rewards the students for past sharing behavior and then asks them to commit to doing it again. Following the students' reply, the teacher adds a note of support which completes the setting component. The statement ends with a consequence describing a performance-dependent academic behavior. It could also be seen as emphasizing that time will be left for other activities.

Dinah, *three days this week* you have MODELED THE BEHAVIOR ASKED FOR IN THE RULES. *Can you do it four out of five?* (SR) *I knew you would say that.* **It should make you feel great** to end the week this way.

Again, the past self-management behavior is described and asked for again. This time the setting component has an embedded change-over-time component. The statement ends with a consequence related to a change in the student's emotional state.

Partial Descriptive Statements

Complete statements, at times, interfere with ongoing instruction or task behavior. The partial statement is the answer to this problem. The component to emphasize is the description of behavior. In the following examples partial condition (CS), reward (RS), and combination statements (CBS) are juxtaposed to help clarify their use over time.

(CS) Please share the paints and brushes.

(RS) Thank you for sharing.

(CBS) Can you continue to share like you did yesterday?

The students know what to do (CS) and what they have done (RS), with the combination statement (CBS) combining these. All are fast and all allow the flow of the classroom activity to continue uninterrupted.

(CS) Nat, can you follow the list of tasks for today?

(RS) Nat, I appreciate your following the list of tasks.

(CBS) Nat, you followed the first five tasks. Can you do it for the last six?

The list of tasks represents multiple behaviors that the teacher has previously identified for the student.

These examples of complete and partial statements give only a brief, limited picture of what statements look and sound like. Chapter 8 illustrates the ways in which such statements are delivered.

PLANNING DESCRIPTIVE STATEMENTS

Before entering the classroom and using descriptive statements as presented in this chapter, it is necessary to plan them the same way you plan an instructional lesson. Often the form of what is said does not exactly follow what was planned, but it functions appropriately to set the occasion or reinforce student behavior. The following planning procedure will help build statements for the classroom.

1. Identify one of your classroom activities (see Chapter 4). This provides a set of SM and task behaviors and a context.
2. Select one of the behaviors and its consequences.
3. Select a student or group within the identified activity as the focus of the statement.
4. Build a complete condition statement. Include:
   a. A reference to the student or group selected.
   b. The identified behavior (SM or task).
   c. One of the consequences.
   d. A request for a commitment, with support for performance. For the commitment, consider:
      1. an open challenge, or
      2. the modeled challenge.
   e. Word the statement so it is in the future tense.
5. Build a complete reward statement. Working from the condition statement, do the following:
   a. Drop the commitment and support for performance.
   b. Add how the behavior could change over time.
   c. Change the tense of the statement to reflect that the behavior has been performed.
6. Build a complete combination statement. Working from the reward statement, do the following:
   a. Add a commitment and support (setting) component that requests the performed SM behavior again.
   b. Add a change-over-time component.
   c. Word the statement to reflect the performance of past behavior and a request for future behavior.
7. Set out all three statements, side-by-side, and edit for brevity and consistency.
8. Build a partial statement for each statement. Consider the following:
   a. Focus on the description of behavior for the condition and reward statements unless implied by context.

     b. Focus on the description of behavior and request it again for the combination statement.

9. Repeat steps 1 through 8 for each activity and several of its SM behaviors. Consider:
   a. Building a few statements each day.
   b. Building with other professionals to keep variety in your statements and fun in the activity.
   c. How much faster you build statements after about a week.
   d. How natural the statements start to sound after about a week.

By following this procedure, you can build statements that apply to some or all of your classroom activities. What remains is the practicing of statements according to rules of effectiveness presented in Chapter 8.

7

QUESTIONS

To operate independently and adaptively on and with the environment, students must be taught to look ahead, to reason about, and to plan their futures. In combination with statements, questions make it possible to teach the inductive thinking behavior that assists them in doing so. This chapter illustrates how questions function, analyzes inductive behavior, and presents a question-based procedure for teaching students inductive thinking. The examples of this chapter are limited to inductive thinking needed by students to manage themselves within a classroom plan. Chapters 13 through 19 expand such behavior into the SM system strategies.

THE FUNCTION OF QUESTIONS

In the most inclusive sense, questions function to set the occasion for behavior and, thus, precede it (Chapter 1).[1] Because a self-manager (as speaker) and task performer (as listener) often live within the same skin or group, an individual or group can set the occasion for a vast range of their own behavior.[2] But they must be taught how to do so.

Questions can set the occasion for two inclusive types of behavior: *remembering* and *reasoning* about the discriminations, operations, or procedures that can be identified or performed. Reasoning divides into two inclusive procedures: *deductive* and *inductive*. SM behavior is concerned with inductive behavior which has a remembering behavior component.

INDUCTIVE BEHAVIOR

As a procedure, inductive behavior has five components.[3] They include:

(1) --------> (2) -------> (3) --------> (4) ---------> (5)

Presenting	Making	Observing	Presenting	Making
Supporting	Prediction	Changes	Confirming	Confirmation
Evidence	Statement		Evidence	Statement

Two *inductive arguments* represent the heart of the inductive procedure. Steps one (1) and two (2) function as the premise and conclusion to the *prediction argument*. Steps four (4) and five (5) function in the same way for the *confirmation argument*.

The first argument necessitates the second because predictions would never improve without confirmation. Working without the latter would be like trying to improve one's tennis stroke without ever seeing how the ball moved through space or where it landed. Your strokes (as predictions) would never improve. In this case, we know the tennis stroke was correct (confirmed) by observing how the ball traveled and where it landed (evidence). The confirmation statement springs from the direct relationship between the prediction, the observed changes, and the confirming evidence.

In complex learning situations, such as experiments, the prediction (often called the hypothesis) is only supported by the observations; moving to statement of confirming evidence (often called the results) is not direct. There may, for example, be conflicting evidence. As a result, the confirmation statements (as conclusions) are liable to be inductively weak.

Every one of the SM system strategies depends on inductive behavior. Planning, for example, first builds a plan (prediction argument) and then evaluates it (confirmation argument). The conclusions to the confirmation argument can, in turn, be used as supporting evidence in modifying the plan (another prediction argument). To teach inductive behavior and reinforce its use, however, we begin at a less sophisticated level.

TEACHING INDUCTIVE BEHAVIOR

When to Teach

We begin to teach students the inductive process during their first days in school. Why? Because from this point on students have to behave inductively to be successful. They must, for example, predict and confirm what will happen next and how they will have to behave managerially and academically. This inductive behavior often appears trivial and goes unnoticed. And perhaps it should be when compared to the inductive behavior of the physical and social scientists with their complex labyrinth of theory and evidence. But our students are not yet scientists, and their fledgling behavior, as the same process, needs instruction to make it precise and automatic. With this foundation they can be taught to make inductive leaps when planning their futures and learning about their world.

What to Teach

The specific content of initial inductive behavior is represented by the elements of the classroom plan (Chapter 4). For any activity, this includes the answers to: (1) Which task do I do? (2) Which materials do I need? (3) When does it start and stop? (4) With whom do I work? (5) Where is it performed? (6) Why do I do the task? (What are the consequences?) (7) How do I do the task? (8) How do I self-manage?

Given the range of classroom activities, the array of learning tasks, the variety of SM behaviors required, the types and direction of consequences, and the changes in classroom plans that occur from day to day and year to year, students need to make an almost infinite number of inductions. Of course, we could limit ourselves to reinforcing appropriate behavior for each in a specific classroom, but it seems more fitting to provide them with an adaptive boost for controlling their futures.

How to Teach

The element that makes teaching inductive behavior possible and relatively easy is a consistent, stable environment. In an environment that has no clear plan, inductive behavior becomes more complex and, thus, much more difficult to teach. By constructing your classroom and instructional procedures as illustrated in this text, you avoid such pitfalls.

In teaching inductive behavior, the goal is to overtize it, to bring the procedure into their verbal world so they can learn it and manage their behavior with it. Eventually, for the individual much of it becomes covert; but to teach it, overtization is required.

Teaching the inductive procedure has four steps: modeling, prompting, testing, and reinforcing statements. The following sections outline the structure and function of the procedure and provide examples. The examples used from step to step are related, so it is helpful to reread them to see the flow of moving through the steps as opposed to seeing a range of applications within a step. Remember that the students have had a history of descriptive statements. The students' replies, simply indicated by SR, have been left out so that you can focus on the procedure. Assume that the replies are appropriate. Chapter 11 covers the correction of inappropriate inductive behavior.

Modeling. The modeling step illustrates the inductive procedure and has two parts: (1) presenting your prediction and supporting evidence, and (2) asking if predictions were confirmed and the confirming evidence. The first precedes behavior, replacing a condition statement, and the second part follows it, replacing a reinforcing statement. The first example is related to activity task behavior.

> Each day you have read the next story and answered the questions which follow. Therefore, I predict we would read story six today and answer the questions that follow. Who agrees? (SR) Please begin.
>
> Everyone, was the prediction about the reading story correct? (SR) How do you know? (SR) Yes, that is the story we read and corrected. Clear thinking.

The first part uses a setting component (Chapter 6) to get students to agree with the prediction. In the second part students participate in the confirmation and supply the confirming evidence. The key to asking for evidence is a simple "How do you know?" question.

The second example models the inductive behavior concerned with activity SM behavior.

> Because you have accepted the mistakes of others, answered questions when asked, raised your hands, and wrote only when asked the last three days, I predict you will do it again today. Raise your hand if you think my prediction is correct. (SR) That's a positive outlook!
>
> Everyone, was the prediction about following the rules correct? (SR) Jake, give me one piece of evidence. (SR) Give me another, Wilma. (SR) Are there any other reasons? James. (SR) Yes, you performed all of those behaviors throughout the activity.

The list of SM behaviors is long and represents the rules of the activity the teacher has been promoting with her statements. Because there are multiple pieces of evidence, a number of students can become involved in their identification and thus the inductive process. If the prediction was disconfirmed, you would still ask for the evidence, but it contradicts the prediction. Move through these statements quickly.

The third example focuses on task performance and its consequence.

> I predict that you will have access to project time. How do I know? Because you will finish your tasks by helping each other as you have done all week. Who thinks they can do it today? (SR) So do I.
>
> Meanhan, was the prediction correct? (SR) Henry, what did you see to support Meanhan's evaluation of the prediction? (SR) Rosemary, can you add other supporting evidence? (SR) Sharp observations; all that evidence supports Meanhan's confirmation statement.

The first step presents the prediction and then uses the "How do you know?" question to get at the evidence. This is simply a variation on the preceding examples. In the second step, Rosemary was asked to broaden the scope of confirming evidence. Notice the partial reinforcing statement at the end.

Prompting. The prompting step functions to facilitate inductive behavior through questions. It has two parts: (1) asking for predictions and supporting evidence, and (2) asking for confirmation and confirming evidence. The first precedes behavior and the second follows it. This step brings the students into the full inductive process. Presenting the confirming evidence is often trivial. For example, if the students predicted they could finish the task on time, the evidence would be the task product by the end of the time. They would simply show the finished problems, project, or whatever. The first example is, again, related to task behavior.

> Zelda, what do you think the group's assignment will be today? (SR) Vernander, how do you know? (SR) A clear prediction and evidence. Please begin.
>
> Sidney, was the prediction correct about the assignment? (SR) How do you know, Karon? (SR) Correct, it was confirmed for that reason.

In the first interaction, the students set the occasion for performing the assignment. As a variation, the teacher could have asked other students to evaluate the prediction and evidence: "Who thinks the prediction and evidence are correct?" The second interaction continues like those in the modeling examples. Every part of the inductive process has been made overt and the partial reward statement at the end rewarded the confirmation and its evidence.

The second example, predicting activity SM behavior, varies the interaction a bit.

> Zelda, what is one thing you would predict everyone will have to do to complete our activity? (SR) Richard, what is another? (SR) Hellen, do you think we can do all these things? (SR) Tonja, what evidence would tell you that Hellen's prediction is correct? (SR) Yes, you have done those consistently over the last few weeks.
>
> Peter, was Hellen's prediction confirmed? (SR) I agree. Foster, how do you know it was? (SR) Excellent, your evidence is accurate and supports the confirmation.

Including as many students as possible in the process helps them to see how other students are thinking, the kinds of predictions they are making, and the evidence they see. Students are provided peer models. Again, a partial statement reinforces part of the inductive process.

The third example, predicting task performance and its consequences, has a few variations from the two previous prompting examples.

> Rita, how do you predict your group will perform today? (SR) Fred, what evidence gives strength to that prediction? (SR) Tina, do you agree with that evidence? (SR) I concur with your predictions and evidence again! Keep it up.
>
> Anthony, was Rita's prediction confirmed? (SR) And Carol, what did you

observe as evidence? (SR) This group is getting sharper and sharper at making and evaluating predictions. That's the way I like to see you reason about the future.

In both parts, the language of inductive behavior is sophisticated and the statement at the end reinforces inductive behavior in general.

Testing. The testing step confirms that students' inductive behavior is operational with little, if any teacher support. As with the other steps, this one has two parts: (1) setting the occasion for their inductive behavior in a very limited way, and (2) asking them about their predictions, confirmations, and the various forms of evidence. The first part comes in various forms. In the true test, you give students what directions they need to begin the activity, without reference to predictive behavior. Anything you say or do that suggests direction for such behavior functions as a prompt. Most predictions are private kinds of things — we say them to ourselves. In the early testing stage a small prompt, in the form of a condition statement asking them to make specific predictions to themselves before they begin, may be used.

The second part of testing is performed after an activity is underway or at its end. You ask students about their predictions and their confirmation. Part or all the steps of inductive behavior can be covered. If students cannot give quick answers to your questions about predictions and evidence, they have not made the predictions and have, thus, failed the test. You need to correct them as indicated in Chapter 11 and, if errors persist, move back to the prompting step.

> Each of you can make a number of predictions about the reading assignment. Please do so and begin.
>
> Marcia, what was your group's prediction about today's task? (SR) Willie, what evidence supported that prediction? (SR) Kim, was the prediction correct? (SR) Greg, what evidence gives support? (SR) Keep up your accurate predictions and evidence spotting.

The second interaction essentially combines the elements of both interactions from the prompting step of the procedure. It evaluates both the prediction and its confirmation. The second interaction could have been broken into two parts. The first two questions could have occurred a little after the start of the activity, and the last two at the end. The same format could have been used with an individual student.

For the second example, predicting activity SM behavior, a small prompt is also used.

> Each of you can make a prediction about what you need to do to finish the activity. Take a few moments before we start to do so. [Pause.] Okay, let's begin.
>
> Penny, what was your prediction? (SR) Denny, what would provide support?

(SR) Ronny, was the prediction supported? (SR) Venny, what did you see that confirmed the prediction? (SR) Did anyone see anything that does not confirm the prediction? (SR if possible.) You all are starting to make strong inductive arguments.

The second statement goes through all steps of the inductive process. A statement that reinforces inductive behavior ends the interaction.

The third example uses a true test. The interest is still in the task performance and its consequences, but there is no reference made to them; thus, no first step appears.

Brian, what was your prediction about how you would do on the task? Are you achieving it? (SR) And what supporting evidence do you have? (SR) Thanks for making predictions and looking for confirmation.

The questions do not cover the full process, but that is not always necessary, especially after the students have been doing it for some time with a reasonable amount of success.

The problem with not using the prompt is that you are not sure which predictions the students may be making. At the same time, it does tell you if inductive behavior is being performed and its extent in content and process. You will discover that most students follow the prediction types you have stressed.

Reinforcing Statements. For many of the previous steps, reinforcing statements were present. Their function was to reinforce the occurrence and accuracy of inductive behavior. Thus, step four can be imbedded in either of the parts of the other three steps. Moreover, your reinforcing statements can evaluate inductive behavior on six points.

1. The relevance of the prediction.
2. The accuracy of the supporting evidence.
3. The supporting evidence-prediction link.
4. The prediction-confirmation link.
5. The accuracy of the confirming evidence.
6. The confirming evidence-confirmation link.

When asked to make predictions, students may not give predictions related to the activity in question (1). When predictions are relevant, the supporting evidence may not be what has happened in the past (2). Even if relevance and accuracy are present, the prediction and evidence may not be related, or linked (3). When asking for a confirmation, what is given may not be accurate or relate to the prediction (4). In turn, the evidence that is given may not be accurate (5). Finally, the confirming evidence may not be related to the confirmation, even if it is accurate (6). Additionally, whenever asking for evidence, remembering behavior can be reinforced.

The use of statements to reinforce inductive behavior indicates that they never stop. They simply focus on different classes of behavior. In the present context, they function as positive evaluations of the inductive behavior. Over time, the students evaluate and reinforce their inductive behavior using your model as as template.

LANGUAGE REQUIREMENTS

The preceding examples did not control for the language used to talk about inductive behavior. For example, the phrase "How do you know?" was used for getting at both the supporting and confirming evidence. Eventually, you want to use the full range of terms related to inductive behavior, including such terms as *premises, conclusion,* and *argument.* Consider the following replacements for the phrase "How do you know?"

What are your supporting reasons?

What evidence confirms that prediction?

What evidence do you have?

Support your prediction.

Identify your confirming evidence.

Why did you make that inference?

What is your supporting evidence?

What evidence supports that evaluation?

Most of these include a part of the language of inductive reasoning. Going from everyday language to technical terms involves pairing the known terms with the unknown. For example:

How do you know, or what is your evidence?

Your statement about what will happen is called a prediction. What is your prediction?

Together, your evidence and your prediction make an argument. What is your argument?

If you start to do this during the prompting step of the procedure, students pick up the language after only a few examples. Additionally, you can teach them the language related to evaluating their inductive behavior, as illustrated earlier in the reinforcing statement section.

SCHEDULING THE STEPS OF THE QUESTIONING PROCEDURE

Do not attempt to implement the questioning procedure across all your activities at once. Start with one and then another, and then work into the rest.

The hardest part of scheduling is knowing when to move from one step to the other. The model step, when used with older students, can be dropped almost immediately. The prompting step usually has to be done over a period of time. The length of that time depends, for example, on the extent to which you are introducing the more sophisticated vocabulary of inductive reasoning, the detail of the evidence you are looking for, the structure of the activity, and the age of your students. One factor can help you judge your pace through the procedure: the correctness of predictions and evidence. If students are making mistakes, back up to the previous step until they are firm. Chapter 11 details the correction of inappropriate inductive behavior.

PLANNING QUESTIONS

Similar to statements, as a procedure to teach inductive thinking, questioning must be planned.[4] Once students know how to make predictions, building questions parallels building statements. But until that time, the model, prompt, and test steps of the procedure need to be planned. Even if you are not using all the steps, it is essential at first to build them all. In doing so, you are preparing yourself for student responses.

1. Identify one of your classroom activities. This provides you with a context.
2. Select an element of the plan that they can make a prediction about.
3. Build a two-part model of the prediction. Include:
   a. For the first part of a prediction, its evidence, and a setting component asking students to commit to your prediction.
   b. For the second part, questions asking if your prediction was confirmed and what evidence there is for it.
   c. A partial reward statement which evaluates appropriate inductive behavior.
4. Build a two-part prompt for the prediction.
   a. Change the first part of the model so students make the prediction and supply the evidence for it.
   b. Change the second part by focusing on different students.
   c. Add a partial or complete reward statement that references inductive behavior.
5. Build a test for the prediction.
   a. If you want a particular prediction, include a conditions statement description as a prompt.
   b. If you want to cover all elements of predictive behavior, include everything covered in the two-part prompt step (4).
   c. Add a complete or partial reward statement referencing inductive behavior.
6. Repeat steps (1) through (5) for other activities and behaviors that can be predicted.

By following this planning procedure, you can build a set of questions that promote inductive behavior. What remains is the practicing of questions according to the rules of effective presentation presented in Chapter 8.

8

IMPLEMENTING STATEMENTS AND QUESTIONS

Using statements and questions within the classroom has three objectives. The first is knowing how to present them so they have a chance to change the probability of students' behavior. They must have clear direction and be more than faint praise. The second is knowing when to present statements and questions so that instructional time is maximized and student work goes essentially uninterrupted. With knowledge of the first two objectives, it is possible to embark on the third: to arrange statements and questions over time to gradually improve the quantity and quality of student SM and academic behavior. This chapter tells you how to achieve all three objectives.

HOW TO PRESENT STATEMENTS AND QUESTIONS

For statements and questions to function as described in Chapters 6 and 7, six presentation rules are important.

1. Believe in the importance of what you are saying.
2. Make your presentation relaxed and positive.
3. Clearly identify the person or group to whom you are talking.
4. Use a positive, varying tone of voice.
5. Keep your presentation short and clear.
6. Match your presentation to the age level of your students.[1]

(1) The planning performed in the earlier chapters should support your belief in their importance. (2) By building and practicing statements and

questions prior to classroom implementation, you take the first step toward a relaxed and positive presentation. (3) To identify the audience, use student names, group names, or other clear designations, and do not forget the value of eye contact. Personalizing statements and questions adds power to your presentation and gains students' attention. (4) The voice changes because the context at times requires the exclamation, the moments to speak softly, and the formal tone when the students have achieved something important. (5) You keep the presentation short by avoiding wandering and repetition. (6) Your style of presentation will evolve. Initially with older students, usually grades seven through twelve, begin presenting statements in a low-keyed and very descriptive manner. Often it is necessary to give them privately. For the younger students, especially those in kindergarten through second grade, tenderness and enthusiasm often go hand-in-hand with clear description. Use friendly social contact, such as the hug, pat, or handshake. These help insure student attention and associate their reinforcing warmth with teacher statements and student behavior.

WHEN TO PRESENT STATEMENTS AND QUESTIONS

Because time and the opportunities to present statements and questions are limited, it is necessary to preplan when to use them. The following sections provide guidelines for presenting them during each portion of an activity or class period.

Beginning an Activity or Class

Complete condition and combination statements set the occasion for an activity; therefore, they are used to get it going. Two examples follow; the first is a condition statement and the second a combination statement.

Here is what you will have to do for reading. [Cover reading procedures.] Who thinks they can follow them? (SR) That's what I thought. This will assist all of you in completing your assignments.

Yesterday all of you completed your assignments early. Can everyone do it today? (SR) I know I can count on your best effort. I know you can do it and earn more time to work on other projects.

The complete prediction step of questioning can replace the preceding statements. Here is an example:

What do you predict you will have to do to progress on your group geography projects? (SR) Jim, what evidence do you think supports that prediction? (SR) Martha, can you add any support? (SR) Together, both of you have given a complete picture of what you will have to do to perform as predicted. Let's go.

Continuing an Activity or Class

When an activity or class is underway, you do not want to break up instruction or practice; therefore, partial statements or their question equivalents are in order. Here are three examples:

How long will it take to do the next five questions? (SR) Great prediction and a hard challenge.

This group has just read half the story in five minutes. John, what is your prediction about the last half? (SR) Faster? Let's see.

Sara, did the group confirm John's prediction? (SR) Yes, you read it in four and one-half minutes.

These examples all mix statement and question components, with the third confirming the second's prediction about reading.

Ending an Activity or Class

At the closure of an activity, you use complete reward or combination statements, or complete confirmation questions. These three examples relate to those given earlier.

Congratulations. You completed your assignments because you followed the activity procedure. [Ask student for specifics.] You have done this every day this week, and that is a first. You have made my teaching tasks very pleasant.

Yesterday everyone completed their assignments early, and today you did it also. Can everyone do it tomorrow? (SR) I know I can count on you to make it three days in a row.

Was your prediction confirmed, Harriet? (SR) What evidence confirms that prediction, Orlando? (SR) Patrick, what evidence can you add? (SR) Your skill at predicting what has to be done helps you get your tasks finished.

One of the most important places to use complete reward statements is at the end of an activity requiring a complex activity procedure.

Libby, you organized your materials, got right to work, asked questions when needed, and followed the directions for completed work. I appreciate such self-management.

These historically related behaviors represent an activity procedure. The teacher summarizes the student's performance, defining and providing a clear picture of her as a self-manager. This presentation could easily be converted to a set of questions.

The foregoing suggestions for using statements and questions are not hard and fast. Statements and questions never stop because new behaviors are constantly required of students—that is the nature of being in a learning environment. Statement and question content changes, but the process of stating and asking continues, as does the process of thinking inductively.

REFINING BEHAVIOR

Even when students begin to manage themselves appropriately and complete their academic work, you usually feel that you could be doing more to improve the performance or quality of their work, SM or academic. You can make this happen when you refine behavior. The *refinement of behavior* refers to a change in (1) the latency of, (2) the rate at which, (3) the duration of, (4) and the accuracy with which behavior is performed. *Refining behavior* is a teaching procedure involving the presentation of statements and questions over time to achieve one or more of these refinements.[2]

In general, we desire to decrease latency and increase the other attributes of behavior. For example, we want students to begin work without delay (short latency), work rapidly (fast rate), continue working throughout an activity (long duration), and work accurately. When these happen, we often refer to such students as well managed and motivated.

The procedure to refine behavior consists of five steps. You can see how the components of statements and questions capture the behavior and expose its refinement. The steps of the procedure follow, along with examples.

Step 1: Set the Conditions for the Behavior to Be Refined

Setting the conditions can involve the use of condition statements or questions. The condition statement can be complete or partial. The questions have the students give predictions about the duration, rate, and/or consistency of their performance. Here are a few examples. Again, (SR) stands for student replies or students reply, whichever is appropriate.

> Sandra, can you improve your supervision of the group by KEEPING ALL THE GROUP MEMBERS ON THE TOPIC? (SR) I agree. Remember to thank those who do and move to another student when someone gets off.
>
> Your worksheets have A FEW EXTRA ITEMS on them today. Who thinks they can do them? (SR) That's my kind of enthusiasm. Let's begin.
>
> This is a difficult task. Who thinks they can organize and supervise themselves THROUGHOUT THE ACTIVITY? (SR) I like that prediction, and I support you all the way. Please begin.

The first asks for a change in the quality, the second asks for an increase in rate, and the third for an increase in duration.

Step 2: Intermittently Observe the Behavior Being Refined

Observe your students' behavior, looking for the refinement requested, and checking their progress against the criteria established in Step 1.

Step 3: Intermittently Present Statements and Questions

As the behavior progresses toward satisfying the refinement criteria, present partial statements or ask questions about this progress. Multiple presentations are required.

> Sara, it looks like your group is really keeping to the topic. Keep it up.
>
> Even with the extra items, you are already more than half finished. At this rate, you should all finish early.
>
> How are you working? (SR) Yes, rapidly. So, are you going to achieve your prediction? (SR) I think so, too.

The context, along with the previous challenges and predictions, would supply the missing details of these statements and questions.

Step 4: Reference the Refinement at the End of the Activity

Use statements or questions to sum up student performance in relation to the behavior being refined.

> Sara, you kept the group on the topic for the whole activity. That is the second time in a row. Good job!
>
> Knowland, was your prediction about doing the extra items confirmed? (SR) How about the rest of you? (SR) You worked rapidly throughout the activity and did it. You're getting faster each week.
>
> Raise your hand if you think you worked quickly and continually to meet your prediction. (SR) It was a hard task and you did it. Can you do it tomorrow? (SR) I will look for it.

At this point, the change-over-time component, as statement or question, is important. The first two presentations provide examples.

Step 5: Over Time, Cycle Toward Refining New Behaviors

As students learn new SM and academic behaviors for group and individual tasks, cycle the intensity of refinement toward these new behaviors. After cycling a number of times, students expect themselves to improve. Their self-knowledge has matured. At this point, change your strategy by asking students how they think they should improve. It is a first step in having them plan their futures.

> John, do you think you have improved your work on addition problems? (SR) Do you think you will do the same with the subtraction problems? (SR) I think you will also.
>
> Zelda, how do you think your backhand should improve? (SR) Yes, the ball should stay closer to the net. You're analyzing your behavior accurately.

In both examples, the students have learned to look at their behavior and decide how it should change. This sophisticated behavior is a consequence of an environment that models the analysis of behavior through statement, question, and refinement procedures.

Once proficient with statements and questions, start to practice refining behavior according to the procedure. At first prompt yourself in the classroom by using a posting that outlines its steps and the types of elements that are refined (see Chapter 10).

EVALUATING THE IMMEDIATE IMPACT OF STATEMENTS

Just how do students think and feel about the content and presentation of statements made to them? Three practical procedures can be used to answer the question.

The first procedure is to take a quick look at the student or group to whom the statement was directed a moment or two after you turn (physically) to something else. If the student's expression is inappropriate, the statement may not have been effective in content and/or style of presentation. The second procedure is to use a trained observer familiar with the procedures in this text. Chapter 22 expands on the use of classroom observers.

The third method is to ask the students directly about the content or presentation. Here are some questions related to content that can be asked at the end of statements.

> Is that request clear?
>
> Do you consider that consequence important?
>
> How many enjoy these challenges?
>
> Do you enjoy hearing how well you have done?
>
> Do you like my pointing out how you have changed?

Many other variations are possible. The following questions ask about the presentation:

Did you like the way I said that to you?

How would you tell Mary what I just told you?

Would you prefer that I talk to you privately?

It is important not to overdo such statements and to restrict them to individuals or small groups.

STATEMENT AND QUESTION DELIVERY CHECKLIST

The following checklist outlines the considerations to be made in delivering statements to students. Once statements are built, this checklist should guide practice and implementation.

1. Does the presentation reflect your belief in the importance of the statements or questions? If so, continue. If not, review your work from Chapters 4 and 5.
2. Does the delivery unambiguously reference the intended individual or group? If so, continue. If not, add a name, eye contact, physical contact, or some combination of these.
3. Is the delivery relaxed and positive? If so, continue. If not, stop worrying about exact wording, practice component by component, and practice with other professionals.
4. Is there variability in your voice? If so, continue. If not, put in some exclamations, practice some with a soft voice, some with a punch, and express your positive feeling about the behavior.
5. Has all the redundancy been cut out? If so, continue. If not, see if you can rewrite it with half the words and do as much.
6. Have you considered the background of your students? If so, continue. If not:
   a. In general, be more reserved with older and more enthusiastic with younger students.
   b. But for specifics, observe students' reactions to statements and questions, have others observe, or question students about content and presentation.
7. Have you considered how you will refine the behaviors of interest? If yes, stop. If no, ask yourself:
   a. How could the behavior improve?
   b. How would you set conditions for this improvement?
   c. How would you intermittently question and reward this improvement?
   d. Which behavior would you cycle to next?

When you have practiced statements and questions so that they satisfy this checklist, you are ready for implementation in the classroom.

9

FORMULATING AND USING
EXAMPLE SETS

To teach the individual discriminations and operations that make up the
SM system strategies, another powerful teaching tool is needed. That tool
is the example set. It brings together a group of examples to teach the
discrimination or operation of interest. This chapter illustrates how to go
about designing and teaching SM behavior with example sets.

The design and use of example sets is not difficult — they are essentially
a modification of the way statements and questions are used. Moreover,
their use saves an immense amount of teaching time and makes it possible
to teach a wide range of sophisticated discriminations and operations even
to very young students.

THE DEFINITION AND FUNCTION OF EXAMPLE
SETS

There are two inclusive classes of examples. *Modeled examples* are instances of a complete or fragmentary contingency (condition, behavior,
consequence). A modeled example illustrates a condition-behavior match
or nonmatch that may or may not include a consequence. When a match is
presented, it is called a *positive modeled example;* when a nonmatch is
presented, it is called a *negative modeled example.* The function of modeled examples is to set the occasion for student learning or change. Usually
a modeled example is simply called a *model,* positive or negative.

The second inclusive class, *test examples,* function to set the occasion for
a demonstration of learning. Test examples are the conditions component
of the modeled examples. If a condition is matching, relative to the class of

behavior being taught, the example is called a *positive test example*. If a condition is related to nonmatches, the example is called a *negative test example*. Usually a test example is simply called a *test*, positive or negative.

An *example set* is a group of examples arranged together, to effectively and efficiently teach, essentially through models and tests, a class of behavior, discrimination or operation.[1] Chapter 2 defined discrimination behavior as classifying (arranging, sorting, or labeling) instances of elements, relationships, or events into more or less inclusive classes. Operations were defined as behaviors that altered the state of the individual or some other part of the environment.

Figure 9.1 provides a possible example set to teach the discrimination "in." This spatial relationship is taught with eight positive and negative examples, presented one after the other. The first four are models, and the

Figure 9.1
Example Set for "In"

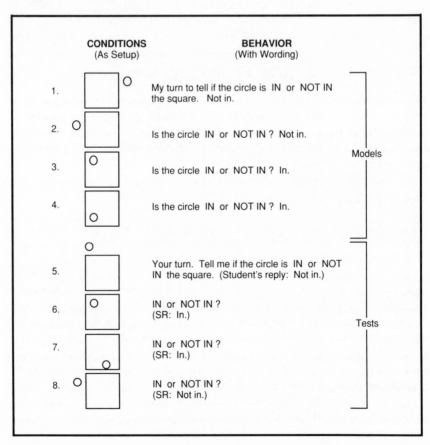

second four are tests. The goal of teaching with example sets is to have students behave correctly under a range of test conditions. Moreover, you often want them to behave under conditions never before experienced. In other words, they need to behave inductively—past learning must set the occasion for appropriate behaving that occurs under conditions different from those already experienced. In Figure 9.1, the four test examples are ones never before seen. If learning occurs, it is because of the four examples modeled at the start of the sequence. The question to be asked is, does the set of examples effectively teach and test the discrimination? To answer that question, this chapter provides the knowledge to arrange and present example sets so you can increase the probability of students learning individual behaviors that are part of the SM curriculum.

FORMULATING EXAMPLE SETS

Two types of example sets must be constructed to teach most discriminations or operations. The first type, *initial teaching,* introduces the learners to the discrimination or operation. The second type, *expansion teaching,* expands the conditions in which the students can behave. The following four steps help you formulate these two types of example sets:

Select the Discrimination or Operation to Be Taught

The discriminations and operations related to activity SM behavior were determined in Chapter 4. The related SM system strategies are identified in Chapters 13 through 18. For the present, two discriminations, "conflict" and "helping," and the two-part operation "offering and accepting help" are used to illustrate the design of example sets.

Design Initial Teaching Sequences

Five rules can help you design your initial teaching example sets, or sequences.[2] Two such sequences are usually used.

Rule 1: Use the Same Setup Across Examples. When the conditions of the examples, both models and tests, share as many elements as possible, they have a common *setup.* By having as many elements in common from example to example, you focus the student on the critical elements and minimize the number of examples needed to model a class. Additionally, students must know the elements (e.g., objects or words) that compose the setup. In Figure 9.1, the setup consisted of a two-dimensional square and circle, both known to young students. The only change in the setup from example to example is the relationship between the square and the circle. It was this change that defined and set the occasion for the discrimination behavior "in" or "not in." For most discriminations and operations, a simple setup can be found.

Rule 2: Use the Same Instructional Wording across Examples. With each example, you talk around it, getting the students' attention, often pointing out the criteria for accepting or rejecting the example as a member of the class, and telling students when to behave. By using the same wording across examples, you increase the probability of learning and its demonstration. The students focus on the models and the tests. They do not have to figure out what is going on. Thus, to make the condition-behavior match as unambiguous as possible, use the same wording across the sequence of examples.

Figure 9.2 illustrates a sequence for the event discrimination "sharing." The A and B brackets point out the wording and setup for the discrimination. The setup consists of a set of verbal examples of interactions among students within a classroom. The wording remains the same across all examples, except for the small change that occurs at the beginning of the test examples. During the test, the students perform the behavior that was part of the teacher's model.

Figure 9.3 illustrates a sequence for the event discrimination "conflict." Again, the A and B brackets point out the setup and wording used in the sequence. The setup consists of verbally presented examples that illustrate classroom events. Even the hypothetical students remain the same across examples. The wording has the same structure across all examples except that beginning with example six the students are being tested. Each test has two parts: the performance of the discrimination and the criterion, or rule, controlling it. The "How do you know?" wording, first introduced in Chapter 8, is used again. Essentially, the rule points the student toward the evidence that makes the example belong or not belong to the class of events called conflicts.

Figure 9.4 illustrates a sequence for the operations "offering and accepting help." Because these two SM operations are part of an interaction, they are taught together. Again, the setup and wording are consistent across examples. For the models, the teacher could play the parts of both the offerer and accepter. For all the conditions presented, helping is possible. For teaching operations, this is always the case. The behavior that occurs within the conditions can be appropriate or inappropriate.

Rule 3: Model the Range of the Class. A class has a diverse membership of instances. This diversity is called its *range*. The range is determined by your instructional interests. You illustrate the range by juxtaposing, or presenting together, the diversity of positive modeled examples, and responding to them in the same way. With discriminations, the same way has a literal interpretation. The same class name is given, as in Figures 9.1, 9.2, and 9.3. With operations, the same way has a functional interpretation in the sense that the behavior matches, or is appropriate to, the conditions of the example, as in Figure 9.4. Juxtaposing a group of three or so positive modeled examples is usually sufficient to illustrate the range.

The C bracket for Figures 9.2, 9.3, and 9.4 illustrate the range for

Figure 9.2
Example Set for "Sharing"

| A: Setup | B: Wording | C: Range | D: Limits | E: Testing |

CONDITIONS (As Setup)	BEHAVIOR (With Wording)
	One way to manage ourselves is by sharing. We share tools, materials, and knowledge so that everyone can keep working on their tasks. Here are some examples.
1. Zenda gives Tonja her only pencil so Tonja can answer her reading questions but Zenda can't.	My turn. Is Zenda sharing or not sharing? Not sharing.
2. During free time, Zenda and Tonja will not let Rendella play Monopoly with them.	Are the girls sharing or not sharing? Not sharing.
3. Henry asks Richard and Urie if he can play the winner in the next game of checkers. Richard and Urie say yes and Henry waits.	Are Richard and Urie sharing or not sharing? Sharing.
4. The four groups performing the science experiment take turns using the only two thermometers in the class.	Are the groups sharing or not sharing? Sharing.
5. Ellen gives one of her pencils to Sharon. Now both can start on the task.	Is Ellen sharing or not sharing? Sharing.
6. Because she was out of the room, Barbara asks Sid for the assignment she missed. Sid says, "Why should I?" and makes a face.	Your turn. Is Sid sharing or not sharing? (SR: Not sharing.)
7. The Purple Group has finished a project on how ants live. They give the class a presentation.	Is the Group sharing or not sharing? (SR: Sharing.)
8. Jim, who has already done the assignment Irene is working on, gives Irene the answers.	Is Jim sharing or not sharing? (SR: Not sharing.)
9. Roland asks Willie and Jermie if he can join them for lunch. They say sure and let Roland in on the conversation.	Are Willie and Jermie sharing or not sharing? (SR: Sharing.)
10. During art Cindy and Stewart fight over using the one box of crayons on the table.	Are Cindy and Stewart sharing or not sharing? (SR: Not sharing.)
11. Jim runs out of paper and Yolanda gives him some of hers. Now both can start on the task.	Is Yolanda sharing or not sharing? (SR: Sharing.)

"sharing," "conflict," and "offering and accepting help." Examples three, four, and five of Figure 9.2 show that sharing can occur between individuals or groups when working on assignments or playing games during free time. All the positive examples fall within the range of events that happen in the classroom.

For "conflicts," the range is again limited to the classroom; examples three, four, and five of Figure 9.3 illustrate conflicts that focus on the

Figure 9.3
Example Set for "Conflict"

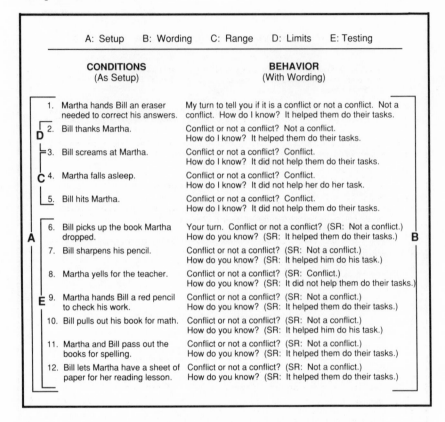

individual and teacher (4) and between students (3 and 5). Even more so than "sharing," the range of "conflicts" presented is restricted by our instructional interest. There is no interest, for example, in having students discriminate the range of conflicts that are of interest to our judicial system. From the point of view of SM teaching, the objective is to get the students to discriminate conflicts so they can be taught to use the intervention strategy of Chapter 18. But an initial base of learning is being given that can be broadened at a later time when some other curriculum, such as social studies, requires it.

For "offering and accepting help," the range is shown by the first three examples in Figure 9.4. The range is again restricted to the subset of events related to the classroom. Additionally, these are not the only operations related to helping. Others, such as "rejecting and accepting the

Figure 9.4
Example Set for "Offer and Accept Help"

A: Setup	B: Wording	C: Range	D: Limits	E: Testing

You already know how to ask for help when working on your assignments. But sometimes we need to offer and accept help. Here are some examples of how to and how not to offer and accept help.

1. This is an example of offering and accepting help. Jim sees that more chairs are needed for the reading group. He says, "Mr. West, should I get some more chairs?" Mr. West says, "Please, and thanks for offering."

C 2. This is an example of offering and accepting help. Jim offers Zelda help by being quiet as she works on her assignments. When she is finished, she accepts Jim's help. She says, "Thanks for letting me do my work."

3. This is an example of offering and accepting help. Zelda sees Jim picking up the books he dropped. She says, "Let me help." Jim says, "I would like that."

D 4. This is not an example of offering and accepting help. Zelda sees Jim picking up the books he dropped. She says, "Jim makes another mess. You sure need my help." Jim says, "Yes, I sure do. It takes a mess to help clean up a mess."

5. Now it is your turn to show me how to and how not to offer and accept help. Betty, how would you offer to give Mark a hand shelving the reading books just before recess?
(SR: I would say, "Can I give you a hand so we can be ready for recess?")
That's it. Now Mark, how would you accept?
(SR: I would say, "I would like that.")

6. Now tell me how you would NOT offer and accept help. Gill, how would you not offer to help Sara shelve books?
(SR: Sara, let me help. You're so slow we will never get to recess.)
Okay. Now Sara, how would you not accept?
(SR: Of course I could use some help from a slow turtle.)

E 7. Again, tell me how to offer and accept help. Timothy, how would you offer to help the rest of the class as they complete the assignments you have already finished?
(SR: I would be quiet and work on my lines for the play.)
And Esther, as one of the class, how would you accept Timothy's help?
(SR: At the end of the assignment, I would say, "Thanks for letting me work.")

8. Now tell me how you would NOT offer and accept help. Valencia, how would you not offer to help the rest of the class as they complete their assignments?
(SR: I would talk to people as they tried to work.)
And Ruth, as one of the class, how would you not accept?
(SR: I would talk with Valencia.)

rejection of help," are important to building helping behavior. Thus, the range is restricted to a particular subset of helping operations (see Chapter 14).

Rule 4: Model the Limits of the Class. For every class there are points at which instances cease being referenced as members of the class of interest. These points are the *limits* of the class. To show the limits of a class, juxtapose examples (conditions) that are minimally different and respond to them in a different way. Sometimes it is not easy or necessary to juxtapose minimally different examples to illustrate the limits, even when we understand exactly what minimally different is. The total set of negative models in proximity with the positive models helps define the limits. The most important concern is the selection of examples.

The D brackets in Figures 9.2., 9.3., and 9.4 point out a limit using a positive and a negative modeled example placed back to back. For all three the conditions are alike, but the behavior is different. Often it is not easy to juxtapose such examples. Doing so may require adding more examples or breaking up a set of examples designed to show the range. For example, in Figure 9.3, modeled examples one and five are basically minimally different. But to juxtapose them, to show a limit, one would have to add another modeled example or break up the three examples that show the range (the C bracket). In the end, the best way to find out if an example set works is to try it out; and remember, two such sets are needed. The second may insure learning, even if the students have problems with the first.

Rule 5: Test the Learner. Once the range and limits of a class have been modeled, *testing* the students follows. This is done by juxtaposing the conditions of examples that roughly fit the range and limits, and having the students respond. These positive and negative tests should bear no predictable relationship to each other, so students cannot guess the answer. The goal is to have the students correctly predict class membership or nonmembership. These examples are, for the most part, new. About five or six different tests are used in initial teaching and may be used more than once to test individuals and groups.

The E bracket in Figures 9.2, 9.3, and 9.4 illustrate the tests. Five to seven tests are used. For "offering and accepting help," the tests alternate between positive and negative examples. With operations, this is acceptable because the students devise the responses that are more or less similar to the models. They are creating something like minimal differences through these alternating positive and negative test examples. For the discriminations, the positive and negative tests are randomly presented.

The five initial teaching design rules guide the building of not only effective instruction but also efficient instruction. None of the sequences presented take more than a minute or so to present, although there may be times when they have to be repeated before students respond correctly for all tests. The set up and wording rules help to insure this. Generally, two initial teaching example sets are used. The second one is used on the following day. One of these sets usually begins with positive examples and the other with negative examples; which one you begin with is not important. Figures 9.2 and 9.3 are *negative first* example sets and Figure 9.4 is a *positive first*. The range and limit rules keep the number of examples to a practical minimum. The tests evaluate not only student learning but also initial instruction.

Design Expansion Teaching Sequences

The initial teaching presentation is effective, but restricted. We want the learner to behave appropriately across a wider range of conditions. The procedure to insure this is called *expansion teaching*. Its use is controlled by following three additional rules.[3] The initial teaching rules are not forgotten. Although the range and limits are not modeled because fewer models are presented, they are considered in selecting the total set of examples. The setup, wording, and testing rules are also followed.

A single expansion can satisfy one or more of the three expansion rules. Modeling and testing are again the inclusive components of expansion teaching. This time, only one or two models are used. An expansion of a class is complete when, in some number of expansion sequences, the behavior is performed reliably within the terminal conditions specified by the curriculum.

Rule 6: Change the Setup. To change the setup you widen the conditions to which students respond. You can do this expansion through events such worksheets, games, or teacher-directed oral activities.

Rule 7: Change the Students' Response to the Conditions. There are many ways the students' response can be changed, especially for discriminations. They can cross out, circle, or underline on worksheets, and can point to, or name the examples during teacher-directed activities.

Rule 8: Juxtapose Different Discriminations or Operations. In everyday life discriminations or operations are made during rapidly changing contingencies. Therefore, we want to expand a student's behavior by embedding it in a range of contingencies. This insures that the appropriate elements of the conditions are setting the occasion for specific behavior. Again, the three main instructional vehicles are worksheets, games, or teacher-directed activities.

For the SM curriculum, the final expansion provides students with the opportunities to make the discriminations and the operations during classroom activities and beyond (Chapter 19). Such expansions meet the requirements of all three rules. But first a less radical set of expansions needs to take place, as the following expansion activities illustrate.

If "sharing" had been initially taught as in Figure 9.2, a teacher-directed expansion would occur after the last of the initial sequences. Here is an example of such an expansion that is teacher directed:

> Give me an example of when sharing would be appropriate during reading seatwork. (SR: Sidney needs an eraser but does not have one.) Martha, if you saw that Sidney needed an eraser, how would you offer to share yours? Tell us what you would say. (SR: "Sidney, if you need an eraser, you can share mine.") Everyone, is what Martha said appropriate? (SR) Sidney, how would you ask Martha to share her eraser; what would you say? (SR: "Martha, would you share your eraser with me, I forgot mine. If she said yes, I would say thank you.") Everyone, is what Sidney said appropriate? (SR)
>
> Now, who can give me another time when it is appropriate to share? (SR) [Continue calling on different students.]

Here, the teacher has the students provide the conditions of the example after a single model.

A second expansion for sharing could be a student worksheet. It juxtaposes other related SM discriminations.

Directions: Read and decide if each example is a conflict, helping, or sharing. Circle the correct answer.

1. Mary sees Martha moving a desk and picks up one side. Martha says, "Thanks."
   Conflict   Helping   Sharing
2. Zelda grabs Ruth's eraser and starts to use it without asking.
   Conflict   Helping   Sharing
3. Timothy and John are taking turns using the ruler to make their graphs for the social studies assignment.
   Conflict   Helping   Sharing

The preceding examples would continue for four to six more examples. This expansion not only expands "sharing" but "conflicts" and "helping" as well. Moreover, it takes a few minutes at most to carry out.

Besides the previous expansion that involves the "conflict" discrimination, others are appropriate. Here is an example of a teacher-directed expansion.

Who can give me an example of a conflict that may occur during our math activity? Ronny. (SR: "Greg hits Mary.") Jim, can you tell me why that is a conflict? (SR: "It stops Greg and Mary from doing their tasks.") Now, Rendella, make Ronny's example not a conflict. (SR: "Greg hands Mary a text that is being handed out.") [Continue with different examples so as many students as possible contribute within about a one- or two-minute period.]

This expansion changes the setup and the response of students. The students provide the conditions of the examples, apply the rule to determine if it is a conflict, give the answer, and then change the situation to make it not a conflict.

The next expansion for "conflict" is again a teacher-directed activity. This time, changes in the setup and wording, and juxtapositioning of other classes of SM behavior occur.

You have learned what conflicts, sharing, helping, and organizing are. I will name one of these classes. You give me an example. Greg, sharing. (SR: "Henry lends me a pencil for math.") Everyone, is that sharing? (SR: "Yes.") Annis, organizing. (SR: "I take out my math book and pencil at the start of math.") Everyone, is that organizing? (SR: "Yes.") [Continue for about one minute.]

This is just the reverse of the worksheet expansion for "sharing." Now the students are providing examples of the classes of interest.

Expansion for operations are a little more restricted. Because the goal is to teach the operation so it occurs in the appropriate place, operation expansions often become similar to the teacher-directed sharing expansion. Consider this example.

> Here is an example of when offering and accepting help would be appropriate during physical education. Helen is trying to carry out the big bag of equipment all by herself. Uoko, how would you offer to help? (SR: "I would say, 'Can I take the other end?'") Helen, how would you accept the help? (SR: "I would say, 'Thanks, I need help.'") Everyone, were the offer and the acceptance appropriate? (SR: "Yes.")
>
> Now who can give me another time when it is appropriate to help? (SR) [Continue for about one or two minutes, calling on different students.]

If the students have been taught to discriminate "helping" as well as the operations of "offering and accepting help," this expansion goes smoothly.

In the end, the final expansion is to perform the discriminations and operations during classroom activities. Here is a final example of how to help that happen.

> Everyone, you have learned about helping. Now, I would like you to start to see where it is needed during the activities of our classroom and then offer help. You know how to offer and accept. How many think they can do it? (SR) I know you can and will be looking for it.
>
> [At the close of the activity.] Okay, did anyone help another? (SR) Yes, Arthur. (SR) Tim, how did you like Arthur's help? (SR) And how did you accept it? (SR) I hope everyone can find opportunities to help or accept help when it is needed.

At this point you can construct your activities to promote the use of SM behavior as illustrated in Chapters 4 and 19. Through refinement teaching, Chapter 8, you can increase the probability of these behaviors in the classroom. Through transfer teaching, Chapter 19, you can increase the probability of these behaviors happening in the everyday lives of students.

Design Correction Procedures

Students will make mistakes when answering your example set questions; they need to be quickly corrected. The final step in formulating example sets is to design correction procedures for each initial and expansion sequence. Because there is an underlying design to correction procedures, this task is not very difficult.

Although the details of constructing correction procedures are covered in Chapter 11, reviewing example sets with potential student errors in mind helps prevent them. Review by asking:

1. Are the students making the kinds of predictions that are necessary for future learning?
2. Have I covered the range and limits of interest?
3. How will the students respond to these test examples given the prior sequences presented?

Knowing which examples you want to cover and predicting how students will respond to them helps you recognize and adapt to student learning problems. Finally, no piece of instruction exists in isolation, and considering its place can help reduce the amount of teaching or any inconsistencies across the discriminations and operations taught.

TEACHING WITH EXAMPLE SETS

When teaching with example sets, three elements of instruction often cause delivery problems. These include how students should respond to tests, how to schedule sequences, and how to include consequences.

Student Responses

During the testing part of the initial teaching sequences and during some oral expansion sequences, students have to respond to your questions. Just how should this be done for an adequate test, one that reliably tests as many students as possible? Essentially, two options exist: calling on individual students or the group. For group responses, a signal must be used. It is best to use a visual signal. A slight pause following the question and just before the signal, gives students time to prepare to respond. The signal is usually a drop of the hand or the lifting of a finger.

Both questioning individuals and groups have their difficulties. When individual responses are used, not all students are tested on each item. For group responses, students may follow the answers of others. In this situation, those who follow are being prompted by the other students and, thus, are not being adequately tested. For the students who follow, simply say, "We must all do it together on my signal," and start over again with the test examples. After a few times, if you are consistent at correcting, they will respond together. To be most effective, begin a sequence with group responses and then give individual turns.

Scheduling Example Sequences

The many individual discriminations and operations to be taught will have to be scheduled, or coordinated over time. Usually, the first expansion sequence follows right after the second initial teaching sequence. The general rule for initially teaching another related discrimination is, wait until the previous one has been expanded for a day or two. Many unrelated discriminations or operations can be taught in one lesson. If a discrimination is causing problems, hold off on the next related discrimination and provide more practice on the previously learned ones, especially the one causing the difficulty. Chapters 14 through 18 illustrate the scheduling of discriminations and operations that are part of the SM strategies.

Consequences

Example sets do not exist in isolation. You provide consequences for how the student behaves relative to the instructional situation and the behavior being learned. Besides the correction consequences for students' errors covered in Chapter 11, reinforcing consequences in the form of statements have a definite place in teaching with example sets. Because of the fast-paced nature of this instruction, only partial reinforcing statements can be given during the presentation. These can reference groups or individuals, and focus on either their management or academic behavior. Here are some examples: "You got it," "Three out of four correct," "Keep it up," "You're really spotting the conflicts," "Mary, can you give me an example like Randy's?" The place for full questioning or complete statements is at the end of the sequence. These statements and questions can focus on following instructions, how well the students did, and how they are changing in learning the discriminations or operations.

PLANNING DISCRIMINATION SEQUENCES AND TEACHING

The following plan guides you through the process of designing sequences and preparing to teach them. It is also a summary of the chapter.

1. Identify the discrimination to be taught. Refer to the results of your Chapter 4 analysis and to Chapters 14 through 18.
2. Design the example to teach the behavior. Consider:
   a. The setup (Do the students know the components?)
   b. The wording (Is it as simple as possible?)
   c. The range (Is this what you are interested in?)
   d. The limits (Change the conditions so a positive becomes a negative example.)
   e. The tests (Can students guess the answer by the pattern?)
3. Decide if classification criteria can be used. Consider:
   a. Simplest, positive wording of the criteria.
   b. Whether students need to be pretaught any of the terms related to the criteria.

4. Build the initial sequences required. Consider:
   a. One negative first and one positive first sequence.
   b. Decide how many examples need to be modeled.
      1. If the student is young and no classification criteria are used, model five to six examples.
      2. If the students are older and classification criteria are used, model two to four examples.
   c. Juxtapose examples to most efficiently show the range and limits of the behavior.

5. Build the expansion activities. Consider:
   a. Changing the setup.
   b. Changing the range of responses to conditions.
   c. Juxtaposing different behaviors.
   d. Using oral or workbook-based expansions.

6. Build correction procedures for both the initial and expansion sequences (see Chapter 11).

7. Teach the initial sequences. Consider:
   a. Using two initial sequences—one negative first and one positive first where applicable.
   b. Testing the students on up to six examples.
   c. Using individual and group response procedures.
   d. Correcting without focusing on an individual student.
   e. Moving quickly from example to example.

8. Teach the expansion sequences. Consider:
   a. Following the second initial sequence with an expansion.
   b. Moving quickly from example to example.

9. Use partial reinforcing statements during sequences and complete statements at the end.

10

FORMULATING AND USING POSTINGS

We set out to teach students a host of academic and SM procedures so they can create changes in their environment. Yet, there is no way to teach how the component behaviors work together through individual example sets as presented in Chapter 9. Another powerful teaching tool is needed. This time it is the posting that outlines the key behaviors or the steps of a procedure so they can be taught as a class, or unit, of behavior. The present chapter provides procedures to formulate and use postings as they relate to classroom activities and their activity-level SM behaviors. With very slight modification, these procedures are used in teaching the SM system strategies presented in Chapters 13 through 19.

TYPES AND FUNCTION OF POSTINGS

A *posting* is a document in outline form that identifies which academic or SM behaviors are appropriate for an activity.[1] To use them, the students must have some basic reading skills. Usually, by the second grade, postings become appropriate.[2]

Postings, as illustrated here, help students follow classroom plans such as those outlined in Chapter 4. In terms of the principles of behavior, postings function similar to example sets: they precede and set the occasion for behavior. They can do this for students or teachers; thus, they are a tool for teaching as well as learning.

Similar to the other tools of teaching, postings do not function in isolation. Reinforcing consequences follow matching behavior (Chapters 5 through 9) and correction consequences (Chapter 11) follow nonmatching behavior. As a result, all principles of behavior and technology come into operation when teaching with postings.

From the perspective of Chapters 3 and 4, five types of postings are relevant to teaching SM behaviors for individual, group, and class activities: rules, goals, activity procedures, classroom procedures, and strategies. Of these, only the first four are examined here. Chapters 13 through 19 provide postings for the SM system strategies.

Rule postings describe the most fundamental SM behavior needed to work in a social environment. They include behaviors such as "take your turn," "use your small voice," "listen to others," or "keep hands and feet to self." Goal postings are a variation of rules; they combine rule level behaviors into more inclusive descriptions such as "cooperate with others" or "finish your work."

Of the two procedure postings, the classroom procedure describes the sequence of activities for a particular day. The activity procedure posting describes the SM steps or jobs, as discriminations and operations, that students perform to facilitate task behavior. Of these two postings, the classroom procedure is always the most inclusive.

Rules, goals, and activity procedure postings inform students of important elements of the classroom plan (Chapter 4). In all cases all types of postings are statements about how one needs to perform to be successful.

FORMULATING POSTINGS

The analyses of Chapter 4 are needed to formulate postings. The formulation procedure has two major steps: determining which locations need postings and making a set of postings for selected locations.

Determine Which Locations Need Postings

Because of the variety of behaviors postings describe and the varied backgrounds of students, different types are best used in particular situations. Several guidelines help to determine which posting is needed in a particular location. These guides will be better understood after completing the requirements of the next section, Make a Set of Postings.

1. If the activity behaviors are performed much like a sequence of steps, use a procedure posting.

The analysis of SM behavior from Chapter 4 illustrated that many complex behaviors are performed in interactive group activities. Many of these behaviors are performed in an almost step-by-step manner, with different group members performing different behaviors or jobs. Under such conditions, a procedure posting would be used.

2. If an activity can be reduced to about five key behaviors that can be performed at any time during the activity, use a rule posting.

In a teacher presentation activity, sitting in one's seat is performed continuously and raising one's hand can be performed at any time during the activity. During activities with these SM behaviors, rule postings are best used.

3. If the set of classroom activities is complex or changes often, use a classroom procedure posting.

These activities represent inclusive behaviors performed in a step-by-step manner. A classroom procedure posting specifies the sequence and times of the activities.

4. If the students have a history of performing the SM behaviors across all classroom activities, use a goal posting.

This does not usually happen unless rules have been used in the past. If you are in doubt, use rules initially.

As these guidelines suggest, more than one type of posting can be used in a classroom or during an activity. For example, if in general students perform the SM behaviors of all but one activity and there is, also, a complex procedure as part of another activity, a rule posting can be used for the problem activity, an activity procedure posting for the complex activity, and a goal posting for the classroom as a whole.

Make a Set of Postings

All postings exhibit three characteristics: They describe (1) the behaviors to be performed, (2) each behavior in a few words, and (3) as few behaviors as possible.

These rules were implicitly followed in Chapter 4 when all activities were analyzed for the behaviors that students had to perform to be successful. Describing each behavior in a few words and using as few behaviors as possible both relate to the principles of commonality and flexibility (Chapter 4). The following examples of goals, rules, and procedures show how to implement these characteristics in postings.

Goals. Goals represent inclusive classes of classroom behavior, take a future perspective, and apply to both teacher and student behaviors. For most situations, only three goals are necessary because three inclusive classes can cover most behavior: individual SM, interactive SM, and academic behavior. Figure 10.1 illustrates three examples.

The first goal of each set, 1A through 1C, focuses on individual SM behavior, with 1C being the most inclusive. The terms for this set come

Figure 10.1
Classroom Goals for Three Activities

GOALS A	GOALS B	GOALS C
1. To supervise my work	1. To plan my work	1. To manage myself
2. To help each other	2. To work cooperatively	2. To work synergistically
3. To finish our work	3. To do our classroom tasks	3. To reach our academic goals

directly from the SM curriculum. The second goal of each set points to interactive SM behavior. Those for 2B and 2C use terms related to cooperative interactions and those for 2A to the possible facilitating effect of the interactions. The third goal relates to academic behavior. Those of 3A and 3B refer to completing the task, but 3C looks at the academic goals previously established by the teacher, individual, or group. When used in this way the academic goals relate to improved performance, to getting more correct answers, or to maintaining a certain score level (see Chapter 8, the Refining Behavior section). Goal 2C, by the definition of synergistic, also refers to academic outcome but in a less direct form.

Rules. Figure 10.2 presents the rules for a teacher presentation and for

Figure 10.2
Rules for Two Activities

TEACHER PRESENTATION ⟶ **PRESENTATION RULES**

1. Putting work away	1. Watch the teacher
2. Sitting in seat	2. Answer questions
3. Looking at the teacher	3. Listen to answers
4. Answering questions when called on	4. Accept mistakes
5. Listening to others' answers	5. Raise hand to ask a question
6. Accepting the mistakes of others	
7. Accepting your own mistakes	
8. Raising your hand to ask a question	

INDEPENDENT WORKSHEET ⟶ **WORKSHEET RULES**

1. Planning one's approach to the work	1. Organize your work
2. Gathering the materials needed to work	2. Attend to your own work
3. Attending to one's own work	3. Use permission procedure
4. Staying in one's own seat	4. Follow directions of manager
5. Using permission procedure to leave seat	5. Finish your work
6. Follow the direction of the class manager	

an independent worksheet activity. On the left are the activity SM behaviors and on the right are the rule postings.

The analysis performed in Chapter 4 revealed eight SM behaviors students needed for a teacher presentation. With the four characteristics for formulating postings in mind, five short rules can almost completely cover the behaviors of the activity. Rule one is a combination of SM behaviors two and three. Rule four is a combination of SM behaviors six and seven. Combinations can occur because they can be demonstrated, or taught, through a few positive and negative examples as shown later in this chapter. SM behavior one was simply left off because it is usually not a problem in most classrooms. If it is, descriptive statements usually can be used to take care of it.

The SM behaviors for an independent work activity, presented in Figure 10.2 and first analyzed in Chapter 4, can also be combined to form a short list of rules. Behaviors one and two become rule one, and behaviors four and five become rule three. Rule five has been added and relates to the activity task behavior. If classroom goals are used, this rule is not necessary. The permission procedure of rule three could take the form of raising the hand for five seconds before leaving the seat. It represents a special activity procedure similar to those outlined in Chapter 4. The idea would be to foster thinking about acting before action; thus, it represents elementary planning behavior. By including it in the rules, students see its relationship to other behavior and the teacher can easily review it in the appropriate context.

In general, five rules are a limit. If there are several worksheet activities or teacher presentations, as would be the case for self-contained elementary classrooms, for example, the same set of rule postings would apply.

Procedures. As stated earlier, procedures function on the classroom and activity levels. Both describe a series of behavioral steps, but at different levels of inclusiveness.

1. *Classroom Procedures.* Chapter 4 defined classroom procedures as the arrangement of activities during a class or day. Constructing classroom procedures begins with a list of the classroom activities (inclusive classes of behavior) and knowledge of their arrangement over time. There may be multiple classroom procedures, because different procedures can be used on different days.

Figure 10.3 illustrates an example. On the top are the classroom activities; below that are the classroom procedures for the various instructional groups. They are derived from the activities and knowledge of the activity schedule. This is the most inclusive description of the behavior of the classroom.

The time indicated on the procedures refers to the start of the teacher-directed element of the subject. Each group is given 20 minutes of teacher-directed instruction for language and reading, and 15 minutes for math. The rest of the reading, language, and math time is spent in independent study. All other subjects are taught to the whole class.

Figure 10.3
Classroom Activity Procedures

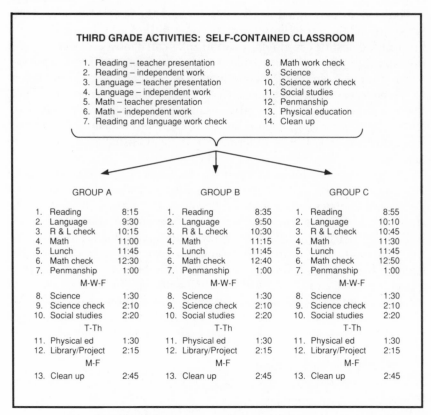

THIRD GRADE ACTIVITIES: SELF-CONTAINED CLASSROOM

1. Reading – teacher presentation
2. Reading – independent work
3. Language – teacher presentation
4. Language – independent work
5. Math – teacher presentation
6. Math – independent work
7. Reading and language work check
8. Math work check
9. Science
10. Science work check
11. Social studies
12. Penmanship
13. Physical education
14. Clean up

GROUP A			GROUP B			GROUP C	
1. Reading	8:15		1. Reading	8:35		1. Reading	8:55
2. Language	9:30		2. Language	9:50		2. Language	10:10
3. R & L check	10:15		3. R & L check	10:30		3. R & L check	10:45
4. Math	11:00		4. Math	11:15		4. Math	11:30
5. Lunch	11:45		5. Lunch	11:45		5. Lunch	11:45
6. Math check	12:30		6. Math check	12:40		6. Math check	12:50
7. Penmanship	1:00		7. Penmanship	1:00		7. Penmanship	1:00
M-W-F			M-W-F			M-W-F	
8. Science	1:30		8. Science	1:30		8. Science	1:30
9. Science check	2:10		9. Science check	2:10		9. Science check	2:10
10. Social studies	2:20		10. Social studies	2:20		10. Social studies	2:20
T-Th			T-Th			T-Th	
11. Physical ed	1:30		11. Physical ed	1:30		11. Physical ed	1:30
12. Library/Project	2:15		12. Library/Project	2:15		12. Library/Project	2:15
M-F			M-F			M-F	
13. Clean up	2:45		13. Clean up	2:45		13. Clean up	2:45

2. *Activity Procedures.* Activity procedure postings, in contrast, describe the SM steps or jobs that occur during an activity. Usually they do not describe all the SM behaviors of an activity. Most group activities—as pairs, triads, or small groups—require activity procedures. Figure 10.4 illustrates the activity behaviors for two activities analyzed in Chapter 4. On the left are the activity behaviors and on the right, the shorter activity procedures focusing on potentially problematic behaviors.

The most difficult part of the seatwork check activity is checking answers (3). The checking procedure is the focus of the activity because it is the activity task behavior; without reliable performance, the workcheck would not accomplish its dual goals of evaluating student work and providing knowledge of results. The rest of the activity can be easily managed by the teacher once work is returned. The procedure also includes behaviors two and four.

Figure 10.4
Two Activity Procedures

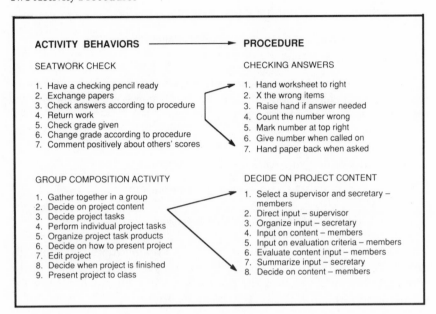

ACTIVITY BEHAVIORS ————————► PROCEDURE

SEATWORK CHECK

1. Have a checking pencil ready
2. Exchange papers
3. Check answers according to procedure
4. Return work
5. Check grade given
6. Change grade according to procedure
7. Comment positively about others' scores

CHECKING ANSWERS

1. Hand worksheet to right
2. X the wrong items
3. Raise hand if answer needed
4. Count the number wrong
5. Mark number at top right
6. Give number when called on
7. Hand paper back when asked

GROUP COMPOSITION ACTIVITY

1. Gather together in a group
2. Decide on project content
3. Decide project tasks
4. Perform individual project tasks
5. Organize project task products
6. Decide on how to present project
7. Edit project
8. Decide when project is finished
9. Present project to class

DECIDE ON PROJECT CONTENT

1. Select a supervisor and secretary – members
2. Direct input – supervisor
3. Organize input – secretary
4. Input on content – members
5. Input on evaluation criteria – members
6. Evaluate content input – members
7. Summarize input – secretary
8. Decide on content – members

The group composition activity in Figure 10.4 illustrates a highly interactive activity procedure. Almost all of the activity behaviors are complex, requiring the further analysis procedure presented in Chapter 4. Thus, all would be appropriately presented as an activity procedure posting. So which one do you use first? The first one. Even though the behaviors of the procedure look complex, they can be taught through a set of simple examples and nonexamples. Moreover, several of the procedures could be designed with commonality in mind. Consider behaviors two, three, five, six, and eight. They could be designed with the same behaviors as the "deciding on project content" procedure, but the academic content would be different. This saves a great deal of teaching time and allows the students to focus on content and not the process. With careful wording, one posting could be used for all of these complex behaviors.

In general, most activity procedure postings have seven to ten steps. If more steps are found, usually one of two things is happening. First, there is too much detail; two or three steps can be combined and still be modeled through examples and nonexamples as outlined later. Second, the original activity behavior represents a combination of behaviors that would be better taught separately. Working with other professionals in building postings is the best way to avoid potential problems: they see your mistakes and you see theirs.

When formulating postings, you often discover other important behaviors or a better way to organize your classroom. This is an outcome of any form of planning—everything keeps evolving.

TEACHING POSTING CONTENT

The teaching procedure consists of four parts; used in combination they insure posted behavior performance. Each of the following parts is based on statements, questions, and the use of examples:

Model: Introduce and Analyze the Posting

The three components to introducing a posting are:

1. Indicate the rationale for the posted behaviors.

The rationale for posted behaviors involves working more efficiently by oneself and with others so tasks can be completed. These are some of the consequences for performing the posted behaviors. The analysis of consequences, performed in Chapter 5, provides others.

2. Model the posted behaviors with examples.

After modeling one or two examples, the students can begin to supply examples. The behaviors can be described or even role-played. Both positive and negative examples should be used, as illustrated in Chapter 9. There is an attempt to show the range and limits of each class of behavior. The number of positive examples presented by the teacher and the students depends on the type of posting. For goals, four to six is sufficient initially, with one or two less for rules, and about two for activity procedures. By juxtaposing the examples for all the outlined classes of behavior, their limits are clearly drawn.

3. Get students to commit to performing the posted behaviors.

Getting students to commit to the posted behaviors requires the use of statements or questions as described in Chapters 6 and 7. The following could be used to close out the initial introduction. Again, the (SR) refers to student replies.

> I feel that these rule behaviors are important for us to work together successfully. By performing them we are showing a high level of self-management skill. How many will try? (SR) Okay!
>
> How many think these goals are something important to achieve? (SR) Can we help each other achieve them? (SR) I will look forward to it, thank you.

A major aim is to keep the introduction short and to the point. It should not take more than a minute or two, including examples. Remember that it is an initial introduction.

Prompt: Conspicuously Display and Review Postings Often

Whenever students can see the posting, there is a better chance of their performing the behaviors. Let the students make up the postings, if time is available. Multiple displays are often useful. For groups working at the same table, the posting can be attached to a small three or four sided form so all can see it at once. This is especially useful for helping students perform new procedures.

You can easily review the postings if they are displayed. Simply talk around it, asking for predictions of which behaviors have to be performed and for positive and negative examples of them. Postings should be reviewed daily until the students can provide examples and exhibit the behaviors consistently. After that, you need only ask them for a few examples, focusing on behaviors they are having trouble performing. Even later, you can restrict review to requests for new examples of the elements of the postings.

The final step is to have the students review the posting behaviors themselves. This is useful if group teaching techniques are used and different postings apply to various groups. The independent review technique needs to be monitored the first time or two. Review should take only 15 to 20 seconds for goals and rules, and only a little longer for procedures.

Test: Fade Postings When Criterion of Performance Is Met

Once the content of the posting is being consistently performed by students, they can be *faded,* or removed. Their removal represents a test and should be based on preestablished criteria. The criteria should be stated positively and based on (1) a high, consistent level of performance, and (2) knowledge of the range of appropriate behaviors. Usually, activity performance is related to the number of weeks during which the posting is consistently followed. The students can be involved in the removal decision and, at times, even the level of performance required. The criteria should be established after the introduction, unless the students have a history of performing posting content consistently. Then it can be done during the introduction. It is important to consider what the consequences should be for meeting the criteria.

Consequences: Present Statements and Teach
Self-Management Skills

When behavior is appropriate, reinforcing statements insure that the behavior continues into the future. So use them in relationship to the posted behaviors. Because postings are to be faded, the change-over-time component of reinforcing statements can be used to describe student progress. Consider these examples:

> Thank you class, everyone accomplished goal two. That makes three days in a row. Do so for six more and we can plan a new set of goals.
>
> Ellis, assisting Zelda the way you did sure was an example of following rule three. You have followed it consistently for three weeks now. Such self-management has helped me to instruct others.

Both have change-over-time components. Notice that the specific behavior was not referenced. That is because the students have a history of giving positive examples of the posting content and, thus, know to what the statements refer.

What happens after the posting has been faded and the criterion of performance met? Here are three guidelines:

1. If activity rule behaviors have been performed to criterion, move to classroom goals.

2. If students have performed to criterion and can or have been taught to plan, they can participate in planning new activities and, thus, postings (see Chapter 16).

3. If postings have been removed and behaviors have been maintained, evolve to other SM behaviors for an activity (enter the SM system strategies).

These guidelines are not mutually exclusive. You can, for example, go to participant planning (2) and at the same time shift from activity rules to classroom goals (1). It must be emphasized that the students have earned the right to participate because they have met the criterion of performance. It is a rite of passage for them; therefore, bring attention to it. Adding a little ceremony helps. Eventually, the SM behavior has to be evolved. At this point, the SM system strategies presented in Chapters 13 through 18 become appropriate.

USING POSTINGS WITH MULTIPLE GROUPS

Teaching students in small groups can be difficult if they do not have the necessary SM skills. If this is the case, postings are an important tool to help you teach them the necessary SM behavior to work independently. Here are two guidelines:

1. Review relevant postings just before students begin working in various groups.

2. Present reward statements or questions to the groups working appropriately.

As indicated earlier, the review must use examples of the posted behaviors. Guideline two requires that you develop the habit of scanning the classroom every few minutes. To give statements or ask questions, you can either comment across the room or take a second to walk over to the group, or you can use student managers to do it. Plan the use of student managers as you would any special activity. It is especially appropriate after students have learned the supervision strategy.

TRANSITIONING FROM ACTIVITY TO ACTIVITY

Many forget that the transitions from activity to activity involve SM behavior. To insure that appropriate behavior occurs here, the positive and negative examples of goals should cover the behaviors and time it should take to make the transition. If goals are not used, transition rules may be formed. This is not usually necessary if you use condition and reward statements before, during and just after transitions.

PLANNING POSTINGS AND THE TEACHING CHECKLIST

Planning Postings

This planning procedure guides you in formulating postings and summarizes the chapter.

1. Decide which types of postings you need for the activity and classroom locations.
   a. If the activity behaviors are performed much like a set of steps, use a procedure posting.
   b. If the activity behavior can be reduced to five or six key behaviors which could be performed at any time during the activity, use a rule posting.
   c. If the classroom activities are complex or change often, use a classroom procedure posting.
   d. If the students have a history of performing the SM behaviors across activities, use classroom goal postings instead of rules.
2. When formulating the posting, include the following:
   a. Behaviors to be performed.
   b. Each behavior in a few words.
   c. As few behaviors as possible.
3. For each type of posting consider the following:
   a. For goals, describe inclusive classes for:

        1. Individual SM behaviors.
        2. Interactive SM situations.
        3. Academic or task behaviors.
    b. For procedures, describe:
        1. The activity procedures—the behavioral steps required by individual or group members to perform the activity.
        2. The classroom procedures—the arrangement of activities and their time requirement.
    c. For rules, describe:
        1. Behaviors that could occur throughout the activity.
        2. Four or five inclusive classes of behavior.

By following these steps, your postings should be relevant and teachable.

The Teaching Posting Content Checklist

When preparing to teach the content of postings, ask the following questions:

1. How should the posting be introduced?
    a. Give a rationale for the posted behaviors.
    b. Describe the behaviors with examples.
    c. Get students to commit to performing the posted behaviors.
2. Have I conspicuously displayed and reviewed the postings often?
    a. Involve the students in giving examples and nonexamples of the posted behaviors.
    b. Review almost daily until the behavior is reliably performed.
3. Have I considered how I will fade the postings?
    a. Establish a criterion of performance for fading the postings.
    b. Decide what to do after fading postings.
        1. If activity rule behaviors have been performed to criterion, move to goals.
        2. If the content of postings has been performed to criterion and students can or have learned to plan, move to a participant planning format as described in Chapter 17.
        3. If postings have been removed and behaviors maintained, evolve to SM system strategies.
4. Have I presented reinforcing statements for appropriate behavior?
    a. Describe the posted behavior.
    b. Show the progress through a change-over-time statement component.
    c. Use the refinement procedure to help focus statements.

11

CORRECTING BEHAVIOR

Students make mistakes. To combat them, correction procedures are needed. Similar to the special activities identified in Chapter 4, corrections are short, positive events sandwiched into ongoing instruction. They represent a revision of your instruction. By correcting mistakes before they become chronic, you make instruction more positive and insure that the learner has the needed skills to continue successfully.

The correction procedures presented here assume that the students are complying with your instruction and that the error is not an outright conflict between individuals. Chapters 3 and 18 illustrate the elements and use of an intervention system to deal with such conflicts. The objective of this chapter is to insure that specific student errors related to the discriminations, operations, and strategies of the SM curriculum can be corrected.

THE ANALYSIS OF CORRECTION PROCEDURES

The Function of Correction Procedures

Correction procedures establish the desired condition-behavior match when the main body of the instructional program has failed to do so. They are designed to stop or quickly follow nonmatching behavior, establish conditions for matching behavior, and reinforce the ensuing correct behavior. To explain this complex activity, all eight principles of behavior and technology presented in Chapter 1 are involved.

A Standard Correction Procedure

All correction procedures can be seen as siblings of a standard consisting of five components.

1. A MODEL of appropriate behavior.
2. A PROMPT to help perform appropriate behavior.
3. A TEST for appropriate behavior.
4. A RETEST for appropriate behavior.
5. A REWARD for appropriate behavior.[1]

Depending on the context, several or all of these components can be used to build appropriate behavior. Except for the retest, all of them have been examined in Chapters 8, 9, and 10 as parts of instruction. In other words, the correction is essentially a representation of instruction, often with additional prompting. The retest is a test that comes at some later point and insures that the presentation of multiple similar examples do not prompt appropriate behavior, making it appear as if students have learned when in fact they have not. In Chapter 9 such context support was called juxtaposition prompting. The retest helps eliminate such prompting. Moreover, the chance to retest is often built into instruction during the second day of initial teaching, and continued through expansion, refinement, or maintenance teaching. Once corrections are made, the teacher must see the following instruction for its retest function as well as its instructional function.

Implementing Correction Procedures

The operational components of a correction procedure are relatively simple. The difficult part is discriminating (1) when to start the correction; (2) what specifically needs correcting; (3) which components of the correction procedure are sufficient to insure the occurrence of appropriate behavior; (4) when to stop correcting; and (5) when instruction needs revision.

The first three discriminations are always in tension. You want to start the correction as soon as possible (1), yet you have to observe enough of the behavior to know what specifically needs correcting (2) so that you can make the correction effective (3). Often corrections have to be repeated more than once. Usually, two or three repeats of the model, prompt, and test are enough (4). If the instructional program is robust, it returns to the behavior multiple times. Essentially you say, "Hey, let's try it again later. You will get it then." By viewing errors and their correction in this light, students are being taught to be resistant to failure, to keep behaving. If they do not get it tomorrow or the next day, even when corrections are inserted, it is time to revise instruction (5). The first four of these discriminations are covered in this chapter. Chapter 22 covers the revision of instruction.

CORRECTING INAPPROPRIATE SELF-MANAGEMENT BEHAVIOR

Interestingly, many of the activity or strategy SM behavior errors can be classified as errors in inductive behavior. The correction components (models or prompts) needed to correct them vary because of the situations in which the behaviors occur. The following identifies the types of errors, the decisions related to correcting each, and examples of applying the necessary correction components.

Inappropriate Replies to Challenges

At times students reply negatively or not at all to your challenge (Chapter 6). Such replies represent inappropriate predictions. The first part of the correction is to (1) model a positive prediction with or without evidence, and (2) reinforce behavior that is congruent with meeting the challenge. Do not enter into discussions about their negative replies because you do not want to reward negative self-knowledge. Here are some examples of the first step.

> You have shown me in the past you are equal to my challenges. I think you can.
>
> I think you can; just start and you will see.
>
> Most of you say you can. So help the others by being a positive example. I know everyone can.

The last statement indicates what can be done in a group situation where only some of the students, maybe only one or two, give a negative reply or none at all. The statement pays attention to those who were positive, yet provides support for those needing it.

When performance related to the challenge is underway, the second part of the correction is used. Here are some examples.

> You just started and already have six problems done. You can do more than you think.
>
> At the rate you are going, you will finish early. I knew you could meet my challenge. So should you.
>
> You have organized the assignment quickly. You know you can do it.

These reward statements help build positive self-knowledge. They contradict the students' first view of themselves. Moreover, the statements are short and keep the atmosphere of the classroom very positive. Later, questions can replace such statements.

The testing element of this correction comes when you give challenges in the future. If students reply in a positive way, your correction has worked. Do not expect everyone to become positive immediately. This correction format may have to be used many times, especially for older students.

Inappropriate Behavior When Failing a Challenge

There are times when a challenge is not met. Getting upset is one response to this situation, especially when students have managed themselves within appropriate limits. Your correction is (1) to reinforce what they did correctly, and (2) to prompt for the future.

> Rendella, you paid attention to your work and almost finished. I know you will finish it tomorrow.
>
> Class, you all organized your materials, helped each other work, and followed all directions. You were so close! I know you will do it next time. Give yourselves a hand for taking a good shot at it.
>
> You managed yourselves very well. I think my challenge was asking for too much. I will give you another try during reading. Is that okay? (SR) I appreciate your accepting my error. Thanks.

The third statement points out a situation that can arise. The challenge was inappropriate. If you see such a situation early on, change the challenge. Show them that your errors can be corrected. When students see success is next to impossible, the probability of inappropriate SM behavior increases dramatically. This type of problem can arise when refinement procedures are being used (see Chapter 8).

Inappropriate Prediction or Prediction Evidence

When students are predicting some part of a plan, you may think a prediction is wrong. Before you correct, the first step is to continue looking at the inductive behavior by making a request for evidence, "I don't know about that, but what is your evidence," or "Could you tell me why you made that prediction?"

If the evidence fits the prediction and is accurate, the student has not understood your question. The second step is to repeat the question, but with the addition of why you are asking for the second time with something like, "I don't think you understood. I asked . . . ," or "You may have misheard. I asked . . . ?"

If the student's prediction and evidence are both inappropriate, go back to the beginning of the questioning procedure (Chapter 7)—model the prediction. The second step is also used if the student continues to make a wrong prediction after you repeat the question.

> I would predict that you can get 18 correct. My evidence is that you have been doing 16 to 17 correct every day, and have become faster each week.
>
> I would predict that you will have to transfer and arrange the texts for the activity. This would allow you to begin the activity.

These components have no immediate test associated with them. The task is to ask for another prediction in the future. This provides a test. If the student or students continue to err, model the predictive process more and have students immediately repeat the prediction and evidence.

A second type of prediction error is appropriate but incomplete evidence. The correction is to prompt for remaining evidence. If it is presented, no correction is needed. If not, model the remaining evidence. Other students can also provide the model. For example, "Robert, can you add evidence to support Vance's prediction," or "You are correct but don't forget . . ."

Again, the test would be given later when other predictions are appropriate. It can come later in the activity or during the next activity, or even the next day.

Inappropriate Confirmation or Confirmation Evidence

Because a confirmation statement and its evidence constitute an argument, as does a prediction statement and its evidence, the correction procedures are similar. If students can make predictions built on evidence, there usually is no problem with confirmations. If their predictions were right, they know it and will tell you. But if they are wrong, they may initially become upset or not reply to the request for confirmation. The correction during this situation is configured much like the correction for inappropriate behavior when failing a challenge:

> You didn't do it, but you worked hard. I predicted you would do it, so I was wrong also. But we were very close to being correct.
>
> You didn't quite finish as predicted. I thought you would. Maybe next time.

Do not elaborate any further; move on to other instruction. The best way to avoid these problems is to reinforce those who give an appropriate negative confirmation of a prediction. After students see that you accept their being wrong, they begin to accept their own mistakes as well. They are beginning to be resistant to failure.

Chapter 16, System Strategy: Planning, explores how prediction and confirmation occur when students plan sophisticated tasks, individual and group. When students can make predictions and confirm them without any problems, they are ready for planning.

Inappropriate Inductive Language

Students' inductive behavior may be correct but their use of inductive language incorrect (Chapter 7). In these cases, you want to separate the form of the response from the content. For correct inductive behavior with inappropriate language, model or prompt the correct usage.

> Correct prediction, but here is how I say it. . . . Now you say it.
>
> Correct, now say it using the terms covered in class.

The first example is a model that asks for a test. The second example is a prompt that sets the occasion for behavior.

If students respond with both inappropriate content and inappropriate form, move back to modeling inductive behavior with desired language. By simply adding "now say it with me" or "now you say it," you are adding the correction for form. Students may have to repeat it two or three times until firm. When applying questioning to a group situation, as is the case during a debriefing, the group can all say it together after your model. Remember that the questioning procedure presented in Chapter 7 was not designed to teach inductive behavior to students with language deficiencies.

Inappropriate Behavior during an Initial Example Set

When initially teaching students to make a discrimination, they can make two errors besides not following a signal or not taking a turn (Chapter 8).

The first is to make a discrimination error. A correction is usually sufficient if you (1) model the answer; (2) test by repeating the item missed; and (3) retest by going back to the first test item and repeating the missed item in context. If errors continue on the second day, a careful examination of the range of examples (content subtypes) involved in the sequences is required.

The second type of error is an inappropriate operation. The students cannot produce the response or produce the answer to the "How do you know?" question. In this case, add a prompt to the previous correction. Essentially, you ask them to "say it with me." When students fail to perform verbal operations such as those involved in "accepting help" or "offering to share" during an initial sequence, the correction is the same.

Inappropriate Behavior during Expansion Example Sets

The errors and the correction procedures for expansion example sequences are the same as those for initial example sequences, with a few minor modifications.

The first modification is in an oral expansion set where students give examples. Here the test is simply to come back to students at a later time in the sequence, and a retest is to come back during a different expansion set of the same discrimination.

Another modification focuses on worksheet errors. If about 85 percent of the items are correct, no correction is needed. After a few expansions, the errors will most likely be even lower. But if errors persist, correct by having students model answers to the first two or three items before they begin an independent worksheet activity.

Inappropriate Procedures Behavior

Many activity strategies and all the SM strategies are procedures. The mistakes that occur are of two types: The first is failing to discriminate when to start a procedure or when to move to another procedure step. The corrections are the same: provide a prompt to get the behavior going. For example, if there is a chance to help, you could say

That calls for help [Point]. Please help.

This is a chance to help.

What is that [Point]?

What should you be doing?

From the first to the last, prompting decreases. The greater the students' background with the activity or strategy procedure, the less the prompting. For moving students forward after the start of a procedure, say "What is the last step of getting help?" or "Don't forget the last step." Elaborate by pointing to the procedure posting or naming the step only if necessary. The test is the initiation or continuation of the procedure. The retest comes the next time the opportunity to use the procedure arises. They should initiate or continue the procedures unprompted. This takes time, and the small prompts are usually needed for some period of time.

The second type of mistake, inappropriately performing an operation of a procedure, can require all parts of the standard correction. At minimum the model and test are needed, with opportunities for retest in the near future. In general, as the students' experience with the procedure increases, the less extensive is the correction. The difficulty with correcting procedural errors is the inability to stop instruction when needed to make the correction. The answer to this problem is the activity debriefing, or review. Here, you point out errors or ask students what they should have done and/or how they should have done it. They can even role-play better ways. The chapters in Part 3 elaborate on activity debriefings.

INTRODUCING AND USING CORRECTION PROCEDURES

A correction procedure is a form of special activity (Chapter 4). As such, students should know what is involved. They can be informed of the steps verbally and provided a few examples. For older students, postings can be used that include the model, prompt, test, and retest steps. Later, during review, ask for a range of examples as illustrated in Chapter 10. An introduction such as the following is appropriate:

> At times you make mistakes. Because you want to do it right and I want to teach my best, mistakes need to be corrected. Here are the steps I will follow to help you get on the road to doing it right.

There is no need to mention directly the reinforcing statements for getting something correct. Just provide them when you model your corrections. Also, a positive tone is pivotal to delivery. In essence, the approach to corrections should be on the order of, "Gee whiz! There is a little problem here. Can we solve it together?" By rewarding students for doing it right the first time, yet presenting mistakes in a noncritical light, you establish a functional level of stress which sets the occasion for what we often call a good effort. It has much to do with making learning a joy.

PLANNING CORRECTION PROCEDURES

Successful corrections, similar to all parts of successful teaching, require planning.

1. Select an activity (Chapter 4).
2. Build an example of a correction related to:
   a. Inappropriate replies to challenges:
      1. Model a positive reply with or without evidence.
      2. Reinforce behavior that is congruent with meeting the challenge.
   b. Inappropriate behavior when failing a challenge:
      1. Reinforce what students did correctly.
      2. Prompt future behavior.
      3. Avoid giving inappropriate challenges.
   c. Inappropriate prediction or evidence:
      1. Continue by asking for the evidence.
      2. If the evidence fits the prediction and is accurate, repeat the prediction request.
      3. If evidence does not fit the prediction or is inaccurate, model the predictive process.
      4. If evidence is incomplete:
         a. Ask if the student has other evidence.
         b. If more evidence remains, provide it.
   d. Inappropriate confirmations or evidence:
      1. Use the same correction as for predictions.
      2. If students become upset or fail to answer when providing a negative confirmation, use the same correction as for inappropriate replies to challenges.
   e. Inappropriate inductive language:

    1. Separate content from grammar.
    2. Model correct grammatical form.
    3. Test by asking for correct form.
    4. Retest with a later question.
  f. Inappropriate behavior during an initial example set:
    1. For discrimination errors:
      a. Model the answer.
      b. Test by representing the item missed.
      c. Retest by going back to the first test item and retest missed items in context.
      d. If errors persist, present another sequence later.
    2. For operation errors, do (1) above and add a prompt.
  g. Inappropriate behavior during expansion example sets:
    1. Follow the format for initial example sets.
    2. For oral expansion sets where students provide examples, the test is to come back to the erring students.
    3. If students have less than 85 percent correct over several worksheets, return to modeling an example or two at the start of the worksheet.
  h. Inappropriate procedure behavior:
    1. If the students fail to discriminate when to perform, prompt the behavior (but as little as possible).
    2. If students inappropriately perform an operational component, model, prompt, test, and later retest.
    3. Use a debriefing if it is difficult to stop instruction to correct inappropriate behavior.
3. Perform step 2 for each activity. Work with other professionals.
4. Introduce your correction procedures:
  a. Model a range of examples and role-play.
  b. Focus on the model, prompt, test, and retest.
  c. Prepare an introduction.
5. Set aside time for delivery practice. Consider:
  a. The quickness of presentation with examples built.
  b. Making the presentation positive.
  c. Practicing with other professionals.

The next step is classroom implementation.

12

THE EVOLUTION OF BEHAVIOR AND THE PROCEDURES OF TEACHING

To teach students the SM system strategies, our talk about behavior and teaching must make another technical advance. Much of this advance has already taken place through the description of initial, expansion, refinement, and correction teaching using models, prompts, tests, and consequences. The present objective is to build on this foundation so that a language covering the evolution of behavior, the process of teaching, and their relationship, emerges.

THE WAYS OF EVOLUTION AND THE TYPES OF TEACHING

The bits of behavior with which a human is born evolve into wonderfully complex repertoires. The suckling-crying-kicking infant becomes the teacher-dancer-comic-parent-lover-humanitarian. How can we put some sense into this behavioral evolution? By building on the analysis performed in Chapter 2. We ask, how can a class of behavior evolve and how can we control this evolution? The answer provides a correspondence between our languages of evolution and teaching, between theory and practice. For each of seven types of change that a class of behavior can undergo, there is a teaching procedure.[1]

Emergence

A class of behavior must first emerge. The *emergence of behavior* refers to performance of the first instances of a class. Releasing a hold on a chair,

Sonja takes her first step. In the presence of a cow, Daniel comes to say, "Cow." Following a feeling from the bowels, Ono comes to use the potty chair. The interaction between our biology, prior behavior, and current environment are the basis for the emergence of behavior.

Initial teaching procedures control the emergence of an elemental class of behavior. An elemental class is the smallest unit or component needed for instructions; it is defined relative to the learner. Instructional environments can be established to teach Sonja to walk, Daniel to say "cow," and Ono to use the potty chair. Likewise much of SM behavior must be initially taught. Chapter 9 illustrates how to teach the discriminations of conflicts and sharing initially, as well as the operations of offering and accepting help.

Integration

The *integration of behavior* refers to the combination of existing classes of behavior to form a new, more inclusive, complex class of behavior. In a most real sense, the inclusive class, as procedure, emerges from subclasses. For example, by combining the identification of premises, their truth or falsity, unstated assumptions, fallacies, conclusions, and the criteria for strong arguments, the inclusive class procedure of argument analysis emerges in Zelda's repertoire.

Integration teaching procedures control this combination. Integration follows the emergence of the less inclusive classes (subclasses). Logically, the ways to combine subclasses lie on a continuum. At one extreme, each subclass is initially taught. After all are learned, they are combined at one time. In this way, the inclusive class emerges all at once. At the other extreme, the subclasses are initially taught one at a time. As soon as each is learned, it is combined with previously learned subclasses. In this way, the inclusive class emerges over a period of time. A middle-road approach is to teach two or three subclasses and then combine them into a more inclusive subclass. This is done until you have a set of more inclusive subclasses that are combined to form the inclusive class of interest. In this way, the most inclusive class comes to life over time in steps or subassemblies.

Which method of evolution is used depends on the learner's history, the complexity of the behavior, and the technology of instruction. Some SM strategies are evolved by combining the steps (subclasses) as they are learned. The overall system of strategies is integrated either by combining the strategies after all are learned or by a variation of bringing them together as they are learned. Chapter 19 focuses on the integration of SM strategies.

Expansion

Once a class of behavior has emerged, it still evolves. The *expansion of behavior* refers to the evolution of behavior through the addition of subclasses to an existing class of behavior. This addition allows the class to be performed under a wider range of conditions, examples, or applications. Sonja comes to walk around corners, up stairs, and down hills; each requires a change in walking behavior. Daniel comes to discriminate cows from a wide host of other animals by using verbal statements, or by pointing, or both. And Zelda comes to analyze longer and more complex arguments across a variety of applications. In a sense, expansion represents moving horizontally on a hierarchy of behavior. Integration represents moving vertically on a hierarchy. Expanded behavior can undergo integration and integrated behavior may be expanded.

Expansion teaching procedures control the expansion of behavior across conditions (as examples or applications). Chapter 9 illustrated that initial teaching restricts conditions to help the behavior emerge. Conditions were then widened by changing the setup and juxtaposing one condition with others. In doing so, the response requirements change. The SM strategies are initially taught in a teacher-controlled context and gradually expanded into the classroom activities to facilitate academic behavior. Chapters 14 through 18 illustrate these expansions.

Transfer

When instances of a class of behavior begin to take place under conditions outside the point of learning (for us the instructional environment), the *transfer of behavior* is said to be occurring. For example, if Zelda continued to analyze arguments presented by other students, politicians, and various media after instruction, we would be witnessing transfer.

Transfer teaching procedures control the transfer of a class of behavior across a range of locations, or life settings, including other classrooms, the school at large, the home, and future work places. Transfer teaching is a subclass of expansion teaching because it controls the occurrence of behavior under new conditions. But with transfer teaching, the teacher is controlling "from a distance." Chapter 19 illustrates the transfer teaching procedures.

Refinement

Newly emerged, integrated, expanded, or transferred behavior is often on shaky ground. Sonja falls down a lot. Daniel identifies horses as cows at times. And Zelda inaccurately analyzes arguments on occasion. All of these can undergo refinement. The *refinement of behavior* refers to changes in the rate, duration, latency, or accuracy with which the behavior is performed. One or more of these may be involved in making the behavior more polished. There is no addition of subclasses of change in task conditions as occurs in the expansion of behavior.

Refinement teaching procedures control the refinement of behavior. For example, the instructional program may help Sonja walk faster (rate) with greater consistency (accuracy) and longer (duration). Daniel may be helped to discriminate cows faster (latency) and with increased consistency (accuracy). And Zelda may analyze arguments in a shorter period of time (duration) and with greater accuracy. Chapter 8 illustrated refining activity SM and academic behavior.

Refinement can be seen as the counterpart of emergence, integration, expansion, and transfer. The latter refer to evolving behavior so students can adapt across a wider range of conditions. Refinement refers to evolving behavior so students can adapt efficiently within a given range of conditions. The difference between novices and masters is primarily in the expansion of skills; the difference between masters is in the refinement of skills.

Maintenance

The *maintenance of behavior* exists when a class of behavior is not changing, or evolving, but remains a part of the repertoire. No change in its subclasses can be detected and it does not appear to be undergoing refinement. The behavior is being kept alive. Sonja continues to walk the same, as Daniel does in identifying cows or Zelda in analyzing arguments.

Maintenance teaching procedures control the continuation of behavior. Often, behavior is maintained by practice or reviews that are essentially retest situations. The number of maintenance events required is directly related to the level of refinement to be maintained. To maintain a world-class repertoire requires an extensive number of maintenance activities of greater duration than compared to maintaining novice-class performance. The difficulty is in determining the spacing or scheduling of maintenance activities. The maintenance of behavior can also be facilitated by integrating it into other behaviors, as is the case when addition is used during multiplication.

Extinction

In the same way a class can come to life, or emerge, a class can come to an end, or extinguish. The *extinction of behavior* has occurred when the conditions for the performance of a class of behavior are present but instances can no longer be performed. Within the school environment, this usually occurs because the conditions for the behavior have not occurred for a long time, the behavior has been punished, or it has gone without reinforcement. Through the use of expansion, integration, transfer, refinement, and maintenance procedures, we can avoid the extinction of appropriate academic and SM behavior.

Correction teaching procedures control, in part, the extinction of inappropriate behavior, or student mistakes. The falls by Sonja, the missed identifications by Daniel, and the incorrect argument analyses by Zelda are all mistakes. If they persist, the conditions may come to set the occasion for inappropriate performance. These mistakes can occur during any type of instructional procedure. The form and simplicity of the correction procedure depends on how fast the instructional system can detect the errors. For example, if the detection does not occur until advanced refinement has taken place, the correction becomes what we often call remediation and may even require a special instructional program or program branch.

From the point where a behavior emerges to the point where it becomes extinct, its evolution can be described in terms of integration, expansion, transfer, refinement, and maintenance. We evolve complex behavior by controlling these types of evolution.

THE ELEMENTS OF TEACHING

Each type of teaching procedure controls a type of evolution by manipulating a set of elements. The four elements common to all seven classes of teaching procedures have been examined in previous chapters: models, prompts, tests, and consequences. Not all teaching procedures utilize all the elements, nor is their form or structure the same. But each element has a common function across teaching procedures.

To evolve behavior, the first step is to manipulate the environment to set the occasion for a desired change in behavior. The elements that do this are the *elements of variation* and include the model, prompt, and test. The second step is to manipulate the environment to select the new behavior, to increase its probability. The elements that do this are the *elements of selection* and include the various forms of consequences discussed in previous chapters. This section examines the function and relationship of these elements.

The Elements of Variation

The model and prompt are the molding force of the teaching procedures. They overtly vary behavior or provide an opportunity for variation. Students imitate models and follow prompts because of past reinforcing consequences.

The elements of variation take many forms. The model can be a performance, a verbal outline, or both. The prompt can be a verbal event that gets a behavior going or keeps it going. The varieties of models and prompts are restricted only by our imaginations and the technology available. Even the statements and questions described in Chapters 6 through 8 are models or prompts. The posting can be either a model or a prompt depending on where it is used relative to a behavior's evolution.

Chapter 9 illustrates the use of multiple models, moving rapidly from one to the next. This allows the student to see the range and limits of conditions that set the occasion for the appropriate behavior. Chapter 10 demonstrates how postings are used to model and facilitate modeling multiple related discriminations and operations within a procedure.

Even with flawless modeling, students are still likely to perform incorrectly or at an inappropriate time. Thus, it is necessary to prompt student performance, often for extended periods of time. The key to prompting is to use as little prompting as possible and to fade it as soon as possible. For most SM behavior, prompting is verbal and informs the student of when and how to perform. Postings are the primary vehicle for prompting once behavior is under way. Prompting can occur at the beginning of the task or during the task. Supply it only when you consider it necessary. If you see a step being missed, a prompt becomes part of a correction procedure. In this way, the same prompt can be part of different teaching procedures.[2]

The testing element is not a molding force; it is designed to provide conditions to determine if the change in behavior has occurred. The change may be under prompted or unprompted conditions. In the examples of Chapters 9, 10, and 11, some behaviors were unprompted during testing. The instruction moved from models to tests. This was the case for the discriminations of conflict and sharing. Others were prompted first and then tested.

In teaching the SM strategies, testing is often done first under prompted conditions and later, after prompts are faded, under terminal conditions. When refinement and transfer procedures are used, testing is done again. Each teaching procedure uses testing. Minimally, all teaching procedures contain a testing element. Moreover, testing is done more than once. Modeling, prompting, and testing usually follow in order; we move toward having students behave under the terminal conditions of our objectives.

Modeling, prompting, and testing all relate to the conditions of instructional contingencies described in Chapter 1. A model points out a complete or fragmentary contingency that sets the conditions for behavior.[3] A prompt supports behavior so a condition-behavior match can be performed. A test presents an opportunity for the performance of behavior under conditions specified in the educational objectives.

The Elements of Selection

In the instructional contingencies described in Chapter 1, selection by consequences increases or decreases the probability of a class of behavior. These consequences can occur under modeling, prompting, or testing conditions. During modeling, they select (reinforce or correct) attending to the model. During prompting, they select behavior under prompted conditions. During testing, they select behavior that imitates the model. Except for the early instances of attending to models, only during prompting and testing is new behavior selected.

THE COURSE OF CHANGE

How can the course, or pattern, of change in an evolving behavior be described? The analysis focuses on the difference in instances of a class over time. As Chapter 8 pointed out, a class changes in its rate, duration, latency, and accuracy. Generally, educational evaluation focuses on accuracy, but the rest of the refinement parameters are also important. Three terms describe the change and pattern in instances over time: *variability*, *trends*, and *stability*. Each is defined in the context of the types of evolution outlined earlier.[4]

The Variability of Behavior

Variability refers to fluctuations in the rate, duration, latency, or accuracy of the instances of a class. Daniel and Ono both ride for a moment, fall down, ride a little or a lot more, and then fall down again. Helda adds the problems correctly one day, gets some wrong the next, and few or many wrong day to day for some period of time. A group supervises itself according to procedures one day, but only does so occasionally for the next week. Excessive variability often describes the relationship between instances of newly emerged, integrated, expanded, or transferred behavior. Although there is always some variability, our instructional goal is to eliminate as much of it as possible, as soon as possible.

The Trend of Behavior

Trend refers to the movement of the rate, duration, latency, or accuracy of the instances of a class of behavior toward some direction, desired or not. Often we desire them to increase. We want Daniel and Ono to ride more and more often without falling down and do so for longer times. We want Tonja and Rebecca to manage themselves successfully for the lengths of their tasks across more and more activities. By definition, the refinement of behavior is occurring, planned or not, when the behavior is trending in the direction desired.

The Stability of Behavior

Stability refers to the absence of variability or trend. The rate, duration, latency, or accuracy of instances are more consistent with each other over time. There is minimal variability and no detectable trend. Eventually, our students identify, ride, and manage almost all the time. Stable behavior, almost by definition, undergoes very little or no evolution. We talk about a behavior's regularity, or of its firmness, or its mastery. Such behavior can be integrated, expanded, or transferred in our quest for evolution.

Variability of instances follows emergence, integration, expansion, and transfer. With time, models, prompts, and consequences, the behavior trends, or begins refinement. If the environment reinforces the desired criteria, the refinement trends in the appropriate direction. It is being selected. When a behavior reaches a state that satisfies the criterion of performance, it is considered stable and the behavior is then maintained, integrated, expanded, or transferred. This is a description of the usual course of change.

THE PROCESS OF TEACHING

For the SM strategies, many skills are being taught at one time, all at different stages of evolution. To keep track of this sequence, to describe the movement through initial, expansion, integration, refinement, transfer, and maintenance teaching you need a detailed day-to-day charting of teaching called a schedule of instruction. Chapters 14 through 18 present potential schedules for teaching the SM system strategies. Although a schedule of instruction is not a procedure to control the evolution of behavior, it is a plan that illustrates the process of teaching and the evolution of behavior. Schedules facilitate both the initiation and the revision of instruction. Chapter 20 illustrates how to build a sequence of instruction that encompasses the SM strategy schedules.

TEACHER EXPECTATIONS ABOUT BEHAVIOR AND ITS CHANGE

Teaching evolves student behavior. You evaluate your teaching and yourself in light of that evolution. But often evaluations are based on a flawed picture of student change. For example, many believe that change must be smooth and continuous. Here are five realistic expectations about the evolution of student behavior.

1. No matter how powerful your instruction or classroom management procedures, expect mastery to take time.
2. With the initial evolution of behavior, expect variability to some degree.
3. When behavior begins to trend, expect variability to decrease.
4. Even after behavior has stabilized, expect an occasional occurrence of inappropriate behavior.
5. Even after behavior has stabilized, expect to maintain it.

With these as the basis of your evaluation, you increase the probability of moving ahead positively and productively. Moreover, when you know what to expect, you are more likely to be patient during the course of instruction and remain composed in the face of day-to-day fluctuations in students' behavior. With an awareness of the course of change, you more fully enjoy teaching and student growth.

SUMMARY

Figure 12.1 summarizes the components and relationship between the evolution of behavior and its teaching. Behavior emerges, is integrated with other behaviors, expands across various activities, undergoes refine-

Figure 12.1
The Correspondence Between the Evolution of Behavior and the Procedures of Teaching

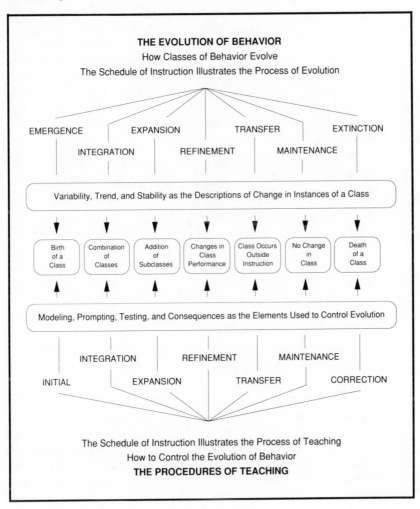

ment, transfers to other environments, and is maintained over time. With each of these changes we see variability, trend, and stability in the behavior. The task of teaching is to manipulate the environment to insure that emergence, integration, expansion, refinement, transfer, and maintenance occur as we desire — reaching a stable state as soon as possible. A schedule of instruction outlines how the teacher goes about evolving behavior. When stability is reached at the time specified by the curriculum, teaching is considered successful. With the picture of evolution presented here, your expectations about student change and the evaluation of your teaching should be realistic.

III

Teaching the Self-Management System Strategies

Part 3 has three objectives: (1) to carefully analyze the components of each SM strategy; (2) to illustrate how they can be initially taught, expanded, integrated, refined, transferred, corrected, and scheduled; and (3) to prepare for their teaching.

13

SYSTEM STRATEGY: ORGANIZING

From the first day of school, young students must manage themselves. Minimally, they need to follow the organization of the classroom by performing the activity SM behaviors identified in Chapter 4. Yet for many, these SM behaviors are radically different from those required of students in the past. Therefore, to insure students' success, we must teach them these required management skills. If they are not learned, academic and SM strategy instruction will be hampered from the start. This chapter presents the procedures to teach activity SM behaviors and the organizing strategy which follows. The importance of such teaching cannot be overstated: It provides students with a model of how they should instruct themselves and others in carrying out their future plans.

ANALYSIS OF ORGANIZING

Chapter 3 defined organizing as bringing together the elements required to perform an activity task. In other words, students have organized when they are in the right place at the right time with the needed materials and tools arranged so that an activity task can begin, continue, or end.[1] At this point, they have achieved an *activity setup*.

Yet organizing is quite dynamic. It is a process of moving from one organization to another, maintaining each as long as necessary, and moving again. With each change in organization (reorganizing), we can say students must adapt. To maintain an organization, we can say they must cooperate.

If students chronically fail to perform the SM behaviors that match the immediate organization, they are classified as anything from being disruptive to having an attention deficit disorder. By teaching as outlined in this chapter, you can increase the probability of avoiding such classifications.

TEACHING YOUNG STUDENTS ACTIVITY
SELF-MANAGEMENT BEHAVIORS

The objective is to teach students to perform activity SM behaviors *without* teacher direction, within the predictability level of the classroom. To achieve this objective, students must be taught (1) to perform activity SM behaviors under appropriate conditions; and (2) to behave inductively relative to the classroom plan. The first means that students can perform the regular and special activities and transition within and between the two as appropriate. The second means that students predict and confirm with whom to work, when to reorganize, which behaviors to perform (academic and SM), how to perform them, where to perform them, and why they are doing so (determine the consequences).

Both initial and refinement teaching procedures are used. With each change in organization, you need to use the same procedures over again. With each change in the classroom plan and from year to year, students require less modeling and prompting to learn.

Initial Teaching

The initial teaching involves modeling, prompting, and testing. Consequences are considered during the discussion of refinement teaching.

The First Day. You begin by modeling each regular activity. Start by setting the conditions for what you are going to teach.

> Our first activity will be reading. I will teach you to read and understand what you read. Here is what you will be able to read later in the year [Display]. Here is how we will do it.

Continue by modeling the steps of the activity SM behaviors. Next, prompt your students through it, doing every step down to passing out the materials. Essentially, you prompt them through an activity with minimal content, doing just enough task work for them to participate in the full activity process. Now, take your students through the rest of the regular activities. Use plenty of statements to reinforce them for following you. With all the activities of a self-contained primary classroom, you will also want to give students a rest period.

Next, introduce, model, and prompt them through the special activities procedures.

> Often during an activity like reading, you will have to sharpen your pencil, or you may need help, or need something to do after finishing with your work. Here is how we are going to do these things.

For each one, both model the behavior and prompt or walk students through it. For the finishing early special activity, outline the options they have. Keep these to a minimum at first.

Rewards and corrections are special activities that represent the conse-quences of the classroom. Chapters 5 and 11 analyzed reinforcing conse-quences and corrections. (Chapter 18, System Strategy: Intervening expands further on corrections.) Introduce them back to back. Start with reinforcing activities:

Special events happen when you are working hard and doing your best. First, I will tell you how much I like what you are doing. Second, you will often spend a few extra minutes playing.

Show them the reward activities. Next, go over a general corrections procedure—model, prompt, test, and consequences. Provide two or three examples illustrating the range of behaviors that need correction and showing how you would correct them. By presenting reward and correc-tions procedures together, students begin to see a range of behaviors that are positive and negative. Each set helps define the other set. By role playing some of these, students begin to see the consequences for appro-priate and inappropriate behavior.

The transitions from activity to activity are also modeled and prompted as just explained. Show them how to move desks, materials, and them-selves from one activity to another. Cover at one time all the transitions that may cause trouble.

Once you have completed these initial models and prompted walk throughs for all activities, do it for real. Present as many activities as the remaining time allows. Keep content minimal. Let them all have time to experience doing the activities and taking part in the "finishing early" activities. Remember that the goal the first few weeks of school focuses on SM skills. The classroom is a complex social experience for which students need to be prepared.

The Second Day. On the second day, do what you did on the first. Just do it a little faster and involve students a little more. The key to this day is to begin asking questions about the classroom plan. Usually, at least one student can answer a question. In the following examples, [COAS] means call on a student, and [COS] means call on students, usually one after the other.

Who remembers what we do first when you arrive? [COAS] Yes, we find our seats for our morning activity. What are those seats? [COAS] That's correct. So let's do it. [Students move into places with you giving only the help needed.] You did that quietly and quickly. That is what I like to see. Thank you. Now, what do we do in our morning activity? [COAS] Okay. That is the main thing. Who can tell me the things you have to do so we can get it done? [COAS] Okay, that is one thing. Who knows another? [COAS] That is an-other important one.

At times things go wrong. What do I do first? [COAS: Role-play an exam-ple.] What do I do next? [COAS: Role-play an example.] What is the next thing I do? Yes, I will take away a privilege. [Role-play an example.] But I know that these things will seldom happen because we will enjoy the work and the privileges. What do I do when you earn the privileges? [COAS] You got it. I will tell you or ask you if you have.

Use plenty of reinforcing statements for inductive behavior, even if it is more remembering than predicting at this point.

The Third Day and Beyond. On the third day, put the initial model and walk through at the beginning of each activity. And then do the activity according to the classroom procedure (Chapter 4). Cover all the special activities at the start of the day. From that point on, reinforce, prompt, or correct the special activity SM behaviors during the activities. Continue to question the students as you move through the activity procedure, asking them what is first, second, and so forth. At the end of the activity, have them predict the next activity and how they will transition to it. Around the fourth day start to call on students without having them raise their hands. After about 10 to 12 days, begin using the full inductive procedure as outlined in Chapter 8. At about this same time you can delete parts of the review that they are getting correct every day, covering them once every few days or so. Concentrate on that which is not firm. At this point, you are beginning to test their activity SM and inductive behavior.

Refinement Teaching

The objective is to achieve stability in the duration, latency, and accuracy of activity SM behaviors and related inductive behavior. It is the variability of student behavior, its day-to-day inconsistency, that contributes to making teaching a burnout profession. You can eliminate this punishing element through refinement teaching.

The elements of refinement are not equally important. Rate is not a concern. You want the inductive and SM behavior to occur only once when required. If it occurred more than once you would be having a problem of accuracy. Accuracy is always desired.

For refining special activity SM behavior, transitions, and inductive behavior, aim for short duration. For most regular activity SM behaviors, such as listening or sitting, reinforce long duration.

Latencies should all be short, with students predicting and performing SM behaviors as soon as appropriate. When they do not, instructional time is lost. By having students predict what is appropriate, you eliminate the need to continually ask them and, thus, help decrease latencies. The result is a visibly different classroom.

Refinement begins after only a few days. Because you are teaching many classes of behavior, refinement teaching begins sooner for some. For example, you begin to refine activity SM behaviors before inductive behavior. Later, the refining of inductive behavior and activity SM behavior become intertwined. As you refine one, the other is also refined. In the following examples, the goal is to illustrate the refinement process. Notice how the examples capture multiple refinement elements, such as duration and latency, in just a few words.

Refining Transitions. Here are some examples of statements that focus on refining transition SM behavior.

> Penmanship is next. To get ready, you will have to get your pencils, move your desks, and take your seat. Who can move their desks smoothly without pushing or bumping into others? (SR) So let's go!

The sequence of transition behaviors is described and followed by examples. The focus is on accuracy. A future set of questions asks for predictions.

> Which activity is next? [COAS] Correct, and what do you have to do to set up for it? [COAS] How will you do it? [COS] Go to it!

As the students begin to transition, partial statements are appropriate.

> Gwen is moving smoothly.
> I like the way Vivian is waiting for Dora to pass.
> This organizing is moving swiftly again today.

The first two statements describe the accuracy of the behavior. The last describes duration and its change-over-time (consistency). As the last students get set up for the activity, the teacher calls for summary statements.

> That was my kind of organizing. No running or bumping, everyone cooperating by taking turns to move into place but doing it fast. I am happy to see it. What about you? (SR)

Next is another summary, but with questions. It is usable when students have been behaving consistently.

> Helen, what did you like about the way you moved to the next activity? [SR] I agree. Is there anything anyone did not like? [COAS] And you have been transitioning consistently for a long time now.

As students start to manage themselves without prompting, summary statements can describe the historical relationship between SM and academic behavior.

> You organized so fast we will have plenty of time for the activity lesson and a little time for our favorite game.

By rewarding students for fast transitions, you are implicitly asking for rate and accuracy (doing it once), and short latency (doing it right away). Referring to one or two refinement components usually gets you the rest. Just vary the ones to which you refer.

The transition behavior for special activities is usually included as part of its procedure. Simply by focusing on the steps of the procedure you can refine the behavior.

> Tina, thanks for raising your hand to ask a question. What is it?
>
> Penelope, I appreciate your flipping up the red card and continuing to work while you waited. How can I help?

After the students are proficient, only the name of the procedure needs to be identified.

Refining Activity Organization. For an organization to continue, students must perform the SM and task behaviors of the activity. The key to refining an activity organization is the historical relationship between SM and task behavior (Chapters 2 and 6). Because of this relationship, either one or their relationship can be referenced. When students can perform the SM behaviors of an activity, the referencing should primarily, but not exclusively, focus on the task behavior.

The following set of statements illustrates refining activity organization, focusing primarily on the duration of behavior and the steps of the activity procedure. Each statement occurs at a later point in the activity. The statements are a little contrived to illustrate the refinement process. The scenario is the first few days of class, and you have just reviewed the organization with them. Begin refinement with a condition statement.

> You are ready to work. How many can keep working for the whole activity? (SR) I am looking forward to it. Let's learn some sounds for reading.
>
> You are impressing me so much with making the sounds that I almost forgot to mention how well you are keeping at it. You are sitting up straight, looking at me and the board, and giving me the sounds when I ask for them. Let's try the sounds again and then add one more.
>
> Because your listening and sounding out were done so well, we are ready to practice putting sounds together. How many think they can watch me, the board, and put sounds together? (SR) I know you can!
>
> Putting sounds together is easy for you. Now, can you continue to do the same kind of work for pronouncing words? (SR) Great! Here is your first word.
>
> Great word saying. Now for the last part of reading, doing the worksheet. Who thinks they can follow the organizational plan while we circle, match, and write sounds? (SR) Okay, so put your finger where mine is [model] and . . .
>
> That is the end of reading. Notice what you have done. First, you said sounds, blended sounds, and pronounced words. Second, you filled in your

worksheet. You did it all without a problem because you followed the procedure of the activity. You made it fun for me. Did you have fun? (SR) Excellent! Who will do it again tomorrow? (SR) I will look for it. Let's give ourselves a hand. [Clap]

These would constitute the major statements in the refinement process. There would, of course, be numerous partial statements such as: "Great sounds." "You're really remembering the sounds." "Very clear." "Right on signal." "That's the way to watch my pointing." As the students begin to identify the elements of the organization prior to the start of the lesson, you shift to an inductive question format. Eventually, short statements in combination with a debriefing (a set of questions about their performance) complete and maintain refined behavior. Such a debriefing is about 30 seconds long and may contain references to other aspects of students' behavior.

For each change in organization, initial and refinement teaching have to be undertaken. Because students are gaining a history of organizing, new organizations are learned much faster. Much less modeling and prompting is needed. They know in general what is required and have been reinforced for it in the past.

TEACHING STUDENTS THE ORGANIZING STRATEGY

The organizing strategy outlined in Chapter 3 included four steps: identifying when to organize, locating, transferring, and arranging. By teaching students to predict when and how to organize themselves and materials across activities, you are implicitly teaching them an organizing strategy. If you want them to efficiently organize complex tasks in any environment, however, overtly teach them a more sophisticated strategy. When this is done, students have a way to talk about and analyze their organizing so it can be planned. You can teach the organizing strategy with or without using postings.

Teaching the Organizing Strategy without Postings

When students efficiently follow the organization of the classroom, you can begin teaching the strategy steps. The organizing terms are overtized by the use of statements and questions. The statements pair student examples of the steps with the name of the steps. This procedure is outlined in Chapter 7's Language Requirements section. Here are a few quick statements that apply to organizing:

I am glad everyone remembered, or IDENTIFIED, that they needed their workbooks for math.

Zelda, thank you for finding, or LOCATING, the book you needed for the lesson.

Everyone put their materials in places that makes work easy. That is called ARRANGING your work.

By IDENTIFYING that you need books, LOCATING them, TRANSFER-RING them to the group, and ARRANGING them as fast as you did, we are ready to begin our lesson. Locating, transferring, and arranging your materials like that is my kind of ORGANIZING. Thank you very much.

These examples indicate the range of statement forms you can use. The last statement would follow only when many statements of the first three varieties had been given over a period of time.

After these forms of statements have been used for a while, students are asked questions that use strategy terms, and asked for their prediction about organizing requirements.

What do you need to IDENTIFY for the math activity?

Who can tell me how you ARRANGE for the math activity?

How will you ORGANIZE for the math activity?

The questions cannot really be answered without discriminating which behaviors comprise the term used. When the last question is asked, the students should have answers that include the terms *locate, transfer,* and *arrange.*

If students fail to use the organizing terms, the correction is patterned after those given in Chapter 11. The first level of correction would be to simply ask them to use the terms. This can also be done as a prompt before mistakes occur.

Would you use the term LOCATE in your answer.

Try again, and this time use all the terms about organizing we have talked about.

If these fail to work, model the answer. During review, you have the best opportunities to bring together the language of organizing and refine their use of it. Once they have it, they have another tool to help them analyze and solve the problems which will confront them.

Teaching the Organizing Strategy with Postings

Teaching students the organizing strategy with postings follows the procedure presented in Chapter 10. The posting would provide a title and then the four steps of organizing: identify, locate, transfer, and arrange.

Because students have a history of organizing and can perform and talk about it in everyday language, there is no need for building individual example sets. Here is how it can be introduced.

For each of our activities you get ready by getting what you need, going to the right place, and getting set to work. We call that organizing. What do we call it? (SR) Yes, organizing. It includes identifying what you need. For math you need your book, a pencil, and paper. Who can give me examples of what they need for reading?

You would continue as discussed in Chapter 10. After about two days, the strategy can be covered by reviewing activities, regular and special, from the perspective of the organizing strategy.

Who can tell me how we organize for reading? Sidney, what do you need to identify?

Similar to all reviews, move quickly. After a few days, students can lead the review. This not only adds variety but also prepares the students to supervise (Chapter 15). In addition, the statement and question procedures used without postings can be mixed into the posting procedure.

SCHEDULE FOR TEACHING ORGANIZING

Teaching students activity SM behaviors begins on the first day of school. Within a week, teaching inductive behavior related to the classroom plan begins. At about the same time, using a mix of statements and questions, the refinement of activity SM behaviors begins. Once inductive behavior is learned, it can be used to tandemly refine inductive behavior and activity SM behavior. At some point—usually six to eight weeks from the start of school—young students should exhibit the full inductive process and consistently perform all activity SM behaviors. At a not-too-distant point, begin to use more pair, triad, and small group organizations. The same teaching procedures are used for each change in organization. With each succeeding year, you have to devote less and less time to the teaching of classroom organizing.

Organizing should be the first SM strategy taught. Kindergarten is a good place to begin although it can be taught at any grade level. With the teaching of the planning strategy, the students can plan how they would organize an activity. At this point, the organizing strategy is paired with the planning strategy to produce an activity organization (Chapter 16).

PLANNING THE TEACHING OF ORGANIZING

To successfully teach students to behave inductively toward and follow your classroom organization, planning is required. Its basic elements follow:

1. Regroup your activity SM behaviors (Chapter 5) in terms of identifying, locating, transferring, and arranging.
2. Plan the steps of initial teaching. Consider:
   a. How you will model the elements of the activity.
      1. The activity procedures and other SM behaviors.
      2. The special procedures.
   b. How you will prompt and later cycle away from an emphasis on activity SM behavior.
   c. How often you need to review.
3. Plan the steps of refinement teaching.
   a. Build refinement statements and questions for activity SM behaviors.
   b. Build refinement statements and questions for transitions.
4. Plan the steps of teaching the organizing strategy.
   a. Do you want to introduce the strategy before students can read? If yes, use the nonposting procedure.
   b. Build examples of statements and questions related to teaching strategy language.

When done, you are ready to teach students to think inductively about and to follow the organization of the classroom.

14

SYSTEM STRATEGIES: HELPING AND SHARING

Students occasionally get stuck on a task or run short of materials. The outcome can be inappropriate behavior. To defuse this possibility, all that may be needed is a little helping and sharing. In this context, helping and sharing represent strategies to maintain appropriate behavior and to avoid inappropriate behavior. This chapter analyzes helping and sharing, and illustrates how to teach them.

ANALYSIS OF HELPING AND SHARING

Chapter 3 defined helping as working with others so that they can continue their tasks.[1] The helper performs just enough of the task with the others to get or keep it moving forward. In this sense the terms *aiding, assisting,* and *supporting* point to the degree of help being provided.

Sharing is defined as letting others use tools or materials so they can start, continue, or end their tasks. Sharing includes three related classes of behavior: reciprocating, lending, and giving. Appropriate sharing occurs when both parties are able to start, continue, or end their tasks. The need for helping and sharing can occur when students are working individually or in various groups.

Helping and sharing are simple strategies with four subclasses, or substrategies, each. The subclasses have four or five component steps that involve the interaction of helper/sharer and helpee/sharee. The basic substrategy and their component steps are as follows. "H/S" means helping or sharing.

1. Identifying → Offering → Accepting → H/S → Thanking
2. Identifying → Offering → Rejecting → Accepting Rejection
3. Identifying → Requesting → Accepting → H/S → Thanking
4. Identifying → Requesting → Rejecting → Accepting Rejection

All four procedures begin with discriminating (identifying) that helping/ sharing is needed. In substrategies one and two the helper or sharer makes the discrimination; in three and four the helpee/sharee makes it. The rest of the helping/sharing components are reciprocal, condition-matching operations between the parties involved.

When the helper/sharer makes the discrimination (one and two), the next step, as the operation component, is to offer to help/share. This step leads to either having the helping/sharing offer accepted (one) or rejected (two). If the helping/sharing is rejected (two), the potential helper/sharer needs to accept the rejection, thus terminating the interaction. If the helping/sharing is accepted (one), the helping/sharing step occurs and the interaction is terminated with a closing "Thank you." by the helpee/sharee.

When the helpee/sharee makes the discrimination (three and four), the next step, as the operation component, is asking for help or a chance to share. If the asking is accepted by the potential helper/sharer (three), helping/sharing occurs and the interaction ends with the helpee/sharee thanking those who helped/shared. If the asking is rejected, the potential helpee/sharee needs to terminate the interaction by accepting the rejection.

There are some minor variations on these procedural subclasses. For example, one starts to help/share as soon as the discrimination is made because it short-circuits a danger or prevents an accident. These can be easily covered in expansion teaching, although students usually adapt to such situations without direct instruction.

TEACHING HELPING AND SHARING

The objective is for students to perform appropriate helping and sharing without the teacher's prompting across the range of classroom conditions (activities). To insure that the behaviors become an automatic part of their repertoires, a wide range of activities need to incorporate opportunities to help and share. The end of this chapter illustrates how to design such activities.

Schedule of Instruction

Table 14.1 illustrates one possible schedule for teaching helping and sharing. The left column presents the instructional components to be taught. The time periods across the top illustrate the relationship of com-

Table 14.1
Schedule for Teaching Helping and Sharing

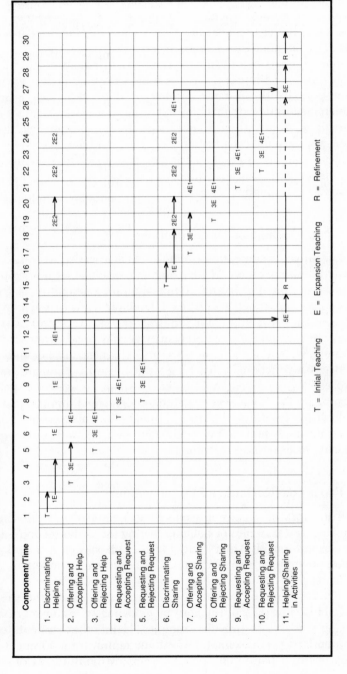

T = Initial Teaching   E = Expansion Teaching   R = Refinement

ponent introduction, but not the exact number of instructional days. The exact number of instructional days depends on the language and reading skills of students. The letters in the cells identify the teaching procedures to be used: T, initial teaching; E, expansion; and R, refinement. To simplify the table, the elements of teaching are not included but are discussed in detail throughout the chapter.

The numbers before an expansion (1E, 4E) indicate a particular expansion form and those after (E1, E4) indicate that all expansions during a time period with the same number are done in a single lesson exercise, which means they are juxtaposition expansions (see Chapter 9). The numbers in brackets in the text, not the examples, indicate cells. For example, [1/2] points to the cell of component one and time period two. Follow the table as you read, so that a clear picture of teaching students helping and sharing emerges. Because this is the first schedule, detailed references are made to it throughout the text.

Initial Teaching of Discriminations

For initial teaching, four example sets are needed—two for helping and two for sharing. Figure 14.1 illustrates an example set for helping. Chapter 9 presented one for sharing. To find alternate examples, walk through your activities as described in Chapter 4. Examples can be used more than once. One of the most important forms of helping is supporting others when they are behaving appropriately managerially or academically (Chapter 3). Examples 1 and 7 of Figure 14.1 fit this subclass of helping.

Begin instruction by teaching students to discriminate helping [1/1]. Proceed as described in Chapter 9. About four weeks later introduce sharing [6/15]. For the young student (preschool through first grade), initially teach two days in a row. For older students (second or third grade) you can simply provide two models and then test with three or four before moving to expansion teaching on the same day.

Expansion Teaching of Discriminations

Two types of expansion example sets are needed. The first is asking students for examples of helping/sharing (1E). The second is a juxtaposition expansion (2E2) that brings together verbally or on a worksheet examples of helping, sharing, or neither (nonexamples). Models are provided in Chapter 9.

The first form of expansion teaching begins on or after the last day of initial teaching [1/2, 6/16]. Start by modeling an example or two and then asking students to provide examples. Have other students confirm the appropriateness of examples. Continue rapidly for a minute, two at most. Repeat this expansion for about a week; by the third day of using it [1/3, 6/17], only tests are needed. Use the expansion until all students can

Figure 14.1
Example Set for "Helping"

One of the ways we manage ourselves is by helping. We help when we work with others on their task just enough so they can continue. Here are some examples.

1. My turn. Everyone in class has just finished the assignment by the end of class. Everyone shakes hands and claps for each other.
   Is everyone helping or not helping? Helping.

2. Zelda sits quietly and reads as Jim finishes his math assignment.
   Is Zelda helping or not helping? Helping.

3. Debra asks Henry how to spell "hammer" during a spelling test. Henry spells it for her.
   Is Henry helping or not helping? Not helping.

4. Debra asks Henry how to spell "hammer" during story writing. Henry spells it for her.
   Is Henry helping or not helping? Helping.

5. Fran's task is to shelve the reading books after the lesson. The last bell is about to ring, so Greg starts to shelve books with Fran.
   Is Greg helping or not helping? Helping.

6. Your turn. Fran is shelving reading books. Greg starts to shelve them also. Fran says, "I can do it. I have plenty of time before the end of class." But Greg continues to shelve books.
   Is Greg helping or not helping? (SR: Not helping.)

7. Jim finishes his math assignment and gives Zelda the thumbs up sign for reading quietly while he finished his math.
   Is Jim helping or not helping? (SR: Helping.)

8. Mary falls down and her books go flying. Selma and Rodney walk right on by without a word.
   Are Selma and Rodney helping or not helping? (SR: Not helping.)

9. Wonda tells Ernestine that she can't get the answer to a worksheet question during story reading. Ernestine gives Wonda the answer.
   Is Ernestine helping or not helping? (SR: Not helping.)

10. Wonda asks Ernestine the answer to a question during seatwork. Ernestine says, "Please ask the teacher."
    Is Ernestine helping or not helping? (SR: Helping.)

11. Cindy carries out the balls and bats for recess.
    Is she helping or not helping? (SR: Helping.)

12. Carlos asks Tina to check his math problem. Tina looks at the answer and then tells Carlos the right answer.
    Is Tina helping or not helping? (SR: Not helping.)

provide examples. As students become firm, spend less time on this expansion, asking for only two or three examples, and move to the juxtaposition expansion form [1/19, 6/19, continued]. Similar to many expansions, this one does not need to be taught every day. How you schedule it depends on the instructional load and students' skill acquisition.

Initial Teaching of Substrategies

Start the initial teaching of substrategies after expanding the discrimination for two days [2/3, 7/17]. Each substrategy of helping/sharing is taught, one after the other [3/5, 8/19, continued]. Chapter 9 illustrated the initial teaching of the offering-accepting, or first, subclass. The others are taught with the same logic, or format. Two initial models are used, followed by a few test (practice) examples. All examples are situations that require helping/sharing. One day of initial teaching should suffice. The models by other students during expansion procedures are strong enough to make up for students who missed initial teaching.

For the older students, a posting of helping/sharing substrategies can be used. All four subprocedures can be presented on one posting, juxtaposed as done in the analysis section earlier. Present one, possibly two, positive examples, and one negative example for each substrategy before testing. There is no need to cover all substrategies at one time.

Expansion Teaching of Substrategies

Two types of teacher-directed expansions are required (3E, 4E). The first proceeds as the one presented in Chapter 9: Pair students, giving each a helper/sharer or helpee/sharee role, provide a situation and ask them to perform the substrategy that was just initially taught [2/4, 7/18, continued], then ask others if all steps were correct. It may be necessary to model one example and prompt the students through the substrategy the first time or two. If small groups are used, two students can perform the substrategy and the others evaluate it, and then change roles. If a posting is used with older students, this expansion can be eliminated.

If parts of the students' interactions are not or do not seem correct, ask students to agree or disagree with the parts. This is the start of a correction. Continue by saying something like, "Not everyone seems to agree with you. You might say instead . . ." Test by coming back to the erring student or students in a few turns.

For the second teacher-directed expansion (4E1), juxtapose different situations with different, substrategies after two or more are learned [2/7, 3/7, 7/21, 8/21, continued]. In this way, the expansion changes as new substrategies are included. By having a student provide a helping/sharing situation and then having students act out the situation for the selected substrategy, the expansion (4E1) includes discriminating helping/sharing [1/12, 6/26]. For a few examples, ask students to make a negative example out of a positive one. This helps them experience back-to-back the different emotional consequences of appropriate and inappropriate helping/sharing.

At the start of all teacher-directed expansions, simply call on students who have their hands raised. After two days, tell students not to raise their hands and simply call on them for participation. Initially, many student answers will be much alike; accept these. But also reinforce for new examples. When students can move through this situation without error, they are ready for the final expansion.

Final Expansion Teaching

The final expansion, 5E, moves the strategies into the classroom activities [11/13, 11/27]. Usually, this begins to happen before the teaching of helping and sharing are complete. Yet, you still want to set the occasion for the strategies. Introduce by saying something like this:

> You know what helping (sharing) is and how to do it. I would like you to do as much of it as possible in our activities. Who will give it a try? (SR)

If you have only a few activities in which you want students to help/share, restrict the request to those of interest.

Technically, the final expansion has an element of integration teaching. Both the discrimination and the operation components are brought together to create the inclusive classes of helping and sharing. Because refinement teaching can take care of combining these components, no specific integration procedure is required.

Refinement Teaching

The refinement of helping/sharing focuses on teaching students to respond to all opportunities without a teacher's request (rate), to do so as quickly as possible (latency), and to appropriately perform all steps of the applicable substrategy (accuracy). Refinement starts almost immediately after the final expansion [11/15, 11/29]. The broken horizontal arrow indicates that refinement may not occur every day. The refinement of sharing would continue beyond time period 30.

The refinement prompt to set the occasion for helping or sharing would come at the start of the day or an activity of interest.

> You know how to help; will you do it if you get the chance? (SR) I know you will keep on the lookout for a chance to help.

Here are some examples of reinforcing statements for helping given to students during an activity.

> Betty, thank you for noticing that Jose needed help and for helping him without my having to request it.
>
> Assisting Zelda in picking up the books she dropped was helpful. I appreciate it very much.

> Cheering each other on like that helps all of you enjoy your work. Such helping is called support.
>
> Jennifer, your offer to help was very polite. As was your acceptance, Gilda. Did you enjoy working together? (SR)

These examples point out various attributes to be refined, and relate to the subclasses of helping: aiding, assisting, and supporting. The same type of statements can be given for sharing. Here are two examples:

> Rachel, lending Terrence your extra pencil showed me you can share your resources when needed without being requested to do so.
>
> Sharing the science materials allowed all of you to complete your projects before the end of class.

Related terms such as *lending* and *giving* can be defined in the context of sharing. Later, these statements can be replaced with questions asking for predictions, confirmations, and evidence related to helping/sharing.

At the end of an activity or day, use complete statements or debriefing to reinforce helping/sharing. A debriefing is a combination of statements and questions related to the behavior and conditions of interest. It is an open-ended interaction.

> John, I noticed you helped Henriette by pointing out the next step in the assignment. What are some of the other examples of helping that were or could have been done during the activity? [COAS] How could Brad and Wendy have offered and accepted help? [COS].

The debriefing helps the students explore their helping and sharing through their inductive behavior. By providing all class members with an opportunity to see how other members perform and support helping/sharing, you are building compatible contingencies in the classroom (Chapter 5) as well as illustrating the range and limits of these strategies. After helping and sharing have been taught, both can be included in the same debriefing.

Beyond the Schedule of Instruction

Once students have a history of being reinforced for helping and sharing, the behavior can usually be maintained simply by providing numerous opportunities to do so. By then the processes themselves generate emotional, structuring, or access consequences that are reinforcing, or intrinsically motivating. Yes, it is necessary to assure students that helping and sharing are appropriate, and to reinforce them for it. But at this point the statements and questions focus on how helping and sharing facilitate the new task behaviors they are learning. Much later, the behaviors are reviewed during the integration of SM strategies and transferred to everyday life (Chapter 19).

DESIGNING ACTIVITIES TO PROMOTE HELPING AND SHARING

The secret to designing activities is not in the physical arrangement of the classroom, but in seeing the classroom as a set of implicit or explicit *rules of interaction*, each of which contributes to the flexibility allowed students in interacting with each other to continue appropriate behavior. The goals, rules, and procedures covered in Chapter 10 explicitly define ways to interact. This is especially true for some of the rules to get help or interact after an activity task is finished. By showing students the range and limits of helping/sharing, you are widening these rules. By stating that students can help and share, you are setting the occasion for them and expressing your approval. These rules are only as good as the opportunities present for helping and sharing. To increase the opportunities, there are two things to do.

The first, to promote sharing, restricts the materials available. You can give them an example of how to do it or wait to see what happens and correct as needed. The second, to promote helping, assigns tasks to individuals that take more than one to do. Similar to sharing, you can either model or simply see if they adapt. In general, be prepared for innovative ways of helping and sharing.

PLANNING THE TEACHING OF HELPING AND SHARING

Before you begin to teach helping and sharing, planning is required. The following outline lists steps that need to be planned:

1. Build example sets for discriminating helping and sharing.
   a. Identify for each activity the range of examples that define the classes of behavior.
   b. Identify for each activity the limits of the classes through examples that are minimally different from the positive examples.
2. Build example sets for each substrategy.
3. Determine if helping or sharing would be problematic in any activity.
   a. Are there any activities where I do not want the students to share or help?
   b. Are there any activities where I am having trouble defining the limits of the class?
   c. If the answer to these is yes for any activity, note it.
4. Construct your teaching. Answer the following questions:
   a. How will I introduce the initial teaching of helping and sharing?

   b. Which expansion procedures will I use for:
      1. Discriminating helping and sharing.
      2. Teacher-directed expansions for helping and sharing. (Two are rec-
         ommended in this chapter.)
      3. Activity expansions. Note the activities in which you do not want
         helping and sharing to occur (item three).
5. Build refinement procedures. Consider:
   a. Condition statements to get the behavior going.
   b. Reward statements during the activity.
   c. Debriefings after the activity or class.
   d. Focusing on rate, latency, and accuracy.
6. Decide on procedures to maintain helping and sharing.
7. Schedule the teaching components.
   a. Decide when discrimination and operation components are to be
      taught for each strategy.
   b. Use Table 14.1 as a model from which to plan, but work out schedules
      by actual teaching days.

After following this planning activity, you will be ready to implement the
teaching of helping and sharing.

15

SYSTEM STRATEGY: SUPERVISING

If today's students are to become the skilled supervisors needed in tomorrow's world, we must teach them a supervising strategy. If this teaching begins at an early age, the chance of making that strategy an automatic and integrated part of their behavior increases. The long-term consequence is a citizenry who can keep tasks moving forward whether working individually or in groups. This chapter analyzes the supervising strategy and presents the procedures to teach it.

ANALYSIS OF SUPERVISING

Chapter 3 defined supervising by a student or group as behavior that interacts with and occurs throughout an activity to facilitate task behavior. Figure 15.1, an expanded posting, outlines the discriminations (as questions) and operations (as statements) of the supervising strategy steps.[1] The class names can be adjusted for students with different vocabulary skills. The components of each step are examined.

Decide on Supervising

Not all activities need to be supervised. When one wants to learn, perform a new task, or work in a group, supervision is usually needed. Once the need has been established (1a), the supervisor next discriminates what supervision is needed (1b). The smart supervisor adjusts to those being supervised and the task being performed. At minimum, a supervisor always monitors task progress. To help students make these two discriminations (1a and 1b), a few guidelines are presented later. These can be used once students have a foundation in supervising. Thus, this strategy step is the last one taught and forms the basis for refining supervision.

Figure 15.1
Supervising Strategy Posting

SUPERVISING STRATEGY

1. DECIDE ON SUPERVISING
   a. Is supervision needed?
   b. What supervision is needed?

2. TELL ABOUT THE PLAN
   a. Who works on the task?
   b. What materials are needed?
   c. When do we start and stop?
   d. Where do we work?
   e. How do we manage and do the task?
   f. What are the consequences?
   g. Give the needed answers.

3. SET ACTIVITY GOALS
   a. What should our goals be?
      • Management goals
      • Task goals
   b. Are the goals possible?
   c. Commit to the goals.

4. DIRECT ACTIVITY FLOW
   a. What needs to be done next?
   b. Give the needed direction.

5. LOOK FOR SUCCESS
   a. What has been done?
   b. What should be done?
   c. Is there success?

6. POINT OUT CONSEQUENCES
   a. What consequences occur?
   b. Point out consequences.

Tell about the Plan

To carry out an activity, students must discriminate the parts of the plan. Each question of step two, 2a through 2f, indicates one of the parts presented in Chapter 4. Since Chapter 13 illustrated teaching students to follow and behave inductively relative to the classroom plan, the present instructional task is to relate this knowledge of the plan to the supervising strategy.

Set Activity Goals

Students need to make predictions about their management and task behavior (3a), to set goals. These often relate to the refinement of behavior.

For example, students may want to start and finish on time, follow specific rules, get so many correct, or cooperate (reciprocal accuracy of management behavior). Yet identifying goals is not enough. Goals must be possible (3b) and, thus, based on evidence. After the goals are clear, students need to commit to them (3c).

Direct Activity Flow

All tasks move forward in time. To keep this movement alive, the supervisor has to predict what needs to be done next as task components are completed (4a). Because the plan indicates ways to get help, the supervisor always has access to appropriate behavior. When 4a can be answered, the needed direction is given (4b).

Look for Success

By making the discriminations "What has been done?" (5a) and "What should be done?" (5b), it is possible to discriminate "Is there success?" (5c). The answer to 5b is directly related to 3a, "What should the management and task goals be?" Once known, the supervisor proceeds to step six.

Point Out Consequences

The answer to "Which consequences occur?" (6a) is a prediction built on the relationship between discriminating potential consequences (2f) and the degree of success (5c). Supervisors should be able to discriminate a variety of consequence types (form, access, and emotional changes) and their direction (self or others) relative to task performance. Once the discriminations are made, the consequences need to be pointed out to those supervised (6b).

Because an activity task is ongoing, the continual application of directing activity flow (4), evaluating success (5), and establishing consequences (6) is often necessary. The skill to do so depends on the extent to which the supervisor can discriminate what constitutes the appropriate behaviors of an activity at any point in time. When the activity involves little SM behavior and has obvious task products, then supervision is simplified. For example, if the task for an individual working alone is to do 30 problems in 30 minutes, half the problems should be done in 15 minutes, if the difficulty of the problems is about the same. For a complex activity where a group of students must plan, organize, or learn extensively, supervision becomes more difficult. The supervisor must look beyond the task product and examine the progress related to the SM behaviors. When this is done, continual progress can be exposed throughout the activity to keep those involved moving forward with enthusiasm.[2]

TEACHING SUPERVISION

The objective is to teach students to supervise themselves individually and in groups. The key to teaching supervision is to see the teacher's classroom supervision as a model. Once students can discriminate the component steps of this supervising strategy model, they are gradually taught to take over the responsibility.

Entry Skills

Before beginning to teach supervising, your students must be able to predict all the predictable parts of the classroom plan, follow it, and read and follow simple rule and procedure postings as described in Chapter 10. Besides being able to discriminate a range of consequences, students should be able to classify consequences by their types, direction, and placement (Chapter 5). This is especially important for older students (grades six through nine). The types of consequences can be taught with example sets that expand the discrimination of consequences across a large array of behaviors.

Schedule of Instruction

Table 15.1 presents a possible schedule for teaching supervision. The components to be taught are on the left. The time periods across the top illustrate the relationship of component introduction, but they do not indicate the exact number of instructional days. The symbols within the cells represent the following: T, initial teaching; E, expansion; I, integration; and R, refinement. The number before a teacher procedure (1E, 1I) indicates a particular procedure. The number after an expansion (E2) indicates that all expansions with that number during a time period are taught in a single lesson exercise, which means that they are juxtaposition expansions (Chapter 9). Horizontal arrows indicate the continuation of a teaching procedure and dashed arrows indicate that the procedure does not need to be done each day.

The following illustrates how the components of supervision, as presented on the left side of Table 15.1, are taught. The bracketed numbers ([2/4]) in the text, not the examples, indicate a cell of the table. The first is the component number and the second the time period. By following the table as you read, a clear picture of teaching emerges.

Teaching Students to Discriminate Supervision Steps

Both initial and expansion teaching procedures are used. During both, you are primarily modeling group, not individual, supervising, even though you are going to teach both.

Initial Teaching. Begin with a short rationale [1/1].

Table 15.1
Schedule for Teaching Supervision

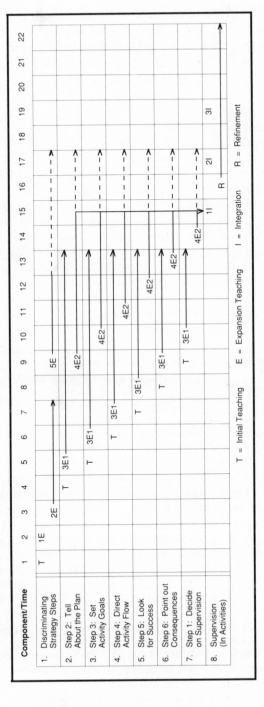

Component/Time	1	2	3	4	5	6	7	8	9	10	11	12	13	14	15	16	17	18	19	20	21	22
1. Discriminating Strategy Steps	T	1E	2E						5E													
2. Step 2: Tell About the Plan				T	3E1				4E2													
3. Step 3: Set Activity Goals					T	3E1				4E2												
4. Step 4: Direct Activity Flow						T	3E1				4E2											
5. Step 5: Look for Success							T	3E1				4E2										
6. Step 6: Point out Consequences								T	3E1				4E2									
7. Step 1: Decide on Supervision									T	3E1				4E2								
8. Supervision (In Activities)															1I	R	2I		3I			

T = Initial Teaching   E = Expansion Teaching   I = Integration   R = Refinement

For each of our activities, I supervise your work. I guide you through the task. Now it is time for you to learn how to take over that responsibility. Here is what I do when I supervise.

Now present a six-step supervision posting that looks like this:

Supervising

1. Decide on supervising.
2. Tell about the plan.
3. Set activity goals.
4. Direct activity flow.
5. Look for success.
6. Point out consequences.

Except for the first step, cover the steps by giving an example or two, and then asking a few students for examples. In the following example of teaching, everything done by the teacher is in brackets: point to supervising strategy [SS], point to supervising strategy—step 1 [SS1], call on a student [COAS], call on students [COS]. What the student does is in parentheses: (SR) student replies or students reply, whichever is appropriate.

[SS1] The first thing I do is to decide what supervision is needed. For example, I may decide to do very little supervising if I think you know how to perform the task. We will go over this step later.

[SS2] Second, you already know about the plan. But I tell you about those parts that you can't predict. For example, yesterday I told you which pages the assignment for reading would cover, and how many questions to answer. Who can tell me some of the things that I told you about the plan today? [COS]

[SS3] Third, I ask you to set your goals for an activity. Yesterday, in reading, I asked you to commit to finishing your assignment. Who can tell me some of the goals that I asked you to commit to today? [COS]

[SS4] Fourth, I direct activity flow, or guide you throughout the activity. In reading I tell you to start, who should read next, and if you have errors. Can anyone give me an example of my directing them during a task? [COS]

[SS5] Fifth, I look for your success. This helps me to tell you just how well you are doing on the task. Yesterday, I looked for how accurate your reading was and how you shared materials during art. What are some of the other things I look at to see if you are being successful? [COS]

[SS6] Finally, I point out the consequences that occur because of your success. For example, yesterday, I saw that the Blue Group had met their goal of having five or less errors each day. This allowed me to tell them that they had earned extra free time. Also, I told Arnold that he had reached his reading goal for the first time and asked him how he felt about it. He said it surprised him. Who can tell me some of the consequences I have pointed out to them? [COS]

This initial teaching is done for two days and concludes with a request for them to observe the steps of your supervision.

Students may make two types of errors when you request examples. First, they will present examples that do not fit the step being considered. Simply point to the correct step in the posting and say, "I think it fits better here [SS]." Or ask others. The second error is no response—the student does not have an example. Just move to another student, but return later for a retest.

Expansion Teaching. Three expansion activities are required. The first, 1E, takes place during the SM teaching activity [1/2]. You have students identify (1) what you have done, and (2) what they have done that fits the supervision steps. You want them to discriminate that they supervise even as you are supervising. Move fast, spending at most one minute covering the steps. After a time, focus on only those steps for which students are having the most difficulty generating examples. This expansion can be done on a worksheet.

The second expansion, 2E, overlaps the first and takes place during the classroom activities [1/3]. The objective is to get students to discriminate supervision steps in a real supervision context. It also gives them a model of supervising under a variety of contexts. As often as possible during an activity, ask students (1) to identify which supervision step you or they just performed, and (2) to predict which step will come next. Prompt with the strategy posting and use partial statements to reinforce. Ask for evidence to clarify.

To correct, give the answer and move on. At first implement this expansion during one activity, but quickly move to others. If for some reason you cannot stop during an activity, do this expansion as a debriefing. The debriefing has the advantage of giving students a better total picture of supervising, but it does not develop in context the inductive behavior element of supervision.

The third expansion, 5E, focuses on teaching students to remember the steps of the supervising strategy [1/9]. The objective is to have them reproduce the strategy posting. After the students start to learn to perform the strategy steps, begin presenting them with worksheet exercises that require filling in the steps and substeps of the strategy that they have learned. A worksheet need only focus on a step at a time, gradually combining them. These worksheet exercises, which take a minute or two, not only insure that students know what strategy steps to perform but also tell you when to fade the posting. Remembering the strategy without error is one criterion that can contribute to earning a supervision award.

Initial Teaching of Supervision Steps

The six expanded steps are taught one at a time. The first step is taught last. The posting in Figure 15.1 can be expanded one step at a time. During initial teaching, performing the substeps is isolated from the classroom activities. For each step, you model, prompt, and test the students under a variety of activity scenarios (examples).

Inform of the Plan. The objective of this step is to firmly tie their knowledge of the plan to the supervising strategy. Present the expanded posting and introduce the strategy [2/4].

> You can now identify the components of supervising that I perform. Now it is time for you to learn to do it. Here is what I think about and do as I supervise you [SS]. Let's look first at "tell about the plan" [SS2].

Have the students read each substep for "tell about the plan." Next point to 2f and explain that you only tell about the parts of the plan that need to be reviewed or are going to change. Now walk them through an activity, such as reading or math, and for each substep question, ask, "So do I need to tell you or not tell you about this part of the plan?" Confirm their prediction and ask for evidence through the "How do you know?" format. To correct, model the answer and repeat. Go over one more activity and repeat for different activities on the next day. Initial teaching should take about two to three minutes.

Set Activity Goals. Introduce and initially teach set activity goals as follows [3/5]:

> [SS3] Here is what I think about and do when I set activity goals. [SS3a] First I ask, "What should our goals be?" [SS3a.] I think about management goals, like following the rules or procedure of an activity. [SS3b] How do I know this goal is possible? You have done it before and you are getting better at it. [SS3c] Once I know the goal is possible, I ask you to commit to it by saying something like, "Who can do it?"
>
> [SS3a.] Also, I think of task goals, like getting nine out of ten reading comprehension questions correct. [SS3b] How do I know this goal is possible? You have done many questions like these and you are getting to be better readers. [SS3c] Because the goal is possible, I ask you to commit to it by saying something like "I think you can do it, do you?"
>
> [SS3a] Your turn. Who can give me a goal for math? [COAS] Is that a task or management goal? [COAS] Everyone, is the goal possible? [COS] How do you know? [COAS] [SS3c] So, how would you ask someone to commit to it? [COAS]

Continue for a few more examples. This step should not take more than two minutes. Repeat on the next day.

Direct Activity Flow. Introduce "direct activity flow" as done for the previous steps [4/6]. Next, present four to eight examples that cover going through the substeps. These examples should cover the range of your activities. Model the first two or three. Here are a few examples.

My turn. In independent reading, Ron has just finished the third of ten comprehension questions. What does he do next? [SS4a] The fourth problem. How does he know? [SS4b] Our plan says to finish assignments. [SS4c] Now he asks himself to do it.

John and Mary have just finished the first part of their cooperative center math activity, but they don't remember what to do next. [SS4a] So, what do they do next? [SS4b] Get help. How do they know? Our plan says to get help when stuck. So what is the next step? [SS4b] To tell themselves to do it.

The Blue Group has just finished group story reading. [SS4a] So, what do I do next? Assign them reading workbook pages and problems. How do I know? Our plan says to give assignments after reading group. So, what is the next step? [SS4b] To tell them which pages and problems to do.

Your turn. You have just finished your comprehension questions. What do you do next [SS4a], Hubert? (SR: Correct the questions.) How do you know, Gilbert? (SR: Because our plan says to correct questions when finished.) [SS4b] So, what is your next step, Roda? (SR: To tell myself to correct it.)

You want to ask a question during study time. [SS4a] What do you do next, Sharon? (SR: Flip up red card.) How do you know, Vinny? (SR: That is what our plan says to do to ask a question.) [SS4b] So, what is your next step, Ronny? (SR: To tell myself to flip up the green card and go back to work.)

To correct students who do not know the answer to the first part, simply link not knowing (as in the preceding second example) with looking at the plan. Ask, "What does the plan say?" If they still do not know, tell them. As Chapter 4 indicated, organizational plans should always include a way for the students to behave appropriately—they can at least use the getting help procedure. Do initial teaching one more day.

Look for Success. Begin initial teaching with the expanded posting and an introduction [5/7]. Next, present six to eight examples that do and do not illustrate success. To answer the "How do you know?" components of the following example set, it is helpful to initially prompt students with a posting of the rules, goals, and applicable procedures (parts of the plan) placed next to the supervising strategy posting.

My turn. [SS5] Math seatwork has just started. [SS5a] What has been done? John has his book, pencil, and paper out and is writing his name at the top. [SS5b] What should be done? Our plan says organize your work first. [SS5c] Is there success? Yes. How do I know? What has been done is what should have been done.

[SS5a] Your reading group has just finished, and the group read the story with only three errors. [SS5b] What should be done? Their goal was to read with five or less errors. [SS5c] Is there success? Yes. How do I know? [SS5a] What has been done [SS5b] is what should have been done.

[SS5a] The language workbook activity is almost over. Winfred, Tina, and Quincina have done 10 of 20 problems and are talking away. [SS5b] What should be done? Our goal is to finish the problems by the end of the activity. [SS5c] Is there success? No. How do I know? [SS5a] What has been done [SS5b] is not what should have been done.

Your turn. [SS5a] Math seatwork is half done and you have most of the problems finished. [SS5b] What should be done, Mel? (SR: To finish by the end of the activity. [SS5c] Everyone, is there success? (SR: Yes.) How do you know? (SR: What has been done is what should have been done.)

Next. [SS5a] Your group is quibbling over taking turns with the equipment. [SS5b] What should be done, Mico? (SR: Our plan says to share equipment.) [SS5c] Everyone, is there success? (SR: No.) How do you know? (SR: What has been done is not what should be done.)

The answer to what should be done relates to the plan, the goals, or both. Because there are three possible answers, one student is asked to answer. The last example may not be appropriate given the preceding models, but it does at this point help to illustrate a range. Repeat initial teaching the next day.

Point Out Consequences. You have modeled pointing out consequences and they have classified this model. Moreover, they have been predicting consequences for some period of time. These two facts simplify teaching. Again, present the posting and introduce this last posting step [6/8]. Next, present three or four examples of activity scenarios similar to the previous ones. Many of the same ones can be used. They show a range of points during the activity in which various consequences could be pointed out.

[SS6] Ronny is successful. He completed all the assignment before the end of the activity. [SS6a] Which consequences could occur because of his behavior? He can go to the finish early area and listen to music or he can sit and read a book in the book nook. Which other consequences could occur? [COS] [SS6b] How could the supervisor point out such consequences? She could say "You're really fast today. Are you going to read a book, listen to music, or what?" What other ways could the supervisor point out the consequences? [COS]

[SS6] Next example. The Green Group is not being successful. They have hardly started their group writing assignment and the time to work is almost half over. [SS6a] Which consequences could occur because of their behavior? They may not finish their assignment and they could get a failing grade. Which other consequences could happen? [COS] [SS6b]. How could the supervisor point out such consequences? He could say, "If you start to focus on your task, you could finish before the end of the activity. I hope you will do that." Which other ways could the supervisor point out the consequences? [COS]

Continue for one or two more examples and repeat the next day [6/9].

Decide on Supervising. Teaching students the "decide on supervising" step is based on a number of decision guidelines. These help students make predictions about substeps 1a and 1b of Figure 15.1

Figure 15.2 presents the guidelines. Guides 1A, 1B, and 1C point to conditions where students must carefully manage themselves. Guide 2A simply means do not supervise steps that can be done by those doing the job. In other words, smart supervisors skip steps when those supervised are reliably doing it by themselves. Yet they minimally look for success, or track progress. Guides 2B and 2C give those supervised a chance to think and perform on their own. Over the long run, these guidelines evolve with the supervisor's experience.

Place the supervision posting and the guideline posting together, and start initial teaching with an introduction [7/9]:

> [SS] During our activities you have been supervising yourselves more and more. Now it is time to become really smart supervisors. [Point to guide posting—GP] [GP1] First, we must ask, is supervision needed? These guides help us in deciding if only some or a lot of supervision is needed. [GP2] Second, we must ask, what supervision is needed? These guides help us decide. Let's see how.

Now present examples, as activity scenarios, that fit your classroom. For the first question of the posting, find four or five examples that require very little supervision and four or five that require more extensive supervision.

> [GP1] Let's find out if supervision is needed. First example. Albert is doing a drawing for fun during our free period. Does he need to supervise his work? Not really. How do I know? [GP1A] He is not trying to learn how to draw, [GP1B] it is not a new task, [GP1C] and he is working alone.

Figure 15.2
Supervision Guidelines

SMART SUPERVISING

1. IS SUPERVISION NEEDED?

   Guide A: Supervise when you want to learn.
   Guide B: New or active tasks need supervision.
   Guide C: Groups need more supervision.

2. WHAT SUPERVISION IS NEEDED?

   Guide A: Only supervise the steps needed.
   (Supervisors always look for success.)
   Guide B: Ask questions when possible.
   Guide C: If the task can be done many ways,
   let those supervised decide how.

Next example The Red Group is trying to do a great job on their group project. Is supervision needed? Yes. How do I know? [GP1A] They are trying to learn, [GP1B] it is a new task, [GP1C] and they are a group.

Next example. The Green Group is doing their group reading as they do everyday. Is supervision needed? Some. How do I know? [GP1C] They are a group and [GP1A] they want to learn, but [GP1B] it is not a new task. So some supervision is needed.

Your turn. Two teams are playing a game during spelling. Is supervision needed? [COS] How do you know supervision is needed? [COS, GPs as needed] Sharp thinking. Yes, they are groups, they are trying to win, and they are active. They know the game, but that is not enough to stop the need to supervise.

Next example. Vivian and Winfred are playing marbles at recess. Is supervision needed? (SR: No.) How do you know that they do not need supervision? [COAS, GPs as needed] Yes, at recess they are just taking it easy and it is not a new task and it is not active enough to be a danger or interrupt the work of others. They are a group, but that is not enough to require supervision in this situation. [Continue for about two more examples.]

Next, move to the second part of the guides. Use the examples requiring supervision just given and about two more. This whole procedure is dependent on your prompting them and following their examples and predictions. Do not be too critical, let plausible answers stand, and ask the others to agree or disagree with the students' responses.

What supervision is needed? These guides help you decide which supervision steps to use. Let's read them together. [Read] Here are some examples.

Remember the Green Group was going to do their reading as usual. Which steps of supervision could be used? Well, they all know the plan by now. So I could just ask them some questions about what they have to do. [GP2B] But I need to look for success [SS5 and GP2A]. [SS6] That will make it possible to point out some important consequences or [SS4] direct activity flow. [Model one more example.]

Your turn. The Red Group also needed supervision for their project. Which steps of supervision do you think would be needed? [COAS] Yes, probably all. Who can tell me how they would do the first step? [COAS] Yes, you could ask questions. [GP2B]. If you wanted to direct the flow of the task [SS3], how would you do it? [COAS] Yes, you may want to let them decide by asking them how they want to do it. [GP2B and C]. Anything else you would want to do? [COAS] How many agree with Teresa? [COS] I agree.

Finish with one or two more examples. You may have to prompt more than these examples suggest the first day or two. If you have used some variety in your supervision and students are firm on discriminating and performing individual strategy steps, they will be able to provide reasons for specific supervising in a short time.

Expansion Teaching of the Strategy Steps

Two types of expansion follow the initial teaching of each strategy step.

First Expansion. The first expansion, 3E, is a worksheet exercise that takes place during the teacher-directed SM activity and follows the day after initial teaching is completed [2/5, 3/6, 4/7, 5/8, 6/9, 7/10]. The worksheet is a paper and pencil version of initial teaching. It presents the same type of activity scenarios (examples) in text form and gives the students the same questions to answer, including the "How do you know?" components.

Each step is initially expanded in isolation, but is then juxtaposed, 3E1, in a single exercise with the previously expanded steps [2/6, 3/7, 4/8, 5/9, 6/10, 7/11]. Thus, scenarios are lengthened and questions are inserted at points where supervisors would perform a supervision step. The same scenarios can be used with slight modification at various points, so a range of individual and group supervising is covered. This expansion continues until all steps are expanded and occurs concurrently with the second strategy step expansion.

With the introduction of the worksheets and at each point where a step is added, prompt the students through the exercise once or twice by asking students to read and answer questions orally before they do it on their own. After the first two steps are juxtaposed, the prompt can be isolated to the new material. During this expansion, keep the strategy and guideline postings in view. Use a workcheck activity to evaluate answers (Chapter 4).

Second Expansion. The second expansion, 4E1, moves supervision into the classroom activities [2/9, 3/10, 4/11, 5/12, 6/13, 7/14]. The objective is to select students to perform various steps of supervision as the activity unfolds. Initially pick one individual and one group activity to implement the expansion. With the individual activity, call on the group or individuals to perform a supervision step as indicated in the following examples. For the group activity, select one that has been designed with you as the supervisor. Here is an introduction.

> [SS] We have been going over examples of how to [name step]. Now it is your turn to ask and answer these questions during our activity. To help, I will ask you now and then these questions or ask you to perform a step [name]. How many think they can do it?

Each time you introduce a step there would be less elaboration. From this point, prompts and reinforcements involve individual or group statements. Here are some examples for individual activities.

> Could everyone tell themselves about the plan. [SS2, Pause] Daniel, what did you tell yourself? (SR)
>
> Everyone, let's supervise. Zelda, could you perform step one? [PTS] Could everyone do step two for themselves?

[Private statement] Ron, are you being successful? (SR) How do you know? (SR) Keep it up. I like success, as I know you do.

[SS3] Please stop and direct the flow of the task.

When focusing on small groups, get the whole group involved.

Everyone, please stop and do step 5 of supervision. [SS5] Answer the first question. [Pause] Answer the second question. [Pause, Point] Is there success as a group? [COAS] How do you know? [COAS] How many agree? [COS] You are thinking! Keep it up.

Later, the prompts telling them to answer the questions can be dropped. The short version would look like this:

Everyone, do step 5 of supervision. [Pause] Are you being successful as a group? [COAS] How do you know? [COAS] Clear thinking.

At the next level, drop the "How do you know?" once they can accurately supervise when you prompt them. By changing the preceding to focus on one student, you have an example for working with individuals within a group.

Integration Teaching

When students can accurately perform individual supervision steps, integration teaching begins [8/15]. Its objective is to insure that students can, on their own, perform the necessary supervision steps so that tasks move forward as planned.

There are only three basic activities where students can fully supervise: (1) groups working on individual assignments; (2) groups working on a collaborative assignment; and (3) individuals working on an individual assignment. To insure that students fully integrate their supervision behaviors, model, prompt, and test students across this range of activities. The ease with which this is accomplished depends on the range of activities over which students have been asked to perform the individual supervision steps.

Supervising a Group Working Individually. This supervision situation is an extension of the getting help procedure discussed in Chapters 4 and 13. Essentially, the helper becomes a supervisor who does not perform the assignment, but supervises the group throughout the activity.

To model this type of activity [8/15], take a group of five or six students and have the others watch you supervising it. They can use observation forms containing the supervision steps to check off the steps performed. It is important to review how they direct activity flow without giving answers. Modeling one activity should be sufficient.

To prompt and test, break the class up into four or five groups and assign one of the members as a supervisor. Rotate supervisors from day to day. To separate the knowledge requirement from supervising, provide the supervisor with an answer sheet. The teacher's task is to move from group to group prompting and reinforcing the supervisor's supervision. Except where intervention procedures are required, interact with the groups only through the supervisors.

Supervising a Group Working Collaboratively. The setup for this situation should be exactly the same [8/17]. If students have been working in collaborative groups, it is usually only necessary to request that they supervise themselves according to the strategy and strategy guidelines. The prompts to supervisors are the activity procedure and the supervision postings. This time the supervisor participates in the task. Again, circulate, prompting and reinforcing appropriate supervision behavior.

Supervising Oneself. Model this situation by sitting at a desk and supervise yourself out loud as you work on a short individual worksheet task [8/19]. Next, prompt all the students through the same activity having them supervise themselves out loud. The last step is to prompt them through a short individual activity where they quietly supervise themselves. Keep the supervision postings in view.

Refinement Teaching

Supervisors adapt when their supervision behavior changes relative to the task and those involved. The objective of refining supervision is to facilitate this adaptation. Most of the refinement of supervision focuses on rate (supervising when needed), latency (as soon as needed), duration (for as long as needed), and accuracy (what is needed). These attributes are refined primarily through prompting with the guideline postings and reinforcing their occurrence across a variety of activities.

Refining supervision begins shortly after the start of integration teaching [8/17]. Initially, prompt activities by requesting students to supervise themselves during all activities. From this point, statements and questions are used to refine supervision behavior.

How many can follow these guides [GP] for smart supervising? (SR) I will be looking.

Jennifer, asking questions like that shows me you are trying to follow the guides. Thanks.

This is a new task, and you are carefully supervising yourselves along the way.

I like the way this group lets each person figure out how to do his or her part. That's smart supervising.

Statements do not need to refer to the guides.

Thank you for informing yourselves of the plan and directing the flow of your work.

Thank you for supervising your own tasks.

The last statement is the most inclusive. Yet it is just as descriptive because it has been extensively defined. Refinement teaching can also be done as a debriefing. Use the supervision posting and the guidelines posting. Ask the students about their supervising and how they are following the guidelines. This is a point to insert reward statements or show and question them about how their individual supervision helped the group supervisor or the teacher.

Finally, when all the students are supervising across activities to the extent planned, it is time for an award ceremony, a rite of passage with special privileges and responsibilities.

Beyond the Schedule of Instruction

Supervision is a skill that is always evolving. From classroom to classroom and year to year, student supervising behavior will be required in new situations and will continue to be polished. Thus, the SM curriculum needs to periodically return to the strategy and guidelines to model, prompt, and test new elements of supervision. This does not take much time and is critical to the continued evolution of supervision behavior (see Chapter 19).

PLANNING THE TEACHING OF SUPERVISION

Before teaching supervision, you must plan what needs to be done and when. The steps of the supervision skills planning operation provide you with a guide. Here are the steps:

1. Analyze your activities (Chapter 4).
2. Analyze your supervising.
   a. Build an analysis matrix with the supervision steps across the top and the classroom activities on the left side.
   b. Review how you supervise activity by activity using the matrix.
   c. Update your analysis as you continue to supervise.
   d. Decide if you are ready to model supervision to students.
      1. Does your supervising consistently cover the range of supervision steps?
      2. If answer is yes, you are ready.
      3. If the answer is no, practice supervision skills.
3. Analyze your students' skill at following and predicting your plans.
   a. If they consistently can, they are ready.
   b. If they cannot, implement procedures in Chapters 7 through 14.

4. Prepare teaching materials.
   a. Make up your postings.
   b. Work out examples appropriate to each component.
   c. Write out introductions to each component.
   d. Write out statements and questions for each step.
5. Prepare details of teaching procedures.
   a. Determine how you will call on students.
      1. During initial teaching.
      2. During activity expansion and integration.
   b. Determine how you will correct students.
      1. During initial teaching.
      2. During activity expansion and integration.
6. Prepare a tentative schedule for teaching.
   a. Decide how much time will be devoted to each supervision component.
   b. Decide which activities will be a part of supervision teaching.
   d. Follow the logic of Table 15.1.

Once you have followed these procedures, you will know if you are ready to teach students to supervise.

16

SYSTEM STRATEGY: PLANNING

Every generation faces new problems that require it to adapt. Within the SM curriculum, the first step in adapting is planning. Because most planning starts with a problem and ends with a solution that did not exist before, it represents what many call the problem-solving process.[1] As human behavior, this process can be represented as a strategy. The question is, do we want students to plan by trial and error, or do we want to teach them a more effective way? Without planning skills, future generations will be unable to save and remake the world they inherit. This chapter analyzes a four-step planning strategy and illustrates the procedures to teach it.[2]

THE ANALYSIS OF PLANNING

Planning begins with a real or potential problem. To eliminate it, students do not start in a vacuum. They work from an existing plan that functions as a model.[3] Solutions spring from changing this model. For most problems, students are only required to adjust a few of the elements or parts of the prior plan. In fact, a solution that solves the problem without changing much is often called innovative.

Models, Planning, and Learning

Before students can engage in planning, they need to be familiar with a number of models. Within the classroom, these models are their regular and special activities. Replanning these activities provides an excellent introduction to the planning process. Student apprentices need some basic skills and reinforcing activities that involve problems that are real to them, that have impact on their daily lives.

Although students plan many activities that involve learning something, the initial use of the planning strategy needs to be separated from the need to learn. If students must expand their existing knowledge base to solve a problem, they must exit to the learning strategy to discover which models exist, how to build and operate related models, or how to evaluate models. When such learning is needed, the process of planning is fragmented. For the present, planning is restricted to problems that use the knowledge base of the individual or group doing the planning.

Individual and Group Planning

Both individuals and groups plan. There are four advantages to group planning. First, there can be a supervisor whose main task is to guide the planning so that the problem solvers can concentrate on evolving a solution. Second, there is a larger knowledge base from which to work. This increases the probability of finding a solution. Third, each participant's contributions prompt and reinforce other contributions. And fourth, the whole planning strategy is overtized. This allows everyone to see the behaviors required in each planning step so that they have a model to imitate during individual planning.[4]

Components of the Planning Strategy

Planning is inductive behavior. The planning strategy as presented in Figure 16.1 helps overtize this behavior. Planning is done in two phases. The first phase, which includes the first three steps, is essentially a prediction argument. The second phase, which includes the fourth step, is a confirmation argument. Along with the observations that occur during implementation, the entire inductive process described in Chapter 7 takes place.

Identify the Problem. Identifying the problem (1) first involves discriminating which model needs changing (1a). The second element in problem identification is why the model needs changing (1b). In general, the changes are to facilitate the task, but at other times they may be to use new resources, or to make the activity more efficient, or to simply change things. Or it may be time for students to begin participant management planning. In general, these examples of a problem encompass the terms *goal* and *objective.*

Design Solutions. When students begin to design a solution or solutions (2), they look at the old plan when asking which changes are needed (2a). As stated earlier, usually only a portion of the plan has to be modified to achieve the desired results (1b). How it can be changed (2b) depends on the knowledge base of the planning group. Other past plans provide background; they help students prompt themselves when they are stuck on how to change some step of a plan.

Figure 16.1
Planning Strategy Posting

PLANNING STRATEGY

1. IDENTIFY THE PROBLEM
   a. What plan needs changing?
   b. Why change the plan?

2. DESIGN SOLUTIONS
   a. What changes are needed?
   b. How can it be changed?
   c. Does anything else change?
   d. Is the plan clear?

3. SELECT A SOLUTION
   a. Does the plan solve the problem?
   b. Does the plan fit the resources?
   c. Does everyone want to?

   [IMPLEMENT THE NEW PLAN]

4. EVALUATE THE SOLUTION
   a. Was the plan followed?
   b. Were there problems?
   c. Is improvement needed?

To discriminate whether anything else changes (2c) requires examining the new plan in light of the changes and asking if other steps are now required or need to be changed. For example, the resources to carry out the changes may also need to be rearranged, added, or deleted. This examination is a class of inductive behavior called systems thinking. When one or two things are changed, other changes are often required. Once all changes are roughed out, the students must make the plan clear (2d). If a new posting can be made and examples given of each step of the new strategy, then it is clear.

Select a Solution. Once one or more solutions are designed, their viability must be determined. To answer whether the design fits the problem (3a), students determine if step 1b is being satisfied. To answer whether the procedure fits the resources (3b), they must determine if the procedure can be implemented with the time, persons, and materials available. If a solution does have impediments, they must be removed to solve the original problem, or another solution must be designed and examined for fitness. By gathering a consensus (3c), students are committing to implementation. At this point, implementation of the new plan begins and phase one ends.

Evaluate the Solution. The second phase confirms if carrying out the plan solved the problem (4). Only if the plan was implemented correctly (4a) can it be evaluated. Given sufficient implementation, the next step is to ask if there were any problems (4b). To determine if problems exist, review each step of the plan in light of the criteria (1b).

If there were problems, it does not necessarily mean that some part of the plan needs changing (4c). It may just require more implementation time, or the partial solution arrived at may be acceptable for now. If the students elect to improve, they return to step two of the planning strategy. Thus, planning needs to be viewed as cyclical. As students change something, they see it again in a new light, and this may reveal a new problem or simply a chance to make things more interesting, efficient, or aesthetic.[5]

TEACHING PLANNING

The objective is to have students, individually and in groups, independently plan classroom activities by following the outlined planning strategy. The teaching of planning, especially the expansions, requires that the students have mastered the supervising strategy.

Schedule of Instruction

Table 16.1 presents a possible schedule for teaching planning. The components are on the left. The time periods across the top illustrate the relationship of component teaching procedures, but not the exact number of days of instruction. The symbols within the cells mean the following: T, initial teaching; E, expansion, I, integration; and R, refinement. A number before a teaching procedure indicates a particular procedure. For example, expansions 1E, 2E, and 3E refer to large group, small group, and individual expansions.

The following sections illustrate how the four components are taught. The bracketed numbers ([1/1]) in the text—not the examples—indicate a cell of Table 16.1. The first is the component number and the second is the time period. Table 16.1 does not indicate content or problem relationships among the first three instructional components. As one moves from phase one of planning to implementation to phase two of planning, the same problem is covered. For example, [1/1], [2/2], and [3/3] all cover instruction related to the same problem. Expansions such as [1/10], [2/11], and [3/12] cover another problem in the same fashion. Following the table as you read helps in gaining a clear picture of teaching planning.

Initial Teaching

All four components of Table 16.1 are initially taught. From planning problem to planning problem, the instructional goal is to move from the initial introduction (model and prompt) toward a test in which the students can ask and provide answers to all the planning strategy questions. This progression from introduction to testing takes about three or four planning problems. In all initial teaching applications, the teacher supervises.

Table 16.1
Schedule for Teaching Planning

Component/Time	1	2	3	4	5	6	7	8	9	10	11	12	13	14	15	16	17	18
1. Planning: Phase One	T1									1E	1E		1E / R	1E / R		1E / R	1E / R	1E / R
2. Implementation		T1		T2	T2		T3	T3			1E	1E		1E / R	1E / R		1E / R	1E / R
3. Planning: Phase Two			T1			T2			T3			1E			1E			
4. Remembering Planning Strategy	T	E →———			R			R			R			R			R	

Component/Time	19	20	21	22	23	24	25	26	27	28	29	30	31	32	33	34	35	36
1. Planning: Phase One	2E			2E / R			2E / R			3E			3E / R			3E / R	3E / R	3E / R
2. Implementation		2E			2E / R		2E / R	2E / R			3E			3E / R			3E / R	3E / R
3. Planning: Phase Two			2E			2E / R			2E / R			3E			3E / R			
4. Remembering Planning Strategy		M			M			M						M				

T = Initial Teaching   E = Expansion Teaching   R = Refinement   M = Maintenance

To shorten the following examples, student responses have been eliminated and abbreviations are used for what the teacher does during the presentation. Everything done by the teacher is in brackets: write on board [WOB]; point to board [PTB]; point to planning strategy [PS]; point to original strategy [OS]; point to new strategy [NS]; point to planning original, or new strategy step two [PS2, OS2, NS2]; call on a student [COAS]; call on students [COS]; continue as above [CAA]. The statements the teacher makes that refer to a planning strategy step are in parentheses. Where needed, the teacher's reply to students fills in the necessary gaps.

Planning: Phase One. The example to illustrate the introduction and first contact with planning is designing a new finishing early procedure, one of the special activities identified in Chapter 4 [1/1].

> You have been following my strategy for finishing early for a long time. You have done it day in and day out. What are the steps? [COS, WOB]

Finishing Early Procedure

1. Get ready for workcheck.
2. Turn up green card.
3. Take out special project.
4. Put work away on signal.

> Besides simply wanting to make it better, why should we change this procedure (1b)? [COS] Yes, I agree that you could do more things and perhaps even help others [WOB].
>
> Here is how effective planning is done. [PS] First, we identify the problem. To do that we ask and answer two questions: [PS1a] Which plan needs changing and [PS1b] Why change the plan? Second [PS2], we design solutions. Third [PS3], we select a solution. Later [PS4], we evaluate how we did.
>
> The first step has been done. What is the answer to, "Which plan needs changing?" [PS1a, COAS] And what is the answer to, "Why change the plan?" [PS1b, COS]
>
> Now let's do step two, design a solution. [PS2a] Tony, please read the first question. [PS1b] What can we change to satisfy our reasons? [COAS] Yes, step three, take out special work is correct.
>
> [PS2b] Now we ask, how can we change it? [COS] You could go to a special place instead of staying at your desks to do your special project or have events like games, or do both.
>
> Okay. [PS2c] Now what else could change? What do we have to do so those who have not finished can keep working? [COS] You are sure seeing how changing one thing changes others. [WOB] You have to get your work ready for workcheck, enjoy yourselves but be quiet, and return promptly when it is time for workcheck. I think it will be necessary for me to give the signal for workcheck two minutes before it starts.
>
> [PS2d] Let's finish step two by making the plan clear. Let's write it out in a procedure like the old one. What would be the first step? [COAS] That is

short and positively stated. What would the second step be? [COS, WOB, CAA] That about does it. Here is our new strategy:

New Finishing Early Procedure

1. Get ready for workcheck.
2. Turn up green card.
3. Go to special area.
4. Select activity.
5. Quietly enjoy activity.
6. Return on signal.

You have found six things to do in a special area. You will have to decide without arguing about who does what. But what do you know how to do? [COAS] Yes, share. How many think it is clear? Let's check it out by doing step three of planning [PS3a]. Does this plan do it? [PTB — criteria 1b] Here is what it has to do. Does it do these things? [COS] Yes, it appears to. But why? [COS] That one is important. You could help each other on other subjects during that time. We have to plan that part very carefully at another time.

Let's polish off step three by asking, does the plan fit the resources? [PS3b, COS] Why? [COS] Yes, we have what is needed for the six activities, but we also have some spaces. Where could we do the finish early activity? [COS] Our library space and project display space are about all we have. That seems to do it for step three.

We will go over the strategy again tomorrow, and plan carefully how you could help each other if you want. Then you can practice it a few times. If it seems to be okay, we will implement it. One last question for next time. What do you do when our spaces are filled and you have extra time? Think about it for next time. But let me add, I like your plan. [PTB — 1a and 1b answers] It fits our resources and seems to solve the problem of giving you more from which to select.

The example points out three important elements in teaching the first phase of planning: you can (1) supply part of the plan; (2) delay part; and (3) present potential problems. In this case, the teacher suggested the "getting ready for workcheck" signal, avoided the part about helping each other, and told them to think about what to do when there was no more space left in the finishing early areas. The teacher could have prompted answers or dealt with all of these, but time and moving through the entire phase one at a time are important during initial planning.

This plan focused on changing the what and where of the old plan. It was probably enough to outline a simple six-step procedure and identify the set of events students could participate in during finishing early time. But for each new planning problem [1/4, 1/7] different elements of a plan may be attacked. These may require more elaborate ways to specify changes in procedure, such as a planning sheet that documents the who, what, when, where, and how of the solution.

Implementation. The implementation objective is to link the two phases of planning with carrying out the plan. It is accomplished in two parts. The first is practicing and reviewing the new plan. This links phase one with implementation. Practice the new plan as you would any new organization. Walk the students through it. Additionally, do it in the context of the planning strategy. Post both the planning strategy and the new plan. It would go something like this [2/2]:

Yesterday you planned [PS] a new finishing early procedure [NS]. Let's go over the new procedure. [PS1b] First, why did we want to change it? [COAS] Second, [PSa2] what changes did you feel were needed? [COAS] Third, [PS2b] how did you change it? [COS] Next, [PS2c] did anything else change? [COS] Does this new plan [NS] seem clear [PS2d]? How many still feel that the new procedure solves the problem [PS3a] and fits the resources [PS3b], and want to give it a try [PS3c]? [COS] Great.

So first let's practice trying out, or implementing, the plan [Point to implementation section of posting]. Here is the situation: Zelda, Oza, and Wonda all finish early at the same time. Everyone, watch them practice following the plan. When you watch you want to do part of step four of planning [PS4], evaluate the solutions. Evaluate means to find out if something worked. Everyone, what does evaluate mean? [COS] When you look to see if something worked, ask the first two questions of step four. [PS4a, b] Let's read them together. [Read] Is everyone ready to watch Zelda, Oza, and Wonda give the procedure a try? Okay, Zelda, Oza, and Wonda, give it a try. [Prompt watching implementation, continue for a few minutes.] Zelda, Oza, and Wonda, here is your two minute signal [Ring bell].

[PS4a] Everyone, did they follow the new plan? [COS] Yes, they did. Now, [PS4b] were there any problems? [COS] Yes, they had trouble cleaning up in time but they did it. Should we give the plan a try this afternoon? [COS] And which questions are you going to ask yourself as you implement the plan? [COS] Yes, [PS4a and 4b]. Only if you ask and answer these can you [PS4c] improve the plan if it is not working as well as needed.

After the first day or two, the worksheet on remembering the plan (component four, Table 16.1) can be introduced and used to start off teaching planning. Then cover step four of planning by asking students questions 4a and 4b relative to the last implementation. With the next plans that are implemented [2/5, 2/8], continue in this latter mode.

Planning: Phase Two. The objective of phase two is to consolidate the observations following initial implementation and to decide whether improvement is needed. This step can be performed from two to five days after implementation has started [3/3]. The time frame depends on the problems encountered during implementation. The following example continues with the finishing early procedure.

We have been performing our new finishing early strategy for four days now. Let's do step four of the planning strategy, evaluate the procedure. [PS4]

Everyone, what does evaluate the solution mean? [COS] Yes, to see if a plan works.

Now for the first question, did we follow the plan? [PS4a] Said another way, did we follow the procedure as we planned it? [COS] I agree, we did that.

So let's ask the next question [PS4b], were there any problems? Did anything go wrong during any of the steps? [PS, COS] Yes, a few times we had to intervene to stop those who were not quiet, and a few times people did not return on time [WOB].

These problems lead us to the last question [PS4c], is improvement needed? [COS] So, you think we have to improve it. Let me ask you two questions. Did we have to quiet people the last two days? [COS] Yes, we did. Second question, was anyone late the last two days? [COS] Not one. If you look at how we improved at steps four and five of the new plan [NS], do we have to change the steps? [COS] Some say yes and some no. If you want to evaluate a plan, to see if it works, give it time to work. [PS4c] But if we had to change the new plan, which step in planning would we have to go to? [COS] Correct, back to step two. [PS] Why? [COS] Yes, we have already identified the problem. [PTB] It is not always quiet so others can work.

At this point you have finished evaluating the plan. If you were to proceed to solve this new problem, you would be returning to phase one. The solution to the quiet problem could involve using supervisors or inserting a step in the plan requesting that everyone supervise themselves. This is how you create planning problems for later initial teaching or expansion teaching.

Remembering Planning Strategy. When students enter planning in the future, postings and your support will not be present. Therefore, they need to remember the steps of the strategy and the definitions of key terms [1/4, continued]. In this case, the key terms are *design, solution, resources,* and *evaluation.* For initial teaching, have the students repeat the steps orally without the posting, and do it a step at a time, gradually combining steps and including definitions of terms. The expansions indicated on Table 16.1 move the remembering to worksheets that contain a blank strategy and ask for definitions of key terms. After initial and expansion teaching, schedule refinement to coincide with the implementation phase of planning. This time, remembering behavior is one of the criteria for a planning award.

Expansion and Integration Teaching

By the time you finish initial teaching, you will be a minimal manager. The students will know the steps of the strategy and be able to find relevant answers to each step. But there is more. You must become the invisible manager by expanding and integrating the planning strategy. The behavior is expanded by widening the range of individual and group contexts (setups) in which it takes place. By expanding across groups initially, the process of planning remains visible, helping the individual acquire the skill.

Additionally, teaching integrates the supervision strategy with planning. The students take over the teacher's role in guiding the planners. There are three expansion-integrations of interest: large group, small group, and individual. For reasons of simplicity, Table 16.1 does not indicate integration teaching.

Large Group Expansion—Integration. At this point, you replace yourself with a student supervisor. Move through the components in the same fashion as initial teaching by first modeling and prompting [1/10, 2/11, 3/12], and then by prompting with some testing [1/13, 2/14, 3/15], and finally by testing [1/16, 2/17, 3/18]. Start by selecting a student to lead the entire class through the planning strategy. A secretary may also be appointed to assist. If your class is large, you may want to change supervisors as they move through each step of the planning strategy. This provides more students with the opportunity to supervise.

It is not necessary for every student to supervise during this expansion. If they see a student model being successful, the probability of their behavior emerging under appropriate conditions is high. They have supervised and they have planned; the two will merge.

Small Group Expansion—Integration. The objective is to insure that all students supervise and participate in planning. Establish groups of about five or six students before beginning [1/19]. Each group should be composed of strong and weak planners—those who have contributed and those who have not. Here are the steps:

1. Give all groups the same problem.
2. Provide a posting of the planning strategy.
3. Provide a planning worksheet.
4. Insure that each group has a supervisor and a secretary. (Inform them that everyone will eventually do each job.)
5. Instruct students in using the planning worksheet.
6. Have them start planning. (Monitor their activity.)
7. At the end of small-group planning, debrief the class by going over the different groups' answers to each planning strategy step.
8. If applicable, build a class-level procedure that can be implemented and evaluated.

By giving the students the same problem (1), you establish an opportunity for them to see that there are many effective ways to solve the same problem. The planning worksheet provides students with an outline for problem solving (2) containing spaces for answers to each element of the planning strategy.

When students have finished the first three steps of planning, debrief the groups as a class (7). Cover the groups' planning steps so that every group has contributed to step one of the planning strategy before going on to step two and so forth. It is important to point out the range and similarities of solutions. To manage this event, call on group supervisors to provide group contributions. Next build a new strategy for the classroom, using the class to select the best answers from those given (8). Pilot the implementation as you did during initial teaching [2/20]. Set up an evaluation at a later time [3/21]. Move toward testing as done with previous teaching [1/22, 2/23, 3/24, 1/25, 2/26, 3/27].

Individual Expansion—Integration. During group planning, most students contribute at least to some extent. When left on their own to plan, individuals sometimes fail. They get stuck. They cannot think of a solution because they lack the needed knowledge base. Thus, it is necessary to start individuals with planning problems that are quite simple. In part, the need to provide individuals with simple problems places its introduction after small group planning [1/28].

A simple problem is one in which the problem solvers have a background. They may have followed the model to be changed, followed similar models, solved problems involving similar models, solved different problems related to the same model, and/or the solution is a matter of convention as discussed in Chapter 4. For example, the finishing early procedure planned during initial teaching is simple: students have extensive experience with it, have planned it, and any solution is largely a matter of convention. By the time you get to individual planning, a great many of your activity procedures fit this definition of simple.

Again, have everyone do the same planning problem. You prompt them through a planning outline similar to that used with small groups. After they have finished planning, debrief them as you did for the small-group expansion, asking for a number of answers to each planning step. If applicable, make up a master plan from the elements suggested. You can use a group vote to decide on elements. Implement and evaluate as appropriate [2/29, 3/30, continued].

Refinement Teaching

Refinement begins during expansion and integration teaching [1/13, 2/14, 3/15, 4/5]. Besides refining remembering skills, its primary aims are to refine both planning and supervision skills. For planning, refinement focuses on the speed of the answers, their relevance to the problem or strategy step, and the cooperative interactions required in groups. The complication is in reinforcing some ideas publicly and not others. Everyone needs to be motivated to plan, but rejecting some ideas before they can be seen as part of the evolution of a solution is inappropriate. The answer is to provide statements pointing out the evolution of contributions during planning. Here are a few examples of refinement statements:

There is no wasting time in this group. You got these reasons very fast, one after the other. Can you move through step two just as fast?

It only took two minutes to do step two, and look at this plan. It looks good to me. Let's try step three on it.

Great planning! Five minutes and we have a new plan for getting help. You had to cooperate and work off each other's suggestions to do that. You're getting faster with each problem.

Notice that we did not use Zelda's idea in the new plan but it helped Verda and Eddy get the steps we used. That is how many plans come about.

Evolving to questions that require students to predict and evaluate the interdependence of their contributions and other refinement attributes is the next step in refining planning behavior.

The refinement of supervision proceeds in the same direction as indicated in Chapter 15—the student supervisor can be prompted and reinforced for keeping the planning task flowing, reinforcing group suggestions, getting all members to contribute, and maintaining cooperative interactions.

Beyond the Schedule of Instruction

Table 16.1 takes you only a short way. The teaching of planning continues throughout the school year and beyond. Planning, similar to supervision, keeps evolving. One step in this evolution is integration with the learning strategy. Another is the transfer of planning into the everyday world of work and leisure. Both are taken up in Chapter 19.

PLANNING THE TEACHING OF PLANNING

Teaching planning requires planning. The following procedure is presented as a guide:

1. Analyze your original classroom organization (see Chapter 4).
   a. List your activities (regular and special).
   b. List those activities that could be replanned without learning.
2. Select planning problems for initial teaching and expansion.
   a. Select three or four for initial teaching.
   b. Select three or four for each expansion.
   c. If you have trouble finding problems for expansion, remember that many will emerge with each application of the planning strategy.
3. For each problem do the following:
   a. Outline the planning of the problem.
      1. Outline the planning strategy on one sheet of paper, leaving space for the answer to each question.
      2. Fill in some of the things you think of for each step.

4. Design the organization for initial teaching of planning and the three expansion-integrations. Consider:
   a. Using the SM activity for initial teaching.
   b. How supervisors and secretaries will be selected for large and small-group expansions.
   c. Using existing groups if they are heterogeneous for the small group expansion.
   d. Providing small group and individual expansions with the same problem.

5. Design initial and expansion teaching for remembering exercises.

6. Build refinement statements and questions. Consider:
   a. The relatedness of their contributions.
   b. The problem relevance of their contributions. (Do this at the end of each planning phase.)
   c. The students' cooperative interaction.
   d. The change in a, b, and c over time.
   e. Refining supervision skills.

7. Schedule your teaching. Consider:
   a. Doing a rough draft until you have done part of initial teaching.
   b. Schedule about 15 minutes for the first few planning sessions.
   c. During expansions, it is not necessary to implement all plans. You can have students walk through it and then evaluate.
   d. Once you have done it, you can improve your schedule.

By completing this procedure, you will be ready to teach. Have fun. You may be amazed at what you will learn from your students about how things can be done.

17

SYSTEM STRATEGY: LEARNING

When students cannot solve a problem, they need to learn to change so that they can discriminate and operate on the world in ways not previously possible. As their teachers, we have two options: (1) to change them so that they have a larger knowledge base from which to work; or (2) to change them so that they can learn independently to solve any of their future problems. Both options need to be pursued. If the latter is given strong emphasis, our students inherit a strategy for discovery that increases the probability that they can learn about, adapt to, and control the world when it is theirs. This chapter analyzes learning as a strategy and illustrates how to teach it.

ANALYSIS OF LEARNING

Student-initiated learning is an inclusive subclass of SM behavior that can be partitioned into three subclasses, each of which can be expressed as a strategy.[1] Students require strategies to learn from text, observation, and experimentation. Because it directs observation and experimentation, learning from expository, content-based text is fundamental and is the focus of this chapter. If students desire to learn the unknown, the first step is the analysis of what is known. Most of our everyday problems are solvable by knowledge that exists in some form of text. Therefore, students who can learn through the use of text take a large step in satisfying their learning requirements.

Learning, Problems, and Planning

In learning from text, a student goes about reorganizing knowledge in relationship to a problem, a question about something for which there is no immediate answer.[2] The student takes one organization and builds another. The first organization, the original text, is analyzed, and a second is synthesized. The process of moving from analysis to synthesis is controlled by the student's learning strategy behavior. Moving from one organization to another changes the student, and this change is overtized by the second organization, making the evaluation of learning possible.

Problems spring from many sources. The most obvious in this context is failing to find a solution during planning. The problem solver may have no model for planning, no knowledge of options for model change, or no knowledge of the consequences for implementing the model to predict correspondence with solution and solution requirements.

Components of the Learning Strategy

Chapter 3 outlined a four-component strategy to learn from text.[3] The objective of this strategy is to guide students in gathering and manipulating text. Figure 17.1, a posting, presents questions representing the major discriminations and operations involved in each step of the learning strategy.

Identify the Learning Problem. Faced with a learning situation, students need some clarification (1). First they ask, what needs to be learned (1a)? It is not always easy to answer. They must come to discriminate the range of possibilities on the one hand, and the subset of possibilities that provides

Figure 17.1
Learning Strategy Posting

LEARNING STRATEGY

1. IDENTIFY THE LEARNING PROBLEM
   a. What needs to be learned?
   b. Why learn it?

2. ORGANIZE KNOWLEDGE SOURCES
   a. What sources could help?
   b. Locate, transfer, and arrange sources.

3. UNPACK KNOWLEDGE SOURCE
   a. Where is the knowledge?
   b. What does the source tell?
   c. Does the knowledge help?
   d. How can knowledge be arranged?

4. PACK KNOWLEDGE FOUND
   a. What knowledge is clear?
   b. How can knowledge be arranged?
   c. What more could be learned?
   d. Go to planning?

immediate guidance on the other. By considering both, students keep the search open to new directions.

The next step is to ask why they want to learn (1b). As with planning, it is a question about the short- and long-term consequences—emotional, restructuring, or access—that occur because of this learning. If the learning is being done in the context of solving a problem, the reasons for planning are applicable (planning step 1b). Answering both step one questions helps propel learners into learning, as does a commitment.

Organize Knowledge Sources. Next, students need to organize the sources that help them find what they want to learn (2). They need to identify which sources could help (2a), such as dictionaries and encyclopedias, and then organize them in the sense of locate, transfer, and arrange (2b). Eventually, this step becomes an integration of the organizing strategy. But initially students must be isolated from much of the organizational element so that their use of the strategy is not fragmented. This requires the preparation of special materials as outlined later.

Unpack Knowledge Sources. With sources in hand, students begin the unpacking process (3). They repeat unpacking for each source or part of a source that could help. First students examine the source to find text elements that could be of potential help (3a). This involves, for example, the use of tables of contents and indexes. Even if students do not know how to use these source components, they are not precluded from using the strategy if the preparation of materials compensates.

The second step in the unpacking process requires students to discriminate what the source tells (3b) and then decide whether it helps them solve their learning problem (3c). The control on this decision relates back to what they want to learn (1b). If the answer is yes, they must arrange the knowledge found (3d). This usually involves skills like outlining or summarizing. Again, your presentation and materials must be congruent with the level of the students' skills at representing what is learned.

Pack Knowledge Found. Once the sources have been unpacked, they need to be packed, or organized, relative to the learning problem. The first element of packing is to discriminate if the knowledge found is clear (4a). If many sources have been searched, some part of the knowledge gathered may be ambiguous or contradictory, or some arguments may appear fallacious or weak. Viewing the knowledge in a set puts the pieces in a different perspective. Problematic items have to be excluded or clarified.

Packing continues by organizing the pieces of knowledge relative to each other (4b). By summarizing, outlining, and diagramming, the students gain a composite picture of what has been learned. Yet the learning may or may not have answered the learning problem. Thus, the next packing step tries to determine the limits of what has been learned relative to the learning problem, and which question they may now want answered given the changes that took place during the learning process (4c). Even though more may need to be learned to complete the answer to the learning problem, there is a point where learning must stop and other behavior must begin. Element 4d is a prompt to remind them that there comes a time to return to planning.

The Learning Strategy and Other Curricula

The learning strategy is a skeleton that needs muscles to function. The muscles are the behaviors, or skills, that students learn in other curricula. Students need to know, for example, how to identify the learning problem, search for and through sources, discriminate what applies and what does not, and organize what they find. Often such skills are called studying, thinking, or researching skills. If the learning strategy is to become functional, such behaviors must be incorporated into it.[4]

Table 17.1 outlines, but does not exhaust, the behaviors that give the learning strategy its strength. They are organized by learning strategy substeps, most of which appear in elementary curricula. Groups one (1b, 3b, 3c, and 4c) and six (4a) require special consideration.

A *Taxonomy of Knowledge*. All the discriminations of group one require a taxonomy of knowledge. If none existed, these discriminations would not be predictions, only guess work. Ten classes of knowledge are indicated. Similar to any taxonomy, there are instances, as text in this case, that are difficult to classify. Usually, this difficulty comes from the ambiguous use and relationships of words, phrases, and clauses. Although the taxonomy is not exhaustive, it encompasses a great deal of knowledge presented in scientific and technical texts. Moreover, many of these knowledge classes are taught within the reading curriculum as thinking skills. What is new at this point is their organization and function within the learning strategy. They help students make the discriminations for steps 1b, 3b, 3c, and 4b of the learning strategy.

All knowledge types indicated in Table 17.1 are about something—a person, place, thing, action, or event. Type one knowledge indicates what something is, or in a strict sense, its class membership. For example, Monopoly® is a board game about real estate, and driving is an action that sets or keeps something in motion. Type two specifies what something does. People sing, dogs bark, and cats purr. Types three, four, and five focus on hierarchical relationships, as explored in Chapter 2. Class/part and class/feature are better known as part/whole and feature/whole. Type six focuses on how something changes, usually in features or parts. For example, living things grow old (the features of life diminish), a stock's value fluctuates, and the sun gets dimmer or brighter. The remaining types are fairly straightforward, given the presentation in Chapters 1 and 2, and are explored through examples in the following teaching section.

The Clarity of Knowledge. The sixth group of behaviors, indicated in Table 17.1, help the learner sort out knowledge that may be problematic. Any one piece of knowledge may be ambiguous. This level of clarity is

Table 17.1
Skills Related to the Learning Strategy

1. (1b) WHAT NEEDS TO BE LEARNED? [Discriminate the type of problem(s).]
    (3b) WHAT DOES THE SOURCE TELL? [Discriminate the type of knowledge.]
    (3c) DOES THE KNOWLEDGE HELP? [Discriminate relationship between 1b and 3b.]
    (4c) WHAT MORE COULD BE LEARNED? [Discriminate if clear knowledge (4a) is
         complete relative to 1b.]

    1. What Something Is   6. What Changes Happen to Something
        (Class Membership)   (Historical: Class Evolution)
    2. What Something Does   7. How Something Happens
        (Class Operations)   (Historical: Procedure, Process)
    3. What Parts Something Has   8. Why Something Happens
        (Hierarchical: Class/Parts)   (Historical: Cause and Effect)
    4. What Features Something Has   9. When Something Is or Happens
        (Hierarchical: Class/Feature)   (Historical: Place in Time)
    5. What Types Something Has   10. Where Something Is or Happens
        (Hierarchical: Class/Subclass)   (Spatial: Place in Space)

2. (2a) WHAT SOURCES COULD HELP? [Discriminate the function of these sources:]

    1. Dictionaries   5. Texts
    2. Encyclopedias   6. Graphs/Charts
    3. Atlases   7. Magazines
    4. Journals   8. Newspapers

3. (2b) LOCATE, TRANSFER, AND ARRANGE SOURCES. [Use these to locate
    sources.]

    1. Alphabetizing   5. Card Catalogs
    2. Indexes   6. Computer Retrieval Systems
    3. Bibliographies   7. Dewey Decimal System
    4. Abstracts   8. Library of Congress System

4. (3a) WHERE IS THE KNOWLEDGE? [Use these to locate knowledge within source.]

    1. Table of Contents   3. Text Headings
    2. Index   4. Key Words in Text

5. (3d) & (4b) HOW CAN KNOWLEDGE BE ARRANGED? [Discriminate how to arrange.]

    1. Outlining   3. Graphing/Charting
    2. Summarizing   4. Schematizing/Drawing

6. (4a) WHAT KNOWLEDGE IS CLEAR? [Discriminate (evaluate) if 3d knowledge is:]

    1. Ambiguous/Unambiguous   3. Fallacious/Sound
    2. Contradictory/Noncontradictory   4. Strong/Weak

directly related to the knowledge types of group one. When two or more
pieces of knowledge are of the same knowledge type, they may be contradictory. If knowledge is structured as an argument, it may break the rules
of deductive or inductive reasoning so that the argument is either fallacious or weak. The four behaviors of this group are part of the inclusive
class known as argument analysis.

Although the present learning strategy stops with sorting knowledge into clear and unclear categories, there is a next step: the reconciling of unclear knowledge. This requires unpacking more text, gathering observations, or performing experiments. Reconciling knowledge involves the inclusive class of behavior known as argument construction. Often it requires moving beyond what is known and, thus, represents an expansion of the present strategy.

Learning Materials

Teaching students to learn has always been problematic because learning is difficult to present as a functional, reinforceable unit of behavior. Learning is often fractured by having students retrieve and sort through materials, or by trying to teach support skills when solving a problem. To avoid such fracturing and to insure that support skills are incorporated once mastered, special materials, or minisources, must be constructed. Minisources eliminate much of the organizational busy work of learning and make up for the students' lack of support skills.

Each minipacket covers a learning problem that can be completed in a relatively brief time. They can be as short as a few sentences or as long as several pages. Each can contain knowledge from one or multiple sources. With such packets, you control the students' application of the learning strategy and their need and use of support skills. Learning is then capable of being selected (reinforced) as a unit of behavior. Moreover, the gradual incorporation of support skills expands learning behavior so that the student can take on increasingly more complex learning problems. A section at the end of the chapter guides the building of minisources.

TEACHING LEARNING

The objective is to have students, individually and in groups, independently learn from text by following the outlined learning strategy. The teaching of learning requires that the students have mastered the supervising and planning strategies.

Schedule of Instruction

Table 17.2 presents a schedule for teaching students to learn. Similar to the other schedules, the instructional components are on the left and the time periods are across the top. The letters in the cells represent the procedures of teaching: T, initial teaching; E, expansion; R, refinement; and M, Maintenance. The numbers before an expansion procedure (2E, 4E) indicate a particular expansion format. The numbers after an expansion (E2, E3), indicate that all expansions with that number during a time period are taught in a single lesson exercise, which means that they are

Table 17.2
Schedule for Teaching Learning

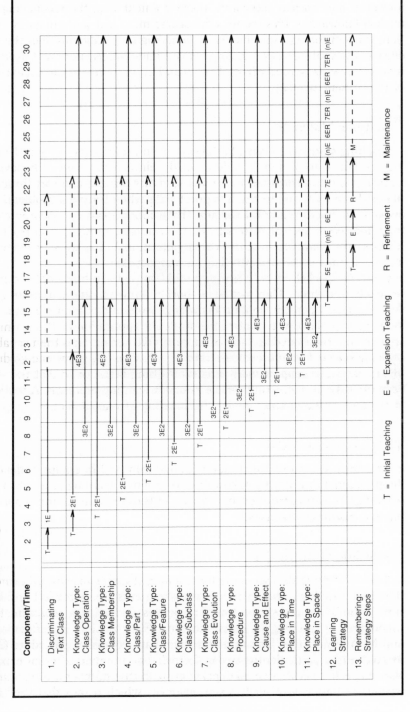

Component/Time	1	2	3	4	5	6	7	8	9	10	11	12	13	14	15	16	17	18	19	20	21	22	23	24	25	26	27	28	29	30
1. Discriminating Text Class	T	1E																												
2. Knowledge Type: Class Operation			T	2E1				3E2				4E3																		
3. Knowledge Type: Class Membership				T	2E1			3E2				4E3																		
4. Knowledge Type: Class/Part					T	2E1		3E2				4E3																		
5. Knowledge Type: Class/Feature						T	2E1	3E2				4E3																		
6. Knowledge Type: Class/Subclass							T	2E1	3E2				4E3																	
7. Knowledge Type: Class Evolution								T	2E1	3E2				4E3																
8. Knowledge Type: Procedure									T	2E1	3E2				4E3															
9. Knowledge Type: Cause and Effect										T	2E1	3E2			4E3															
10. Knowledge Type: Place in Time											T	2E1	3E2		4E3															
11. Knowledge Type: Place in Space												T	2E1	3E2	4E3															
12. Learning Strategy																T	5E		6E	(n)E	7E		(n)E	6ER	7ER	(n)E	6ER	7ER	(n)E	
13. Remembering: Strategy Steps																T	E	R				M								

T = Initial Teaching E = Expansion Teaching R = Refinement M = Maintenance

juxtaposition expansions (Chapter 9). Horizontal arrows indicate the continuation of a teaching procedure and the dashed arrows indicate that the procedure does not need to be done each day.

The following illustrates how the components of learning, as presented on the left side of Table 17.2, are taught. The bracketed number ([2/4]) in the text, not the examples, indicate a cell of the table. The first is the component number and the second the time period. Follow the schedule as you read so that a clear picture of teaching students the learning strategy emerges.

Teaching Knowledge Types

Although it is beyond the scope of this text to illustrate the teaching of support skills, the initial and expansion teaching of the knowledge-type discriminations are outlined because they are prerequisite to the initial teaching of the learning strategy.

Initial Teaching. Teaching students to discriminate the knowledge types begins by teaching students to discriminate what a single sentence of text is about [1/1]—its subject. Next, the ten knowledge types are initially taught one at a time [2/2 through 11/11]. All these discriminations are taught through example sets such as those illustrated in Chapter 9. Present models and tests for two consecutive days. The content of these sets needs to be within the students' knowledge base. By the beginning of the third grade, students have an extensive repertoire across all knowledge types. For example, they know many classroom procedures and why they perform them, besides discriminating a wide array of features, parts, and types of things. Staying within their repertoire of knowledge allows initial teaching to begin at an early point in the students' education.

Table 17.3 presents the key wording and a few positive examples for each knowledge type. The wording pivots around discriminating the two features that determine knowledge type membership. The presentation of these examples can be on large flash cards or on worksheets. The range of grammatical forms should initially be limited. Table 17.3 presents many examples with the same content back to back but in reverse grammatical form to show how the same knowledge type can be presented in very different forms.

The wording used in Table 17.3 is primarily nontechnical. The technical terms, in parentheses, can be taught from the start or introduced during expansion teaching. The procedure would be much the same as for introducing the technical vocabulary for inductive behavior, as described in Chapter 7.

Expansion Teaching. Expansion teaching has two goals: (1) to widen the range of text that students can discriminate as belonging to a knowledge type, and (2) to insure that students can discriminate between knowledge types. The first deals with the grammatical forms a knowledge type can

Table 17.3
Wording and Examples for Knowledge Types

KNOWLEDGE TYPES	WORDING	EXAMPLES
* Something (Class – Not a Knowledge Type)	All text is about something. My turn. [Read] What is the text about? Eyes. Say the whole thing. [Pause] The text is about eyes. Next... Your turn. Read. [Pause] What is the text about? [Signal] (SR) Yes. So say the whole thing. [Pause, Signal] Next...	1. Eyes are for seeing. 2. Bats fly at night. 3. Muscles and bones are part of the body. 4. People have muscles and bones.
1. What Something Does (Class Operations)	All text tells about something. Some tells what actions something does. Here are some examples that tell what actions something does. My turn. [Read] What is the text about? Some muscles. What is one action of some muscles? To pull.	1. Some muscles pull. 2. Some muscles pull bones. 3. In the sunlight, many flowers bloom. 4. With good food and exercise, muscles will grow.
2. What Something Is (Class Memberships)	All text tells us about something. Text can also tell what the something is. Here are some examples of text that tell what something is. My turn. [Read] What is the text about? Dogs. What is a dog? An animal. I will say the whole thing. A dog is a thing that is an animal. Next...	1. Dogs are animals. 2. A clock is a machine used to tell the time. 3. The bicycle is a machine to take you places. 4. Ice is frozen water.
3. What Parts (Class/Part)	All text tells us about something. Text can also tell what parts something has. Here are some examples that tell what parts something has. My turn. [Read] What is the text about? Shoes. What parts do shoes have? Heels and soles. I will say the whole thing. Shoes are things that have the parts heels and soles. Next...	1. Shoes have heels and soles. 2. The parts of the shoe include the heel and sole. 3. A chair has three parts: legs, seat, and back. 4. An airplane has wings, body, and tail.
4. What Features (Class/Feature)	Here is something new about what a text tells. A text can tell what features something has. Here are some examples that tell what features something has. My turn. [Read] What is the text about? Some shoes. What features do some shoes have? Shiny and black. I will say the whole thing. Some shoes are things that have the features shiny and black. Next...	1. Some shoes are shiny and black. 2. Everything has shape. 3. Shape is a feature of everything. 4. An elephant's skin is thick and rough. 5. The skin of an elephant is thick and rough.
5. What Types (Class/Subclass)	Here is another thing that a text can tell. A text can tell what types there are of something. Here are some examples. My turn. [Read] What is the text about? Shapes. What is the whole? Shapes. What are the types? Triangle, circle and square. I will say the whole thing. Shape is the whole that has the types triangle, circle, and square. Next... [Read] What is the text about? Triangles, circles and squares. What is the whole? Shapes. What are the types of shapes? Triangles, circles, and squares. I will say the whole thing. Shape is the whole that has the types triangle, circle, and square. Next...	1. Shapes include triangles, circles, and squares. 2. Triangles, circles, and squares are three types of shapes. 3. The three types of rock are sedimentary, igneous, and metamorphic. 4. There are six senses: seeing, hearing, smelling, feeling, tasting, balancing. 5. The four food groups include meat, grain, dairy, and vegetable.
6. How Something Changes (Class Evolution)	Here is another thing that a text can tell. A text can tell how something changes. Here are some examples. My turn. [Read] What does the text tell about? The baby. How does the baby change? It gets bigger. I will say the whole thing. The baby can change by getting bigger.	1. The baby is getting bigger. 2. Growing old and dying are changes that happen to all living things. 3. Living things grow old and die. 4. Wood expands in water.
7. How Something Happens (Procedure, Process)	Here is another thing that a text can tell about. A text can tell how something happens. My turn. [Read] What happens? Making bread. How does making bread happen? What is the first thing? Mixing the ingredients. What is the second thing? Kneading dough. What is the third thing? Shaping the loaf. What is the last thing? Baking it in the oven. Next...	1. Making bread involves mixing the ingredients, kneading the dough, shaping the loaf, and baking it in the oven. 2. There are four steps to baking bread: mixing the ingredients, kneading the dough, shaping the loaf, and baking it in the oven.
8. Why Something Happens (Cause and Effect)	Another thing a text can tell is why something happens. Here are some examples. [Read] What happened? The boy had energy. [Underline] Why did the boy have energy? Because he ate. [Circle] Next...	1. The boy had energy because he ate. 2. Because the boy ate, he had energy. 3. Bones move because muscles are flexed. 4. Flexing muscles causes bones to move.
9. When Something Happens (Place in Time)	Another thing a text can tell is when something happens. My turn. [Read] What happened? The sun rose. When did the sun rise? Early in the morning. Next...	1. The sun rose early in the morning. 2. In the early morning, the sun rose. 3. The sun will rise at 6:45 tomorrow.
10. Where Something Happens (Place in Space)	Another thing a text can tell is where something happens. [Read] What happens? Flowers bloom. Where do flowers bloom? In the garden. Next...	1. Flowers bloom in the garden. 2. A garden is a place for flowers.

take and the second with juxtaposing the different knowledge types. To achieve these two goals four expansions are required.

1. Add grammatical forms across content areas.

Initial teaching covered three or four grammatical forms. The forms of single sentences that clearly represent a knowledge type are limited. Some of these were presented in Table 17.3. Students need to discriminate these forms over a range of content and be able to do so at a fast rate. Model each new form that is introduced and then expect to prompt for a day or two. All grammatical forms should first be introduced as an expansion to the something, or class component of Table 17.2 [1/3]. This expansion, 1E, would involve five to ten worksheet items each day. After the majority of forms have been introduced, the expansion is done on an intermittent basis. This expansion, if part of a school-level program, would take several years to complete (Chapter 20).

2. Discriminate juxtaposed knowledge types.

As soon as two knowledge forms have been initially taught, juxtaposing knowledge types can begin [2/4]. As more knowledge types are learned, they are included. Generally a worksheet exercise, 2E1 on Table 17.2, with six or seven items is sufficient. This means that not every knowledge type is juxtaposed every day once most have been learned. Include only those that have been most recently initially taught or expanded grammatically, those that are causing the students the most problems, and those that have not been practiced for the longest time. This expansion must be done virtually every day, with models and prompts used whenever new knowledge forms or grammatical forms are introduced. Even though students have been introduced to the grammatical forms in the 1E expansion, they need modeling and prompting again.

A critical juxtaposition format includes discriminating types that are often confused. One such group includes what something is, how it changes, what it does, and which features it has. A second group is what parts, features, and kinds something has. A third group is why and how something happens. Only juxtapose sentences with a single knowledge type. To help students reconcile types that are problematic, juxtapose examples that are minimally different in content.

The cow is big. (Class feature)

The cow got bigger. (Class change)

The cow is an animal. (Class membership)

The cow jumped the fence. (Class operation)

The expansion format could present them one after the other or all at once (as on a worksheet). After students correctly discriminate knowledge type, you would ask them the two questions that discriminate knowledge type membership. This confirms that student predictions were not guess work.

3. Discriminate changes in knowledge type.

This juxtaposition expansion format, 3E2, begins after several knowledge types can be discriminated [2/8]. It uses a kernel piece of text that is changed a little at a time. The changes involve (1) adding details but not changing the knowledge type; (2) changing the knowledge type by adding text; and (3) changing knowledge type by modifying the last addition to the kernel. Here is an example.

Bats fly. (1)

Bats fly to hunt. (2)

Bats fly to hunt for food. (3)

All over the world, bats fly at night. (4)

Bats fly without hitting objects. (5)

The addition of text may produce a sentence with more than one knowledge type as illustrated in items four and five. This variation will have to be modeled and prompted with care. The text kernel does not have to remain exactly the same. The wording would first ask if the knowledge type changed. If it did not, ask which detail was added. This helps illustrate the relationship between knowledge types and literal comprehension type questions. In example three, the answer would be "what bats hunt for." If the knowledge type changed, ask for the incorporated type and then ask students how they know. This build up expansion is usually done on a chalkboard or overhead projector with only one example presented at a time.[5] Six to ten examples are sufficient. This expansion needs to be performed on a daily basis until shortly after all knowledge types have been initially taught, unless the learning strategy is a school- or district-level program.

4. Discriminate the knowledge type or types for a passage of text.

A passage of text, as two or more sentences, can represent one knowledge type or several. When this happens, students need to discriminate what many would call its main idea. By discriminating the knowledge types within a passage, they have the first step of a procedure to determine the main idea. The second step is to combine knowledge types into a sentence that summarizes the knowledge. Here is a simple example.

(1) We use a getting help procedure because we can do our tasks faster. (2) Getting help has four steps. (3) First, raise your hand. (4) Second, wait to be called on. (5) Third, show the helper your problems. (6) And fourth, follow the directions given.

The main idea would be something such as "why and how to get help." It is in this case a combination of two knowledge types. By leading the students through text to discover the knowledge type (or types) and then summarizing them in terms of the text, the students are provided a procedure to get the main idea. If they perform it on a day in and day out basis with two or three examples that vary across content, they can very rapidly determine with which knowledge form passages deal. This is a critical skill in searching sources to discover what they tell.

Initially this expansion, 4E3, is done as a teacher-directed worksheet with two or three sentences as passages that are within the knowledge base of the students. Later it can be an independent worksheet that asks the "How do you know?" questions. Students can do this expansion in pairs and small groups with the text on flash cards that have the answers on the back. Begin this expansion after students have learned several knowledge types that have undergone expansions 2E and 3E [2/12].

Teaching the Learning Strategy

To a great extent, the teaching of learning parallels the teaching of planning. Initial teaching uses a large group format which is followed by expansion-integrations involving the supervision strategy with groups and individuals. There are two differences. First the large group teacher-directed procedure continues intermittently because of the need for support skill incorporation. Second, the learning strategy is performed in one time frame, at least initially.

Initial Teaching and Support Skill Incorporation. Initial teaching begins after all knowledge types have been taught [12/15]. The students should be proficient at analyzing two to four sentence passages for knowledge types (expansion 4E). Proceed similar to planning: over several learning problems, move toward testing. As support skills are incorporated, expansion (n)E, add prompts at the appropriate points to insure success and then fade them as quickly as possible.

The following example illustrates the second or third application of the learning strategy for students in about the third grade. Everything done by the teacher is in brackets: write on board [WOB]; point to board, [PTB]; call on a student, [COAS]; call on students, [COS]; point to knowledge type posting, [KT]; and point to learning strategy step, [LS2b]. Student replies have been omitted to shorten examples. The teacher's statements provide background where needed.

Here is our strategy to help you learn on your own [LS]. Like the others, it has a number of steps. By following them you have a good chance of learning what you want to learn.

Let's give the strategy a try. [LS1] You begin by identifying the learning problem. [LS1a] You do this by answering the question, what needs to be learned? For today let's learn how muscles work [WOB]. [KT] What type of knowledge are we going to look for in text to answer how muscles work? [COAS] Yes, how something happens [WOB]. [LS1b] Next we ask, why learn it? [COAS] You could be curious. You may also want to do it because you are stuck during planning.

In the future, when (1a) is connected with planning, the parts-of-a-plan poster (Chapter 16) would also be presented. This poster would be used to help them formulate their learning problem, which often has multiple components. From their first problem statements, you want them to see that all problem statements are decomposable or can be focused on from several directions. In doing so, you help them to see the range of possible knowledge types that assist them in the selection and search of sources.

Now for step 2, organize knowledge sources. First, you ask, which sources could help? [LS2a]. You have learned about dictionaries and encyclopedias. Which of these could help answer the question of how something works? [COAS] Yes, the encyclopedia. So, we have identified a source. There may be others but for now that is enough. The next thing we do is organize the source. [LS2b] What does organize mean? [COS] So you next locate, transfer, and arrange the source. Because we have encyclopedias in the room, that is not too difficult.

Students who start the learning strategy very early will not be able to make many, if any, predictions about which sources apply. You can show them the text, telling them where it came from. As students learn about new sources, they can become part of an ever-expanding posting to prompt step 2a predictions.

[LS3] Now for step 3, unpacking knowledge source. First, we ask where is the knowledge in the source? [LS3a] Who can make a prediction about where to look in the encyclopedia for how muscles work. [PTB, COAS] Yes, under M for muscles. That is volume 13 in our encyclopedia set. [Hold up] The minisource you have has two pieces of text with pictures from encyclopedias.

TEXT 1: (1) The human body has over 600 muscles. (2) About half of these have names. (3) There are three types of muscles: skeletal, smooth, and cardiac. (4) Skeletal muscles are connected to skeletal bones. (5) Smooth muscles are found around the intestines, blood vessels, and stomach. (6) Cardiac muscle is found only in the heart. (7) Picture 1 gives the names and locations of a few muscles of the body. [Picture not presented.]

Look at text one [LS3b] to see what it tells. Jennifer, please read the first sentence. Stephanie, what does it tell in terms of knowledge types [KT]? Yes, what parts something has. [PTB] Does that tell about what you want to learn? [COAS] No. But let's read on. [COS to read remainder of paragraph] Ozzie, what type of knowledge does most of this text tell about? Yes, what kinds there are of something. In this case the kinds of muscles.

So, [LS3c] does this knowledge source help answer the learning problem [PTB]? [COAS] It does not appear as if it does. [LS3d] But let's outline it for practice and because it is about muscles and just may help. [Draw a tree diagram of types of muscles on board with students.]

TEXT 2: (1) The skeletal muscles move bones (2) They work in pairs to move a bone. (3) As one muscle contracts, or gets shorter, it pulls on the bone to move it. (4) At the same time, the opposite muscle relaxes, or gets longer. (5) Picture two shows the movement of the lower arm when the biceps muscle of the upper arm contracts and the triceps muscle relaxes. (6) Picture three shows the movement of the bone when the triceps muscle contracts and the biceps muscle relaxes. [Pictures not presented.]

Because we have another piece of text, we do step three again. [LS3a] We already know where the source is, so we begin with what the source or text tells. [LS3b] Let's read text two. [COS to read paragraph] Do any sentences help answer the learning problem? [COS] Yes. [LS3c] Which sentences help? [COS] All but the first seem to help answer the learning problem. So let's outline how muscles work. [Outline on board with students.]

The speed and difficulty of teaching step three is directly related to the students' skill at discriminating the types of knowledge sources at the multiple sentence level and arranging text.

We have unpacked our text and found out what they tell. [LS4] Now we pack the knowledge found to see just what has been learned. [LS4a] First you ask, is the knowledge clear? This question is asked for each piece of knowledge. Remember, if you can tell its knowledge type or types, then it is clear. [PTB] Look at the outline of the first text. [COAS] Is it clear? [COAS] How do you know? Yes, it tells which types of muscles you have and where they are. Now, look at the second text outline. [COAS] Is it clear? [COAS] How do you know? Yes, it tells how muscles work to move bones and gives an example.

[LS4b] The next question is how can the pieces of knowledge be arranged? Look again at our pieces to see if they fit together some way. [PTB] You know the types of muscles. And how skeletal muscles work. Now, how do these two pieces fit together; how are they related? [COAS] Yes, skeletal muscle is only one type of muscle.

[LS4c] So what more could be learned? The learning problem is, how muscles work [PTB]. Do you know how all kinds of muscles work? [COS] Correct, you don't. What more could be learned? [COAS] Yes, how smooth muscles and cardiac muscles work [WOB]. This is a new learning problem that you can learn about at another time. All learning leads to other learning problems. Learning is never done. That is a rule of learning. [LS4d] But it is often necessary to stop learning to return to planning so that what you learn can be put to use.

The construction of sources needs to carefully consider just how the knowledge pieces could be related (4b) and what more there is to learn (4c). Often the learning problem can be answered in a fairly complete manner. When this is the case, simply ask students what they would want to learn given what they have just learned. They will supply many examples without any degree of prompting.

Expansion — Integration Teaching. As with planning, expansion-integration teaching is designed to move you from being a minimal manager to an invisible one by having the students supervise themselves while learning. The design of learning groups is identical to planning, and minisources are needed.

Expansion 5E on Table 17.2 indicates large group integration of the learning strategy [12/17]. It is only performed a few times. Expansion 6E [12/20] and 7E [12/22] indicate small-group and individual expansion-integrations. Each is done several times consecutively until students can manage at a close to independent level. At that point these formats would be used in an alternating fashion [12/25 continued]. The support skill expansions, (n)E, would occur when new support skills can be incorporated into the learning strategy [12/19, continued].

As your students become more sophisticated at learning, it becomes increasingly difficult to reduce the learning problem to something that can be completed in one sitting. The answer is to review the steps completed when the learning exercise is continued. This is good strategy for any learner. What you will find is that their questions become more refined — they have a better view of where they are going. Moreover, it reinforces them for what they have done.

Remembering Strategy Steps. The last component on Table 17.2 is teaching students to remember the learning strategy steps. As with the other strategies, the learning posting will not always be around. Initially it is done orally and then expanded via worksheets. Refinement and maintenance follow. When students can quickly state the steps and provide key definitions, the learning strategy posting can be faded.

Refinement Teaching

Both knowledge types and the learning strategy need to be refined. For knowledge types, prompt and reinforce the rate at which discriminations are made. Refinement begins shortly after the introduction of each expansion. Refinement teaching is not indicated on Table 17.2 for knowledge types.

The refinement of the learning strategy depends on two elements: success and the solution of problems of interest to the students. Both of these are connected to the construction of the minisources discussed later. Refinement procedures begin after the expansions have been introduced [12/25 and 12/26 continued]. The statements and questions used to refine learning skills focus, similar to the other strategies, on the speed (latency) and rate of contributions, their accuracy, and the relationship of contributions.

Beyond the Schedule of Instruction

Similar to the other schedules of instruction, Table 17.2 is only a beginning. Eventually, the students' use of the learning strategy has to include organizing sources and integrating it with planning. At this point, student activities look like they always have. They may spend a week planning a project and writing a report, learning as they go. Yet there is an immense difference. They are guided by a set of strategies that previous generations did not have. Their probability of success and resistance to failure is increased manyfold.

DESIGNING LEARNING MATERIALS

Minisources are designed to be completed in a short interval, allow for success, and be of interest to the students. The first insures that the students work through the learning process. The second and third insure that the process can be strongly reinforced. Follow these steps to make the design of minisources easier.

Step 1: Select Topics of Interest to the Students

Many of the topics can be obtained from the science and social studies curricula. Remember that in large measure interests are a function of the social environment. Reinforcing students with success and positive social interactions in a topic area increases the probability of their activity in that area. Later they venture into topic areas teachers suggest because they have been reinforced for following them in the past.

Step 2: Establish the Learning Problems for Each Topic

Many of the identified topics can be broken into numerous learning problems. For example, the topic "dental hygiene" can include the procedures to brush and floss the teeth; the kinds, features, and operations (functions) of teeth; and their growth and decay. Each of these can become a separate minisource.

Step 3: Select a Time to Teach the Strategy

The learning strategy may become part of your reading program or be inserted somewhere within your language arts program.[6] No matter where you place it, you need to assign a daily time frame of about 20 minutes. Because it replaces part of existing instruction, no extra time is added to the curriculum. Over the long run, teaching SM learning skills makes it possible to accelerate instruction.

Step 4: Arrange Learning Problems on a Time Line Relative to the Teaching of Support Skills

This two-part time line establishes (1) the limit of support skills incorporated in a minisource to complete a learning problem; and (2) the point at which to incorporate new support skills into learning strategy teaching. Additionally, the learning problems of a topic area can be grouped into small blocks that can become several minisources.

Step 5: Build Each Minisource

Include everything they need to complete the learning task, keeping in mind support skills, vocabulary, reading level, and lesson time frame. You may want to number the lines of text to facilitate instruction. As topics get longer, a cover sheet that summarizes each strategy step helps keep track of progress. When topics begin to take more than one lesson, a summary sheet helps review the work to date.

Designing the learning sources takes a great deal of time and effort. Make it easier and more enjoyable by working with other professionals.

PLANNING THE TEACHING OF LEARNING

The following procedure can help you plan the teaching of learning:

1. Design example sets and worksheets for teaching knowledge types.
2. Design minisources. Consider:
   a. Selecting topics of interest to students.
   b. Establish the learning problems for each topic.
   c. Select a point for teaching the learning strategy.
   d. Arrange learning problems on a time line relative to support skill teaching.
   e. Build each minisource to fit within student skills.
3. Design the organization (setup) of your teaching.
   a. Decide when and how to introduce knowledge types.
   b. Decide when and how to introduce the learning strategy.
   c. Decide how to choose supervisors and secretaries.
   d. Follow the steps for expansion-integrations.
4. Build refinement procedures. Consider:
   a. The rate at which knowledge types are discriminated.
   b. The relevance of their contributions and the students' cooperative and supportive interactions for learning strategy.
   c. The change in *a* and *b* over time.

5. Schedule your teaching. Consider:
   a. Scheduling about ten minutes a day for knowledge type teaching and worksheets.
   b. Scheduling about 20 minutes for the learning strategy.
   c. Following the logic of Table 17.2.

18

SYSTEM STRATEGY: INTERVENING

People resolve conflicts in a variety of ways. These range from informal discussion to negotiation to mediation to arbitration to judicial and legislative decision. As the degree of formality increases, the individual's contribution to the resolution decreases, as does the chance of a win-win outcome. Today's crowded courts testify to the individual's lessening role in resolving conflict.[1] If our students are to become citizens who resolve their conflicts in mutually beneficial ways, we must teach them to do so. This chapter analyzes intervention behavior and illustrates how to teach it.[2]

ANALYSIS OF INTERVENING

Intervention Strategy as a System of Justice

An intervention strategy is founded on a system of justice, a set of decision rules that dictates the reward or punishments citizens are to receive for their conduct or behavior. For us, this system of justice is documented in the Constitution of the United States. The Fourteenth Amendment, which focuses on the rights of due process of law and equal protection under the law, has the greatest impact on the design of an intervention strategy. Anything we build must be designed so that due process and equal protection continue to be provided to our contemporaries and those who follow. This is true even when the system's citizens are students.[3]

The principle of due process demands that (1) the law must be fairly administered; (2) persons accused must be informed of their rights; (3)

persons bringing the charges must not be allowed to judge the case; and (4) the law must be so worded as to give adequate warning of the behaviors that are prohibited. Equal protection prohibits sex, age, race, or religious discrimination in applying the law. It requires that the discrimination of conduct be independent of the type of individual and based directly on the law.

Besides satisfying these rights of students, a classroom intervention system needs to: (1) allow them a greater degree of self-determination in conflict outcomes; (2) improve the probability that they reach an equitable and lasting settlement; and (3) increase instructional time in the long run.

Conflict, as inappropriate SM behavior between individuals, is caused by one or more of three things: the students do not know which task to perform, they cannot perform the SM or academic behaviors required, or the task assigned is not rewarding or does not provide access to a reward relative to those involved. In other words, if the social environment does not at some point powerfully instruct and reinforce student SM and academic behavior, the chance of a lasting resolution is threatened because the causes of conflict remain.

Thus, an environment that instructs and reinforces appropriate academic and SM behavior is the counterpart of an effective intervention system. By pursuing both parts, we teach students not just to stop and resolve conflicts, but to avoid them as well.

Components of the Intervention Strategy

Chapter 3 outlined a generic four-step intervention strategy involving stopping the conflict, finding a better way, settling the conflict, and documenting it. Students use this strategy no matter which form of intervention is performed—arbitration, mediation, or negotiation. Only one feature changes from form to form: the degree to which those involved participate in the conflict's resolution. As students move from arbitration to negotiation, they perform a larger share of the strategy components. Figure 18.1, the posting for arbitration, indicates the discriminations and operations of the intervention strategy.[4]

Stop the Conflict. There are three discriminations to this step: classifying the behavior as a conflict (1a); deciding whether more intervening is needed (1c); and deciding whether the conflict is one that should be resolved at the school level (1d). Once the behavior is classified as a conflict, a simple operation is required to stop it (1b). Documenting the conflict, step 1e, occurs only if more is needed (1c). The items to be filled out on the document card can be indicated as numbers in parentheses as they are in Figure 18.1 (see steps 1e, 2e, 3e). The content of the document card is discussed later.

Find a Better Way. Conflicts evolve. During this evolution, each party could have performed differently at some point to avoid, stop, or lessen it.

Figure 18.1
Intervention Strategy Posting: Arbitration

ARBITRATION STRATEGY

1. STOP THE CONFLICT
   a. Is it a conflict?
   b. Stop the conflict.
   c. Is more needed?
   d. Can we take care of it?
   e. Document. (1–4)

2. FIND A BETTER WAY
   a. What are some better ways?
   b. Select a better way.
   c. Perform the better way.
   d. Commit to the better way.
   e. Document. (5, 7)

3. SETTLE THE CONFLICT
   a. Is a settlement needed?
   b. What settlements fit?
   c. Select a settlement.
   d. Perform the settlement.
   e. Document. (6–9)

Students could change in what they say and what they do toward each other. Identifying these behavioral options contributes to the construction of better ways (2a). If all parties contribute to finding better ways from the perspective of changing their own behavior, they avoid the error of searching for the first cause and increase the probability that they will agree on a better way (2b), perform it (2c), and commit to it (2d). Practicing behavioral options is akin to a defensive driving course—it helps decrease behavioral accidents. This step is performed whenever a conflict requires more (1c) and ends by documenting the better way (2e).

Settle the Conflict. At times, classroom conflicts, similar to their legal parents, require a payment for damages. Step three begins with deciding if a settlement is needed (3a). Those who make this determination need some form of criteria from which to work. Suggested criteria are presented later. If the criteria for settlement are met, the next decision, which settlement fits the conflict, is required (3b). This decision is even more difficult than the first. The only way to make the determination is to work through multiple examples of conflicts as indicated later. The more the students participate in steps 3a and 3b, the easier it is to select (3c) and to perform (3d) a settlement. The final element of this step is again documentation (3e).

Document the Conflict. Documenting the conflict is involved in each step of conflict resolution because the extent of the settlement is related to the disputants' history of conflicts. Thus, students, teachers, administrators, and parents need an accurate accounting. Substeps 1e, 2e, and 3e each indicate what to document in relationship to the following list:

1. The names of the disputants.
2. Time and date of conflict.
3. A short description of the conflict.
4. Names of those who stopped the conflict.
5. The better way selected.
6. The settlement option selected.
7. Name of the person who will monitor the practicing of the better way and settlement.
8. Signature of the disputants.
9. Monitor's indication that the better way has been performed and the settlement satisfied.

The document card can be a five-by-seven note card with each of these items listed in a form the students can read and understand. For step one, items one through four are completed if more is required (1b). If not, a card is not filled out. As step two comes to a close, items five and seven are filled out. For step three, the rest of the items are filled in even if no settlement was needed. For the items that are not applicable, just put in a little check or an "NN" for not needed.

BUILDING A CONTEXT FOR TEACHING INTERVENTION BEHAVIOR

The first step in building a context for intervention teaching is establishing an initial classroom intervention procedure. From the first day of school, make it explicit and congruent with the four strategy steps outlined earlier. An intervention procedure is a correction procedure that can be introduced and reviewed similar to the other special activities (Chapters 10, 11, and 13).

> If there are times when you are not getting along with each other, like hitting another or not waiting for your turn, I will have to do something about it. There are four things I do.

Now go over the steps, providing one or two examples of each step. No more elaboration is needed for young students. Each day's review adds a little so that students begin to discriminate the steps of the procedure. If the students can read, use a posting such as the following:

Conflict Strategy

1. Stop the conflict.
2. Find a better way.
3. Settle the conflict.
4. Document the conflict.

The second step in building a context for teaching establishes an *intervention docket* activity, a special time set aside to settle those conflicts that do not require immediate attention (and most do not) and to review those that do. As conflicts occur in the classroom, the teacher quickly stops them and fills out the first three steps of the document card (unless the intervention requires immediate settlement), placing it in an intervention docket box.

During the intervention docket activity, the teacher uses the intervention strategy to resolve the conflicts or review their resolution and to practice better ways. The intervention docket has two advantages: (1) it allows the students to see the teacher model the arbitration form of the intervention strategy; and (2) it provides a context to gradually bring the students into performing the intervention strategy themselves.

TEACHING INTERVENTION

The objective is to have students, within the limits of the school intervention system, resolve their own conflicts by following the outlined strategy. The teaching of the intervention strategy requires that students have mastered the supervising and planning strategies.

Schedule of Instruction

Table 18.1 presents a possible schedule for teaching intervention behavior. The components and strategy variations are on the left. The time periods across the top illustrate the relationship of component teaching procedures, but not the exact number of instructional days. The symbols within the cells mean the following: T, initial teaching; E, expansion; I, integration; R, refinement; M, maintenance. A number before the teaching procedures indicates a particular procedure. The bracketed numbers ([1/1]) in the text, not the examples, indicate a cell of Table 18.1. The first number is the component number and the second is the time period. Follow the schedule as you read so that a clear picture of teaching intervention behavior emerges.

Teaching Strategy Components

Eight components are the key to the intervention strategy variations. The first six include discriminating the following:

Table 18.1
Schedule for Teaching Intervention

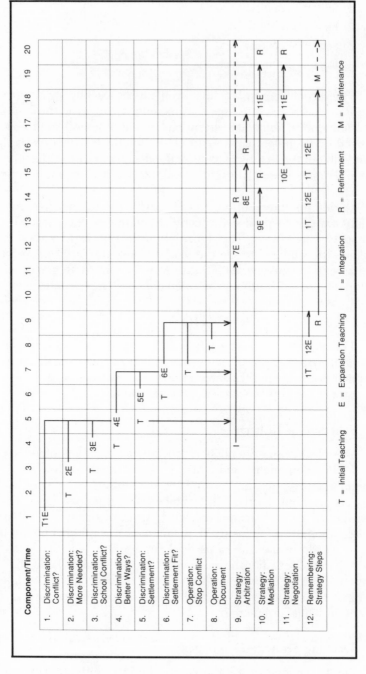

Component/Time	1	2	3	4	5	6	7	8	9	10	11	12	13	14	15	16	17	18	19	20
1. Discrimination: Conflict?	T1E																			
2. Discrimination: More Needed?		T	2E																	
3. Discrimination: School Conflict?			T	3E																
4. Discrimination: Better Ways?				T	4E															
5. Discrimination: Settlement?					T	5E														
6. Discrimination: Settlement Fit?						T	6E													
7. Operation: Stop Conflict							T													
8. Operation: Document								T												
9. Strategy: Arbitration				I								7E	R	8E	R	R				
10. Strategy: Mediation													9E		R		11E		R	
11. Strategy: Negotiation															10E		11E		R	
12. Remembering: Strategy Steps							1T	12E	R			1T	12E	1T	12E		1T	M	M	

T = Initial Teaching   E = Expansion Teaching   I = Integration   R = Refinement   M = Maintenance

1. Conflicts from nonconflicts.
2. Whether to continue the intervention once the conflict is stopped.
3. Conflicts that are settled in the classroom from conflicts that need to be settled at the school level.
4. Possible better ways from inappropriate ones.
5. Possible settlements from those that are not.
6. Settlements that fit the conflict from those that do not.

The last two components are operations: stopping the conflict and documenting it. The following presents examples of teaching each component. As in previous chapters, brackets indicate what the teacher does: point to intervention strategy [IS]; point to intervention strategy item, [IS2]; point to board [PTB]; write on board, [WOB]; call on a student, [COAS]; call on students, [COS]. What the students do is in parentheses: (SR), student replies or students reply, whichever is appropriate.

Discriminating Conflicts. Chapter 9 presented an example set for "conflict" and "not-a-conflict." That same format can be used here [1/1]. Because they give positive and negative examples of following classroom goals, rules, or procedures, students only have to connect these with the term *conflict*. Thus, you can start with the same examples as used then, model only two or three, and test by asking for examples. If you have been using the word *problem* instead of conflict, you may start as follows:

[IS] I have been telling you about what I think is a problem. Conflicts are problems between people. For example, Jose hits Martha with a book, making her cry. Conflict or not a conflict? Conflict.

Another example. Sidney picks up a book that Rachel dropped and hands it to her. Conflict or not a conflict? Not a conflict. [Move to testing.]

Your turn. Zelda refused to take her turn in group reading for the third time in a row. Tell me, conflict or not a conflict? [Pause, COAS] (SR: Conflict)

Next. Ronnie gives Wonda a sheet of paper to do extra math problems on. Tell me: conflict or not a conflict? (SR: Not a conflict.)

After a few of these tests, expand (1E) by asking students for examples of conflicts [1/1]. If they have problems giving them, extend your example set on the next day before asking for their examples. After the second day, ask for a few examples with each intervention review. Eventually, the range of conflicts will be covered.

Discriminating Conflicts for Further Resolution. Some conflicts are so minor that just stopping them is adequate. But at least five factors help determine whether further action needs to be taken. More is needed if:

1. The conflict occurs again during an activity, across activities, or across days.

2. The conflict interrupts the task behavior of others.
3. Those involved have a history of conflicts.
4. The conflict damages property.
5. The conflict puts anyone in danger.

If one or more of these factors is present, there is a need for further resolution. Introduce the discrimination in the following manner [2/2]:

> I have been deciding whether more is needed once a conflict is stopped. Soon you will be making that decision. Here are five kinds of evidence I look for to help me decide if more is needed. [WOB]
>
> 1. Is the conflict occurring again?
> 2. Does the conflict stop work?
> 3. Do those involved have many conflicts?
> 4. Was something damaged?
> 5. Could someone have been hurt?
>
> If the answer to any of these is yes, more may be needed.

Now model three or four examples of conflicts. For each, ask if more is needed. Answer using a "How do I know?" format and pointing to the factors written on the board (or on a posting). Some of your examples will involve more than one factor. Simply mention all of them. Next, present examples to students and have them classify and indicate factors controlling the classification.

By the second day [2/3], expand (2E) by asking one student for an example of a conflict and ask another if more is needed and why. Leave the factors posted for a long time; they will be used for other teaching. Eventually ask for an example or two every few days.

Discriminating Conflicts for School Intervention. Most schools have defined a set of behaviors, at various levels of inclusiveness, that require a school intervention. If this is the case, teach the discrimination by handing out the list or reduce it to four or five inclusive classes and write them on the board [3/3]. Next, ask for specific examples. Here is how it might go.

> There are some conflicts that we don't take care of here in the classroom. The principal's office will take care of these. Here is a list of conflicts that will go to the office [WOB].

Now go over the list with the students, building examples that fit the list and could happen in the classroom. After two days of prompting examples, expand (3E) by asking for examples of conflicts from one student, and from another ask where it will be resolved [3/4].

Discriminating Better Ways. Because students can provide positive and negative examples of goals, rules, and procedures, teaching them to find better ways is relatively easy. The negative examples of goals, rules, and procedures are the conflicts and the positive examples are the better ways. Starting with two or so conflicts that have already been identified, model better ways. Next, ask students for examples of conflicts and corresponding better ways. Prompt until students can give better ways that show how all involved parties could change [4/4]. If you want to use a "How do you know?" format for better ways, the answer for positive examples would be phrased something like, "It allows them to continue, and all parties are satisfied."

> One of the best ways to take care of a conflict so it does not happen again is to find a better way. If Deloris and Marty push and shove to get in the lunch line, a better way would be for Deloris to offer to let Marty go first. A better way would be for Marty to offer to let Deloris go first. Or they could apologize and flip a coin. [Continue for one more example.]
>
> Okay, your turn. If Andy grabs the bat from Cynthia during a game so he can bat first, what would be a better way? [COAS] Yes, Cynthia could suggest they flip a coin. Who has another better way? What could Marty do? [COAS] Yes, he could stop and give the bat back to Cynthia. Who has a conflict we can find a better way for? [COAS—continue.]

Over the next several days, do one or two examples per day. After that, expand (4E) by asking for one or two examples of a conflict and then a few better ways for each [4/5]. Continue until students are firm on finding better ways for a wide range of examples.

Discriminating Conflicts That Require Settlement. To teach students to discriminate conflicts that require a settlement, assemble a set of classroom conflict examples that could or could not involve settlement. The factors that govern whether a conflict requires a settlement or not are the same as those that govern determining if the intervention strategy needs to continue beyond stopping the conflict. The difference is that each piece of evidence has a weight. At some point, the evidence tips the scale toward settlement. How much conflict is necessary before a settlement is needed? The answer for some conflicts is easy, but there are many cases where it is not.

To teach this discrimination successfully, begin by modeling how you move from the evidence to the conclusion to settle or not settle [5/5]. If you have been using the questioning strategy and the language of inductive behavior (Chapter 7), it can be included here. Proceed as follows:

> I have identified a number of examples of conflicts that require settlements. But as you take over the intervention strategy, you will have to make the decision as to whether a conflict requires a settlement. When I make the decision, I consider five types of evidence. [WOB]

1. If those involved have many conflicts.

2. If the conflict has occurred before.

3. If work was stopped.

4. If things are damaged.

5. If people could be hurt.

For example, if Zed, who has had very few conflicts [PT1], refuses to read during group reading for the first time [PT2], I would not require a settlement. Why? Because he seldom is involved in conflicts [PT1], has never done it before [PT2], and it does not really slow us down [PT3]. If he did it again, I might try to help him find a better way, but if he continued the next day [PT2], I would require a settlement.

Next, suppose Riff took Nancy's pencil and broke it. I would choose to settle the conflict because it broke something [PT4]. It did not stop work very much [PT3] because she had another pencil. Also, he has not done it before [PT2], but I still think a settlement is required.

Would you require a settlement if Jim fell asleep during reading seatwork? [COAS] Who knows why? [COAS] Can anyone add to that? [COAS]

If Ethel and Bobby pushed and shoved on the playground, would you require a settlement? [COAS] Who knows why? [COAS] Can anyone add to that? [COAS]

During all these examples, continue pointing to the listed factors. If other factors are suggested that fit, put them on the board, too. After a few days of this, expand (5E) by asking students to give conflict examples and determine whether a settlement is needed and why [5/6]. Keep the posting of factors displayed. Voting on student arguments helps build consensus among students.

Discriminating Settlements That Fit the Conflict. Finding settlements that fit the offense has never been done to the satisfaction of all citizens or done consistently by those who administer the law. To bring a little consistency to your classroom and to teaching students to administer classroom law, you do two things: specify the possible settlement options and make an attempt to specify the criteria of why a particular settlement was made. The options in most classrooms include: (1) loss of free time; (2) separation from others during a lesson; (3) a letter to parents; (4) loss of awards; (5) loss or delay of access to reinforcing activities; (6) payment for damages; and (7) some combination of these six options.

For initial teaching, you would give the options and then a few examples of what you would do [6/6]. Start by writing the options and the criteria for requiring settlement on the board (or as two postings).

Thus far I have made the decisions as to what a settlement for inappropriate behavior should be. Now you must begin to make those decisions. You have seen some of my settlements. Here are the options and here are the general reasons for them [PTB]. Let me give you some conflicts that require settlement and see if we can figure out what to do.

First, let's say that Arnold has been asked several times to stop interrupting others, but he has continued to talk when others are given the chance to speak. Ki, what would you do? Which settlement do you think is appropriate? (SR: He should be separated from the group for one day and lose his free time that day.) Why do you think that is a just and equitable settlement? (SR: Because if he kept it up, we would all end up getting very little from the group work.)

Wilba, what do you think? (SR: Well, I think he should lose a privilege, but if he is separated he will not learn what the group is learnng.) What about you, Valencia? (SR: I think we should have him spend his individual project time on something that would help the group move faster on their work because he has slowed us down. Then I would send a letter home to his parents.)

Valencia's statement requests restitution from Arnold. In the classroom, payment usually takes the form of access to a task the student does not want to do and is done at a time that involves loss of access to something rewarding. The students of the class are usually quite good at figuring out what is punishing and what is rewarding for another student. Conflicts that may entail large-scale restitution are usually taken care of at the school level.

During your interaction with the students, prompt by moving back and forth between the options and the factors controlling settlement. Your task is to relate the evidence, options, and possible just settlements. Consistency in making just settlements requires that students work through many examples, noting the extent to which their decisions are consistent with those of the past. Use a voting procedure to let everyone participate, but always go back to why they selected a particular settlement. It forces them to consider the evidence of an individual case and builds their inductive behavior. By having them confirm one another's input, expansion (6E) occurs [6/7].

Stopping the Conflict. Stopping the conflict is a simple procedure that has two parts. The first involves eye contact, if possible, and a statement such as, "Please stop and follow the rules." The second part is a signal like the flat hand over the heart, as in pledging allegiance. Only one statement and signal should be used. Using more than one signal creates problems in observation and the detection of inappropriate signals. Practice this operation as you did the helping and sharing operations [7/7].

Filling Out the Document Card. Filling out the document card can be practiced as you work through examples of conflicts that do or do not require settlement [8/8]. Introduce filling out the card when they are firm on working through settlements. Give students copies of the card and have them fill it out as you go over examples. Using an overhead projector with the outline of a card provides them with a model or confirmation of their documenting.

Teaching the Intervention Strategy Variations

Teaching students SM skills extensively reduces the number and severity of conflicts. As a result, teaching intervention strategy variations requires the use of conflict scenarios, similar to those for teaching the discriminations. Use a cast of imaginary students. Another technique is to extend existing conflicts with "what if" additions. Here, real situations are modified so that more or different steps of intervention are performed.

Arbitration. As the component discriminations and operations are learned, they can be integrated into the arbitration strategy format during the intervention docket activity [9/5]. Just before this point [9/4] the arbitration posting, Figure 18.1, is introduced.

> Up until now, I have been intervening whenever there is a conflict. Now it is time for you to start doing it. Here are the main things I do [IS] when I have to deal with a conflict. You can already do some of them. You will learn the rest over the next few weeks. How many are ready to resolve their own conflicts?

For each arbitration, review the conflict as initially documented, asking students if it is a conflict (1a) and if more is needed (1c). From this point on, prompt the students to make the discriminations they have been taught. As you work through examples, involve as many students as possible. Let each do a substep. Ask different students about evidence and conclusions. Move very quickly. Ask others if they agree. A voting procedure can be used to gain consensus.

Arbitration at this point requires a word of warning. The first few times the students make the decisions in real situations, there can be dramatic emotional consequences for both those making the decision and those receiving it. The stronger the students' background in the other SM strategies, the less severe these consequences will be. Students treat their intervention responsibility with definite concern and consideration from the start. Close teacher supervision is required to insure just settlements and truncate possible aversive consequences.

As soon as students learn to make all the discriminations and perform the documenting operation, expand (7E) by selecting a student arbitrator to lead the class through the arbitration strategy [9/12]. A secretary can be selected to document the outcomes. Keep all related postings in view.

When the students have learned to stop conflicts, fill out the document card, and consistently implement the arbitration strategy during the docket activity, they can begin to stop conflicts during activities [9/14]. This expansion (8E) involves stopping the conflict, filling out the document card, and placing it in the docket box. Emphasize that stopping conflicts is a privilege earned with the fair administration of the arbitration procedure.

Mediation. The mediation (9E) expands the arbitration by involving the disputants in the resolution of the conflict and by using the arbitrator as a mediator [10/13]. The goal is to have the disputants make the decisions. The mediator's task is to prompt those in conflict toward an equitable resolution. These prompting operations have been added to the expanded posting. Figure 18.2 presents the mediation strategy expansion.

Although the posting appears to be complex, it is composed of discriminations and operational components that both the disputants and the mediator can already perform. The posting is worded from the perspective of the mediator. Steps 1c, 2c, and 3d require that you work out a procedure to deal with students who do not comply with the procedure or who are

Figure 18.2
Intervention Strategy Posting: Mediation

MEDIATION STRATEGY

1. STOP THE CONFLICT
   a. If it is a conflict, stop.
   b. Ask, is more needed?
      If disagreement, decide.
      If nothing more needed, exit.
   c. Ask, can we resolve conflict?
      If disagreement, decide.
      If not, document and exit.
   d. Document. (1–4)

2. FIND A BETTER WAY
   a. Ask, what are some better ways?
      If they fail to answer, provide ways.
   b. Ask, which better way do you select?
      If they can't, select.
   c. Say, please practice the better way.
      If they refuse, document and exit.
   d. Say, please commit to the better way.
   e. Document. (5, 7)

3. SETTLE THE CONFLICT
   a. Ask, is a settlement needed?
      If not needed, document and exit.
      If they disagree, make decision.
   b. Ask, what settlements fit?
      If none found, suggest some.
   c. Ask, which settlement do you select?
      If they can't, select.
   d. Say, please carry out the settlement.
      If they do not, document and exit.
   e. Document. (6–9)

involved in a conflict that requires school-level intervention. The simplest is to document and inform you.

Your task is to first introduce and model the mediator's role and then select students to mediate. The introduction informs students that it is time for them to take an even more active part in resolving their conflicts. Give the mediator and the class a copy of the posting. When prompting students through the posting for the first time, point out that they are asking the disputers to do what the arbitrator did before, and that if the disputers cannot, the mediator does it as the arbitrator did. Stress that the mediator must give it several tries. Primarily, you focus on the mediator by guiding him or her in prompting the disputants in answering the strategy questions.

Although you reserve the right to alter student decisions or put a decision to a class vote, let student intervention behavior take its own course. Explain this to students from the start. You can use a debriefing to examine their intervention decisions. It contributes to refining strategy behavior as discussed later.

Negotiation. As students in conflict come to carry out the requests of the mediator, they are moving closer to negotiation (10E). To facilitate that movement, introduce the negotiation strategy [11/15].

The negotiation posting, Figure 18.3, has no new discriminations. Students in conflict are asked to negotiate with the posting as a guide. Walk them through it the first few times. If possible, focus initially on conflicts that do not require a settlement, only a better way. The probability of success is increased and the members of the class learn that negotiation can work.

A *Final Expansion.* The intervention docket activity is instructionally necessary, but it breaks the flow of conflict resolution. The final expansion aims to reinforce conflict resolution as a unit.

As students became proficient at arbitrating conflicts, they were allowed to stop and document conflicts as they took place (expansion 8E, [9/14]). The final expansion (11E) extends this behavior [10/18, 11/18]. You have two tasks. The first is introducing the expansion to the students, informing them that they have earned the privilege of mediating and negotiating their conflicts as they occur. The second is to prompt the use of mediation and negotiation in conflict situations.

To facilitate the second task, you can do two things. The first is to add a question to the stopping of conflicts. The person stopping the conflict asks the parties, "Do you want to negotiate or mediate now, or wait for the intervention docket?" If all parties in conflict elect to negotiate or mediate they exit to an appropriate setting to do so. If they reject both, the document card is filled out and placed in the intervention docket box.

The second thing to do is add a negotiation/mediation table where those who elect one of the two intervention formats can go to carry out the resolution. The table should have all the postings involved in making

Figure 18.3
Intervention Strategy Posting: Negotiation

NEGOTIATION STRATEGY

1. STOP THE CONFLICT
   a. Congratulations for choosing negotiation.
   b. Ask, is more needed?
      If disagreement, get help.
      If nothing more needed, exit.
   c. Ask, can we resolve the conflict?
      If disagreement, get help.
      If not, document and exit.
   d. Document. (1–4)

2. FIND A BETTER WAY
   a. Ask, what are some better ways?
      If none found, get help.
   b. Ask, which better way do you select?
      If none selected, get help.
   c. Practice the better way.
      If someone refuses, document and exit.
   d. Commit to the better way.
   e. Document. (5, 7)

3. SETTLE THE CONFLICT
   a. Ask, is a settlement needed?
      If not needed, document and exit.
      If disagreement, get help.
   b. Ask, what settlements fit?
      If none found, get help.
   c. Ask, which settlement do you select?
      If disagreement, get help.
   d. Carry out the settlement.
      If someone does not, document and exit.
   e. Document. (6–9)

---

intervention discriminations and document cards. If a table is not used, those in conflict should have a way of saying, "We are in negotiation or mediation" and have access to appropriate postings at least until they have shown that they can remember the strategy steps. Helpers can also be used. Anyone who has settled a conflict through negotiation could be put on a helper list. The class can elect helpers, or you can establish criteria related to classroom academic and SM performance.

Remembering Strategy Steps. As with the previous strategies, students need to remember the strategy steps. For initial teaching use oral exercises and then expand to worksheets [12/7, continued]. The initial teaching and expansion procedures are the same for remembering the three types of intervention strategy postings (1T, 12E) except for content. Because of the infrequency with which conflicts may occur and the complexity of the strategy variations, it is necessary to use maintenance procedures fairly frequently.

Refinement Teaching

As students begin to take over the steps of each intervention variation, consequences focus on rewarding them for quickly identifying conflicts and stopping them (latency), and on the appropriateness (accuracy) of implementing the rest of the strategy steps. Here are a few examples of refinement statements.

> Thank you for stopping that conflict so fast. What is the next step?
>
> I think that is a fair settlement. It fits the criteria.
>
> You are doing a good job of coming up with interesting, better ways.
>
> That is the third time in a row this class has mediated its own conflicts. Keep it up.

After students become consistent in their intervention performance and consistently remember the steps of at least the arbitration strategy, an intervention strategy certificate and ceremony are in order.

Beyond the Schedule of Instruction

Becoming proficient in arbitration, mediation, and negotiation can take years. Thus, each year requires that these variations be refined. Because each class has an intervention system, involving students in its planning and review helps the refinement of intervention behavior. The intervention docket provides a useful format for future intervention systems. Moreover, the development of a school-based intervention system offers a vehicle for expanding intervention skills (Chapter 20).

If schools start to teach SM at an early age, conflicts as we know them today will be greatly diminished. Students who come to resolve conflicts in the very early stages will replace them with what we might call planning problems. At this point intervention behavior melds with planning, where problems are predicted and solutions of avoidance are designed and implemented. The long-term consequence is to move the classroom, school, and society closer to becoming nonviolent.

PLANNING INTERVENTION TEACHING

Before intervention teaching can begin, careful planning is required. The following procedure helps guide that planning.

1. Identify the intervention history of your students.
   a. If they have been taught all strategy forms, set an early time to plan this year's intervention components (Go to 4, see Chapter 16).
   b. If they have received some strategy teaching, design a review and establish an initial system that starts at that point (Go to 3).

   c. If they have no strategy teaching history, design a beginning initial intervention procedure, with or without posting (Go to 2).

2. Design the teaching of the basic intervention discriminations. For each discrimination:
   a. Select examples.
   b. Design a format for teaching.
   c. Design expansion activities.
   d. Design correction procedures.
   e. Build postings.

3. Plan the overall format for teaching intervention. Consider, for example, evolving from the initial intervention procedure to using the intervention docket.

4. Plan the details of each component of the intervention system. Consider for example:
   a. How conflicts will be stopped (wording and signal).
   b. How mediators will be selected for the intervention docket.
   c. How students will access and use the negotiation/mediation table.
   d. How the documentation card will look and be filled out.
   e. How disputants can get help while resolving a conflict.
   f. How you will use documentation secretaries and mediation helpers.
   g. How settlements will be monitored/reviewed by you.
   h. How students could be involved in planning (*a*) through (*g*).

5. Plan the introduction of each intervention component.

6. Build conflict scenarios. Consider:
   a. Using a cast of imaginary characters.
   b. Use "what if" expansions of classroom conflicts.

7. Plan a teaching schedule. Use Table 18.1 as a model.

19

TEACHING FOR INTEGRATION AND TRANSFER

Two instructional objectives remain: to insure that the SM strategies become a system of behavior and that they are implemented in contexts outside the classroom. The first is achieved through integration teaching procedures and the second through transfer teaching. This chapter provides those procedures.

INTEGRATING THE SELF-MANAGEMENT STRATEGIES

Integrating the SM strategies requires modeling, prompting, testing, and consequence elements.

Modeling

Modeling takes two forms. First, model the strategy relationships through a posting such as Figure 3.1 in Chapter 3. The analogy to riding a bicycle is appropriate. The steering, balancing, pedaling, and braking performed depend on the road and the others using the road. As these conditions change, so do the component behaviors of bike riding. If they do not, accidents occur.

Second, model thinking about SM behavior as a system of strategies. Prior to activities and during debriefings, set the occasion for and review students' SM behaviors at the systems level. Use the system posting to point out what they have to do or did.

Prompting

Prompting takes place in two locations. The first is during reviews and debriefings. Almost immediately after you model the analysis of their SM behavior as a system, prompt students to review and debrief their SM behavior as a system of strategies. The review helps them make predictions at the systems level and the debriefing helps them confirm their SM behavior at that level.

Second, prompt during activities. The basic prompt question is, "Which strategy is next?" Their thinking can be evaluated with a "How do you know?" question. If students cannot answer, prompt them to look at the system posting.

Testing

True testing occurs during fairly unstructured individual and group activities when students are given new problems to solve requiring a range of SM strategies to carry out. If activities have evolved to incorporate the use of SM strategies, the probability of success is insured.

Additionally, a specific set of individual and group problems can be designed to specifically test students' use of the SM strategies. The foundation for such activities is the product-oriented problem that requires planning and learning. These activities can be used as a criterion for SM awards.

Consequences

Task success, teacher statements and questions, awards, and access to student management positions are all reinforcing consequences that follow appropriate use of the SM strategies. By the time strategy integration teaching occurs, students should be able to predict and confirm task success. Teacher statements and questions continue to focus on exposing task success and the extent to which it impacts all those concerned. Access to classroom and school management positions should play a large part in reinforcing the integration of the system strategies. By using classroom and school management positions as consequences, transfer teaching facilitates integration teaching.

THE ANALYSIS OF TRANSFER

Transfer refers to the performance of learned behaviors in noninstructional environments.[1] The transfer of behavior is a problem of expansion teaching—you want to extend the range of the behavior.[2] Unlike the expansion procedures used so far, you cannot model, prompt, reinforce, and correct behavior in the transfer environments. Yet it is possible to teach students to transfer their SM behavior.

In a practical sense, transfer procedures fall into two classes.[3] First, there are the verbal procedures that by using statements and questions establish equivalences between the conditions and consequences in the nontransfer and transfer environments — from classroom to school to home.[4] For example:

> Wilber and Karen, you two have just intervened to stop your conflict. Where else could you intervene in the same way to resolve arguments? (SR) In both cases you would get back to your tasks faster.

The statement points out an equivalence across two environments, asks the students to predict an equivalence in conditions, and ends by indicating an equivalence in consequences across environments.

Second, student management systems can be used to promote transfer. They can exist at both the classroom and school levels, and are designed to widen the range of SM applications and provide rewarding consequences. These management system tasks promote transfer because they are equivalent to everyday tasks in many ways. The remainder of this chapter provides you with a strategy to plan for transfer and procedures to insure it.

A STRATEGY FOR PLANNING TRANSFER

Planning for transfer parallels planning a classroom organization, its SM behaviors, and consequences. Altogether, eight steps need to be taken; the first four support the verbal transfer procedures. All eight are involved in building classroom and school student management systems. Each is outlined.

Determine Locations and Activities

There are three inclusive locations (environments) of interest: classroom, school, and nonschool. To determine the activities of each, walk through them as done in Chapter 4.

In the classroom location, identify the teacher's management activities. These might include monitoring, organizing the library, extra-activity management, grading papers, filling out reports, or operating equipment.

The school involves a host of locations. First, there are those related to each type of school manager that includes, for example, the principal, assistant principals, deans of instruction, secretaries, building engineers, lunchroom personnel, and counselors. Second, there are student-related school locations that include, for example, the lunchroom, school grounds, student lounge, the auditorium, the library, and any other place where students meet in an organized fashion.

Nonschool locations are the most distant from the point of initial SM teaching, yet they are the place where we would most like students to apply their SM skills. There are three types of nonschool locations: transitions to and from school, the home, and places of employment.

For the classroom and school activities identified, you want to go back and make a preliminary determination of which things the students could do with a little training. Even if other professionals or the students themselves are to make these determinations as part of the classroom or school management systems, you need a "thinking about it" list so that you know what to expect. One of the purposes of this list is to determine possible titles for students involved in the activities. For example, in the classroom you may have activity planners, getting help monitors, equipment organizers, class representatives, intervention mediators, library managers, extra-activity organizers, or recess supervisors. At the school level you could assign titles like safety supervisor, grounds planner, building engineer helper, library organizer, cook helper, and school court judge.

Determine Each Location's Activity Behaviors

Walk through each activity trying to reduce it to a single procedure. Because the classroom is well known to you, walk through it in detail. At the school level, the personnel performing the activities should do the analysis. They should only have to work on those activities tentatively targeted for student involvement. The nonschool activities can only be analyzed generally with no attempt to reduce them to a procedure. Do not attempt to design postings.

Determine Activity Consequences

Similar to Chapter 5, you consider the types, direction, and placement of consequences for each activity. All school manager activities, directly or indirectly, allow other students access to activities. This access involves continuing an activity or entering into another activity. The extra-school location activities of home, leisure, and work are not as easy to analyze. Hypothesize the positive and remember that reciprocal consequences are very important in these extra-school locations. By performing SM behavior, students are reinforcing others. In turn, they are often reinforced.

Determine Equivalences Across Locations

Now step back and take a look at the behaviors across location activities. Just where are the same classes of SM behavior appropriate and what are the consequences that could reinforce the behavior? First, look from the classroom to the school and nonschool locations. Second, look from the school locations to the nonschool locations. You are always looking toward the more distant locations or to future locations in this analysis.

You can analyze the behaviors at the more or less inclusive levels, although it is easier to do it at the more inclusive SM strategy level. During all this analysis, keep in mind that others should be working with you, that you do not need to analyze all possible locations and activities, and that you are not trying for an extreme level of detail. You are looking for overall patterns of condition, behavior, and consequence (contingency) equivalences.

Determine Student Training Procedures

Who is going to train students to perform the classroom and school management tasks? The answers are different depending on when student training is to occur. Initially, training needs to be done by the personnel performing the task. (How to train the school personnel to do this is a problem taken up in Chapter 22). Once a student is performing the task to criterion, the next student can enter. At this point the prior student can become a manager/trainer for the new student. The adult looks on, prompting when necessary. If the activity has been reduced to a posting, the student trainer has a built-in guide.

Determine Criteria for Earning Management Positions

Student management positions are access consequences contingent on other behavior. Establish the SM and academic behavior that controls the access. For a classroom management position, students should perform task, activity SM, and strategy SM behavior before they can enter a management position. For a school management position, they should perform to criterion on all classroom task, SM, and management behaviors. Academic grades and intervention documentation are key data for determining if a student can assume a management position. The academic requirements are often task specific.

At the elementary level, classroom management positions can be phased in during the second or third grades, and school-level positions can start at about the fourth grade. At the middle and high school levels, students can be part of almost every task. By high school they can be involved in both the activities and their planning.

Determine the Selection Procedure for Entry

There will be more students who reach criteria than available management positions. This requires listing students who have earned positions. Publishing this list is the first phase of access. By having a portion of job time where student trainer and student trainee(s) work together, the length of time in the position increases. You want students to perform the task long enough to become proficient. Your first determination will be guess work. By figuring out how many times each position changes per year and finding a total, you get the number of management positions you have available each year. At the school level, every student should have a chance to participate at least once during a semester or year.

Determine Evaluation Procedure for Management Positions

First, evaluation is based on job-related skills. Second, review the punctuality of and the questions from the students filling the position. These help you evaluate the structure and function of the activity task. The students may find the job impossible to perform. And third, provide students with private and public knowledge of the evaluation.

VERBAL TRANSFER PROCEDURES

Three procedures are presented; they can be used independently or as a unit. When used as a unit, you maximize the probability of transfer. Their aim is to teach students to discriminate equivalences across locations and to prompt and reinforce students' attempts at managing themselves in these locations.

Describing Equivalences

This procedure describes equivalences in behaviors and/or consequences across locations.

> The way you are waiting your turns in the lunch line is the same way you will have to wait to see the exhibits at the museum.
>
> Supervising yourself to get your seatwork done can be used at home to finish your studying so you have more time for your own projects.
>
> By helping Gary with his assignment, everyone finished on time. By helping at home, you can often begin family activities sooner.

The first example describes the equivalence of activity level SM behaviors across school and nonschool locations. The second and third examples describe equivalences in behaviors and consequences across locations.

Asking About Equivalences

This procedure, similar to the questioning procedure presented in Chapter 7, teaches students to think inductively about their SM behavior. It has three steps: (1) describe or ask about student SM behavior; (2) ask where else they could use this behavior; and (3) confirm and ask for consequences in locations identified.

If the student does not see any equivalences, correct by giving the answer and retest later, or continue to use the described equivalence procedure. If the equivalence appears wrong, ask for supporting evidence, (why they would use the identified SM behavior in the given location). If it is wrong, give the answer and retest later.

The steps of the procedure can vary. In the following examples, the numbers in brackets indicate the steps of the procedure and the [V] indicates a variation.

[1] The supervision step of questioning yourself about your success has helped each of you to do an accurate job. [2] Where could it be used at home? (SR) [3] During study and helping your parents are two good ones. How would these help? (SR) Yes, accuracy will end up here, also.

This interaction follows the procedure step by step; the following interaction is a slight variation.

[1V] You have just intervened, stopped your conflict, and as a consequence quickly returned to your task. [2] Where besides the classroom can you try that same procedure? (SR) [3] What do you think would happen if you tried it? (SR) [V] But if the other person did not know the procedure, you would have to help them through the steps.

The first variation adds a consequence. The second variation is a warning that concludes the interaction. In the case of interventions, it is an important variation for the safety of the student.

Another variation is to have the students identify specifics about how to perform a SM behavior in another location. Their response represents evidence for the application of the SM behavior.

[1] What have you done in the lesson? [COS] [2] What could you learn about at home? [COS] [3V] Yes, and how would you learn about your hobbies at home? [COS] You're sure getting to know where and how to manage yourselves.

These examples and variations represent only a glimpse at the behaviors, consequences, and locations to which the questioning procedure can be applied to influence transfer.

Request and Confirm

The request and confirm procedure follows the use of one of the first two verbal transfer procedures. The steps include: (1) describing or asking about uses of SM behavior (previous procedures 1 or 2); (2) requesting students to commit to performing the behaviors in the transfer location; and (3) confirming transfer of the SM behavior. The first two steps are essentially a combination statement or question. The third is the confirmation element of the questioning procedure (Chapter 7). At a later point in time, you confirm the request or commitment to performance [3], asking for the details and the consequences of performance [3A]. This step can optionally include a reward statement element for carrying out the behavior requested [3B]. Here is an example of the first two steps.

[1] Where could you use your supervision skill? (SR) [2] Will you do it there? (SR) I will ask you how it worked tomorrow.

Now for the second interaction, step three.

[3] Who used their supervision skills to help them do their homework? (SR) [3A] Willie, tell me how you used it. (SR) So, what happened? (SR) [3B] I am glad it was such a help to you.

Often you can continue this step by asking several students in a row for examples. After using the procedure a few times, students give consequences without being asked. They begin to see the SM skills as problem-solving devices, so they begin their example by telling how it helped them.

Implementing Verbal Transfer Procedures

Verbal transfer procedures can be implemented after the students have come to perform any of the SM strategies. The procedures can focus on individuals or groups.

There are at least two easy ways to apply the request-and-confirm procedure. The first is to use it during an activity debriefing.

[3A] Who can provide an example of supervising themselves or others in their home? [COS] [3B] Those are a great set of applications. That is clear thinking.

[3A] Who can give me a good example of how they managed themselves outside of school? [COS] [3B] Those are interesting uses of your management skills.

The second technique supplements the first. It involves the addition of a matrix, or chart, that on the top horizontal axis lists many of the transfer environments. On the left vertical axis are the SM strategies the students have learned. Thus, on the grid each SM skill and transfer environment has a space in which student examples can be noted by name or initials.

This second technique helps to see who is transferring SM skills, which skills are being transferred, and to which locations they are being transferred. Thus, the grid provides a full range of data to evaluate your transfer teaching. For example, if a square remains empty or has few names, you can return to using the full request-and-confirm procedure which emphasizes applying the untransferred SM skill to the appropriate locations. You can ask students for specifics of how to apply SM strategies in these locations. Criteria for marking cells may have to be developed.

IMPLEMENTING STUDENT MANAGEMENT SYSTEM PLANS

You have planned a classroom or school-level management system to facilitate transfer. Now you want to implement it; the following guidelines can help.

Evaluate the Existing Student Management Components

Student management systems exist in every classroom and school. Almost every school has a student council or government, and delegates a number of tasks to students. These should be reinterpreted in terms of the SM strategies. As a consequence, your talk about these tasks will become congruent with the management language of this text. You will be surprised at the extent of the existing systems.

Start Small

The preceding transfer planning may show that there are many things that can be done, but start with one thing. At both the classroom and school levels, this can be a student planning committee that is an arm of the student council. At the classroom level, this can involve participant management planning with the entire class.

Provide Staff Training

All staff members must be given a general picture of the project and their part in it as well as the skills they need to perform. For those who will be training and monitoring student managers, the way to start both the motivational and skill aspects of training is to involve them in planning student management tasks related to their professional function. Chapter 21 details training procedures.

Establish an Implementation Sequence

An implementation sequence represents your goals for putting the classroom and school management curriculum into operation. Establish a time line showing when tasks will be included. Begin by starting small and expanding out as training occurs. With a planning committee, establish a matrix with the left axis identifying the tasks (which keep evolving) and the top horizontal axis identifying progress. The progress can be divided into date of conception, selection of planning committee for task or area, initial task plans, final okay, initial start-up, and first evaluation.

Market the Management Systems

Marketing the system to students and staff begins with the initial introduction to the student management system. There are two keys to following up on initial marketing efforts. The first is task refinement through reevaluation. Students and the staff managers compare what the task procedure says and what they found while doing the job. The second is expansion through the addition of new tasks, involving more students. In both, participants see how they can restructure the environment through individual and group contributions. Changing things markets the system by keeping it growing and fresh.

SUMMARY

To successfully use the procedures presented in this chapter, you must plan as carefully as you have for teaching SM skills. The following planning outline functions as a guide:

1. Decide when to integrate and transfer SM behavior (see Chapter 20).
2. Design integration procedures. Consider doing the following:
   a. Reestablish postings for all strategies that have been taught.
   b. Build a system display similar to Figure 3.1
   c. Introduce SM as a system.
   d. Review and debrief activities at the systems level.
   e. Build statements that prompt moving from one strategy to another and reinforcing students for doing so.
3. Decide the extent of your transfer procedures. Consider:
   a. Verbal procedures.
   b. Classroom management systems.
   c. School management systems.
4. Plan transfer procedures.
   a. Determine activities for each location.
   b. Determine which activities for the classroom and school can be performed by your students.
   c. Determine which behaviors are required for these activities.
   d. Determine the access and other types of consequences for these activities.
   e. Determine the contingency equivalences across locations. Consider:
      1. Working from the classroom to other locations.
      2. Working from the other locations to the classroom.
   f. Determine student training procedures. Consider:
      1. Start-up training being done by staff.
      2. Follow-up training being done by students.

3. How many students can be trained at once.

4. Using Chapter 21 for planning staff training.

g. Determine SM and academic criteria for earning management positions.

h. Determine the selection procedure for the position earned.

i. Determine the evaluation procedure for each position. Consider:

1. Performance related to position posting.

2. Student participation.

5. Build statements and questions for each transfer procedure.

a. For the description procedure, describe a classroom SM behavior and the equivalent activity of use and, optionally, the consequences.

b. For the question procedure, describe SM behavior, ask where it could be used, and confirm and ask for consequences in identified locations.

c. For the request-and-confirm procedure, use the describe-or-ask procedure to start, request that students transfer the behavior, confirm the use of the SM skill, and optionally reinforce performance and ask about consequences.

d. Vary these procedures.

6. Select a transfer procedure implementation site. Consider:

a. Where you will implement.

b. How you will implement.

c. Consider delivering the transfer statements with the same truthfulness, sincerity, and consistency as you have for all statements and procedures learned.

7. Implement the classroom and school management systems.

a. Evaluate the existing student management components (Chapter 22).

b. Start small—the heart of controlling the system's evolution.

c. Provide staff training before start up (Chapter 21).

d. Establish an implementation sequence.

e. Market the management system—keep it young (Chapter 22).

When these planning tasks have been completed, you are ready to implement the integration and transfer procedures in your classroom or school.

IV

The Self-Management Program

When the teaching of SM moves beyond the individual classroom and into the school or district, new problems arise. For success across this wider scope, these problems must be addressed and procedures provided for their solution. That is the agenda of Part 4. Chapter 20 guides the planning of a SM curriculum that applies to a classroom, school, or district. Chapter 21 tackles the problems of implementing a schoolwide or districtwide SM program. And Chapter 22 presents a strategy to adapt your SM program to problems.

20

PLANNING THE
SELF-MANAGEMENT CURRICULUM

The preceding chapters have provided the building blocks of a SM curriculum. The next step is to plan how they can be assembled to fit classroom, school, or district resources. This chapter guides the curriculum planning process, describing when and how to teach your SM curriculum. The major product of this plan is an instructional program with daily lessons and exercises. This program makes it possible to plan teacher training and to adapt the SM curriculum to meet the needs of the community (Chapters 21 and 22).

ANALYSIS OF SEQUENCING

A curriculum, as represented by the instructional program, sequences teaching over time to evolve student behavior. This section analyzes the types of sequences that need to be designed and the resources that influence their design.

Types of Sequences

Figure 20.1 illustrates the six types of sequences.[1] An *exercise sequence* indicates the organization of the elements of teaching for an instance of a teaching procedure. Any instance of a teaching procedure is composed of any number of models, prompts, tests, or consequence elements. The preceding chapters have illustrated the variety of arrangements they can take. The exercise sequencing question is: How can the elements of teaching be organized so that an instance of a teaching procedure is effective?

Figure 20.1
Types of Sequences and Influencing Resources

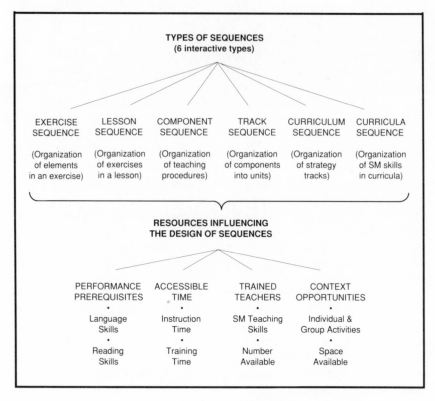

A *component sequence* specifies the organization of teaching procedures for the teaching of a skill component. In other words, it specifies when and which teaching procedures can be used to teach any behavior or strategy. The components to be taught are listed on the left of the schedule of instruction tables in Chapters 14 through 18. The arrangement of teaching procedures are indicated in the cells of the tables. The component sequencing question is: How can teaching procedures be organized to insure the effective teaching of a skill component?

A *track sequence* represents the organization of all component sequences that can be viewed as a unit. The components need to be arranged to facilitate learning. In the present case, the major tracks correspond to all the components of a SM system strategy. The basic track sequencing question is: How can the component sequences be organized to insure effective instruction of all skill components?

A *curriculum sequence* details the organization of the track sequences. The seven strategy track sequences make up the heart of the SM curriculum sequence. There are several ways sequences can be arranged. A *linear curriculum sequence* teaches one track sequence at a time. A *multiple curriculum sequence* teaches more than one track at a time. Additionally, a *spiral curriculum sequence* returns to the tracks of the curriculum each year for further expansion. For example, when you use the system strategies in subject areas outside the point of their early instruction and for the student management systems, you are spiraling by applying the strategies under new and more complex conditions year after year. These options help answer the basic curriculum sequencing question: How can the track sequences be organized to efficiently teach all tracks?

To determine which type of teaching will take place for which skill components, look down the curriculum sequence for a particular day. This vertical picture of each day's teaching plan is a *lesson*. A lesson consists of exercises. An *exercise* represents an instance of a teaching procedure and contains the content of instruction. A lesson is usually made up of several exercises from various components and tracks. The *lesson sequence* is the organization of all the exercises to be taught in a day or single period of instruction. The basic lesson sequencing question is: How can the exercises within a lesson be organized to meet the constraints of the instructional environment and promote effective instruction?

A *curricula sequence* details the organization (starting time, ending time, and total time) of all curriculum sequences. Relative to the SM curriculum, the curricula sequencing question is: How can the SM curriculum be organized relative to other curricula to facilitate their instruction?

In planning the SM curriculum, all six sequencing questions have to be answered. Because of the interdependence of the sequences, this is not always an easy matter. Modifications in one sequence lead to modifications in others. To facilitate planning, many sequencing examples have been provided in previous chapters and guidelines follow.

Resources Controlling the Design of Sequences

The lower half of Figure 20.1 outlines the resources that control the design of sequences and, thus, the instructional program. Four types of resources are important.

Prerequisite performance skills specify which general level of background skills is needed before a curriculum can be taught. The teaching of SM requires that students have a certain level of language and reading skills. These are the performance dependencies outlined in Chapter 2.

Accessible time is the time allotment given to the curriculum in total or to daily lessons. A time allotment exists for all curricula. It is no different for SM. Yet the SM skills have an impact on the other curricula to an equal if not greater extent than reading skills do. Thus, providing time for their teaching at an early point may reduce the time needed later in other curriculum areas.

Trained teachers are those who have the skill to deliver the curriculum within the time, context, and instructional resources provided. Without enough trained teachers, no curriculum can be taught effectively. Chapter 22 examines the area of teacher training in detail.

Context opportunities, the fourth resource, refer to the physical space, its arrangement, the number of students, and the classroom activities provided. To successfully teach the SM strategies, individual and interactive activities are needed. This often requires an efficient use of space for the students involved. If such context opportunities do not exist, they must be designed.

A STRATEGY FOR CURRICULUM PLANNING

The following strategy outlines the process of planning a SM curriculum, from selecting your SM curriculum components to integrating it with your other curricula.[2]

Select Self-Management Curriculum Tracks

The entire SM curriculum does not have to be taught. For example, you may decide not to teach part or all of the intervention strategy because of certain beliefs or community feelings about such matters. For those who work with students for only one academic year, it will be necessary to drop major parts of the intervention and learning strategy, and it will not be possible to achieve independence in student planning.

Establish a Curriculum Time Frame

Next, determine a tentative starting and running time for teaching. Three guidelines are provided.

GUIDELINE 1: Start in kindergarten.

GUIDELINE 2: If implemented in kindergarten, allot about 15 minutes per day for six years.

GUIDELINE 3: If implemented at the middle- or high-school level, allot a one-year course at the earliest grade possible (i.e., seventh or ninth grades).

Early elementary implementation accelerates academic instruction from the beginning. Implementation at the middle- or high-school levels can be an extension of an elementary program or an initial one. If it is an initial program, the sequence is essentially a collapsed form of that used for the elementary level. The introduction would present the strategy system as illustrated in Figure 3.1. All of the strategy postings would be displayed and covered in the sequence suggested later. The students' initial tasks could be their homework from other classes. Later, they could work on individual and group projects of interest to them, planning their own activities as they go. In the end, the students should be managing the class while the teacher acts as a resource and teaches skills related to the learning strategy. Of course, limits would be placed on topics.

When the program is an extension of the elementary program, the middle- or high-school courses offer advanced SM and management skills. Each strategy step is expanded, and management activities are devised for the practice of these skills. For example, the intervention strategy steps can be modified so that extensive legal and procedural elements involved in formal arbitration, mediation, and negotiation can be taught. The learning strategy can be expanded to include techniques of observation and experimentation. Additionally, this class can be a training ground for classroom and school management positions.

Design Component and Track Sequences

The component sequences for each strategy track were shown in the scheduling tables in Chapters 14 through 18. Now, lay out the components in detail to specify the days of instruction. Next, organize the component sequences into track sequences. Arrange the components into tracks following the scheduling models. This initial arrangement will undergo some alteration as the other curriculum design steps are performed.

GUIDELINE 4: Build in safety factors.

Teaching, similar to the other technologies, requires safety factors. Although this text has made suggestions on how many days to teach a strategy component, the wide variability in resources demands that extra instructional days be inserted when in doubt. The goal is for all students to learn. Remember, it is easier to accelerate through material than it is to figure out what is wrong and hastily construct the materials needed.

Design Exercises

Now, design the teaching exercises for each filled cell on your track charts. Two things make this task manageable. First, examples of content and procedure have been provided throughout the text. Second, many of the procedures are redundant—what is done from day to day is the same except for content. There are two guidelines to follow in producing these exercises.

GUIDELINE 5: Provide enough of the procedure so that a few seconds of scanning will allow teaching to proceed.

If teaching a set of examples, simply put in the wording for the first example, list the examples, and outline the correction procedure. If teaching a strategy, number what you want to say by the step numbers of the strategy. The posting will help with the rest.

GUIDELINE 6: Design exercises so that they are fast-paced and short in duration.

The shortness of an exercise is relative to the type of teaching. An initial teaching exercise of a discrimination should take less than a minute. An initial teaching exercise for planning will take ten to twelve minutes, but the pace of the instruction is fast—students are providing answers or making predictions every few seconds.

To keep all the exercises in order, put each on a separate sheet and file by component in the order listed on the curriculum sequence table. At the top of the exercise sheet name the exercise by track, component, and type of teaching (e.g., initial teaching, expansion).

Design the Curriculum Sequence

The next step is to arrange track sequences. Stagger them across the curriculum time frame selected earlier. To get a picture of this sequence, map it out on a wall by putting a time line across the top and numbering it for the school days. Now arrange your track sequences. It yields an interesting blueprint. By looking down the sequence (as a schedule at this point) for any day, you can see the lesson exercises to be taught on that day.

GUIDELINE 7: There may be no perfect curriculum sequence, but there are many that will work.

Many sequences are possible. The resources controlling them need to be considered, as do the number of exercises each day.

GUIDELINE 8: Initially introduce only one SM strategy at a time.

Although the various components of more than one track may be taught at one time, the initial or integration teaching of strategies should be done one at a time. Several strategies, for example, can undergo expansion or refinement at one time. Guideline nine clarifies further.

GUIDELINE 9: Order the introduction of SM tracks as indicated in Table 20.1

Organizing, helping, and sharing are taught first. Without these behaviors, instruction is ineffective. Supervision helps students work in groups and,

Table 20.1
Self-Management Curriculum Sequence

CURRICULUM TRACKS	GRADE LEVEL						
	K	1	2	3	4	5	6
ORGANIZING	TER	ER	R	M ————————————→			
HELPING	TE	ER	R	M ————————————→			
SHARING	TE	ER	R	M ————————————→			
SUPERVISING			TEIR	ER	R	M ————→	
PLANNING			TEIR	ER	R	M ————→	
LEARNING		X	X	TER	IR	R	M →→
INTERVENING			X	TER	IR	IR	IR
SM SYSTEM				IER	ER	ER ————→	
CLASSROOM MANAGEMENT			ZE	ER	ER	ER ————→	
SCHOOL MANAGEMENT					ZE	ER ————→	

T = Initial Teaching
I = Integration Teaching
M = Maintenance Teaching
X = Component Discriminations Teaching
E = Expansion Teaching
R = Refinement Teaching
Z = Transfer Teaching

therefore, needs to be taught early. Planning helps make students independent learners, but it is dependent on supervision skills. Learning is the next strategy taught, although the teaching of knowledge-type discriminations should begin in the first grade. The intervention discriminations can begin in the second grade. Integrating the strategies begins in the third grade. The transfer of behavior at the classroom and school levels begins in second and fourth grades with verbal transfer procedures gradually starting at an earlier point.

Design Lesson Sequences

Everything necessary for each day of instruction, or lesson, has been designed. The next step is to organize the exercises of a lesson. This provides a lesson sequence. First, go through the exercise files and organize one set by day. Second, check the teaching time of these exercises to see if it falls within the lesson time frame. If the teaching for any day cannot be easily done within the daily time frame, the options are to change the time frame or change the lesson. Doing the latter requires going to the track sequence to see if some minor shifting can be done. At the same time, make the same changes in the curriculum sequence table and the exercise file. On each exercise indicate the lesson day.

Third, organize the lessons for teaching. Use ring binder notebooks and enough separators with tabs to distinguish every five days of teaching. At this point, group more than one exercise on a page, if desired. Leave plenty of room for notes on problems, successes, or interesting student responses. Number the order of each day's exercises once arranged. Arrange exercises according to the following guidelines:

GUIDELINE 14: Arrange component exercises before strategy exercises.

This means that the individual discriminations and operations related to SM strategies are done first, followed by strategy teaching. In the middle-school class devoted to SM teaching, following this guideline becomes most important. The initial fast-paced exercises get the class moving from the start. The next guideline occurs within the organization established by the previous one.

GUIDELINE 15: Do initial teaching first, teacher directed expansions second, and then independent expansions.

This means put the newer exercises first. The numerous independent expansions of the learning strategy components are done during reading.

GUIDELINE 16: If a component is initially taught and undergoes its first expansion in the same day, put them back-to-back.

Initial instruction occurs for two or more occasions. By doing the final initial teaching exercise just before the first expansion, you are setting the occasion for success on the latter.

GUIDELINE 17: Activity-based SM strategy expansions and integrations occur during the appropriate activity.

Not all SM teaching can be done during a SM lesson time. Much of it occurs in the context of academic activities. This final formating guideline acknowledges that SM teaching has to be coordinated with the other curricula.

Design Academic Curricula Integrations

In Chapter 19, one goal was to create context opportunities (activities) to promote the use of the SM strategies as a system of behavior. Once this behavior is firm, the design task is reversed. Now context opportunities are created so that learning other curricula content can be facilitated by the student's use of the SM strategies.

To design these curricula integrations, first select the points at which the various strategies are firm enough to be used in content area teaching. This is determined by examining the SM curriculum sequence. Second, ask how the teaching of each content area can be changed to take advantage of student SM behaviors so learning can be accelerated. Individual and group activities are needed. Finding these requires a collaborative staff effort by those who know the SM curriculum and content area subject matter. A walk-through procedure can be performed across subject areas to find activities. Not all subject areas are equally suited to group strategy skills.

Design Procedures to Facilitate Teaching

It is important to have a clear, easy-to-follow lesson format. This is especially important for SM teaching because it requires that SM skills be used during the teaching of academic subjects. To insure success, a simple four-step procedure can be used.

First, take the day's lessons out of the ring binder. Second, write on the board the key points you want to make (a self-posting). Third, tell the students these points and have them remind you. Fourth, put the strategy postings up around the room. By prompting yourself in these four ways, you insure success.

With your daily lesson layout you can adapt to emergencies, take up where you left off when special activities interrupt your plans, and insert notes when having difficulty with some teaching procedure.

During the first year, you will make many revision notes as you teach; these help the revision process. To manage the revision task, allot time to revise a lesson or two every few days of the last half of the year. See the revision on the lesson level as a lesson-by-lesson task and not the planning of a whole year's activity to be undertaken at one time. If revision is done with other professionals, the task can be completed faster, be more enjoyable, and further improve the quality of instruction.

SUMMARY

The goal is to have a SM curriculum that has as little ambiguity as possible and that fits within a particular system of curricula. The following is a summary of the points made in this chapter to achieve that goal.

1. Select the strategies you want to teach.
2. Establish a curriculum time frame. Guidelines:
   a. Start in kindergarten.
   b. If implemented at kindergarten level, allot about 15 minutes per day.
   c. If implemented at the middle- or high-school level, allot a one-year course at the earliest possible grade.

3. Establish component and track sequences. Guideline:
   a. Build in safety factors.

4. Design exercises. Guidelines:
   a. Provide enough of the procedure so that a few seconds of scanning reminds you how to proceed.
   b. Design exercises so that they are fast-paced and short in duration.
   c. Identify each exercise by track, component, and teaching type.

5. Design a curriculum sequence. Guidelines:
   a. There may be no perfect curriculum sequence, but there are many that will work.
   b. Initially teach only one strategy at a time.
   c. Order the introduction of the SM strategies as indicated in Table 20.1.

6. Design daily lesson sequences. Guidelines:
   a. Arrange component exercises before strategy exercises.
   b. Do initial teaching first, teacher directed expansions second, and then independent expansions.
   c. If a component is initially taught and undergoes its first expansion on the same day, teach them back-to-back.
   d. Activity-based SM strategy expansions occur during the appropriate activity.

7. Design academic curricula integrations. Consider:
   a. The point at which the SM system of strategies can be used to accelerate learning within other curricula.
   b. The opportunities available within each subject. (You may have to design some group activities, and some areas will not be as conducive to group work.)

8. Plan your student management systems. Consider the points presented in Chapter 19.

9. Adjust the preceding components to fit each other and the factors that control planning decisions.
   a. Skill dependencies.
      1. Performance prerequisite skills.
      2. SM prerequisite skills.
   b. Resource availability.
      1. Accessible time.
      2. Trained teachers.
      3. Context opportunities.

Once your curriculum is planned, you are ready for instruction at the classroom level. If you are implementing the SM curriculum across a school or district, Chapters 21 and 22 provide the guidelines needed.

21

IMPLEMENTING THE
SELF-MANAGEMENT PROGRAM

Carrying out a successful school- or district-wide self-management program requires detailed planning and careful supervision. This chapter illustrates how they can be performed.[1]

ANALYSIS OF IMPLEMENTATION PLANNING

An *implementation plan* is five distinct but interactive plans. The *curriculum development plan* identifies the personnel, location, and time frame for planning the SM curriculum illustrated in Chapter 20. The *curriculum utilization plan* determines how the constructed curriculum will be put into operation. Because of limited resources, implementation is often done in stages, taking up to several years to carry out the program across the entire school district at any one grade level. With each year there is an expansion of the program.

The *teacher training plan* builds the behavior needed to teach and administer the SM curriculum. It answers seven questions:

1. Who can do the training?
2. Who will be trained?
3. Which skills will they need to be trained in?
4. How will they be trained in each area?
5. When will they be trained?
6. How long will they be trained?
7. Where will they be trained?

The *adaptation plan* outlines the personnel, methods, and time frame for monitoring, evaluating, and revising the program as it evolves from year to year. This plan is examined in Chapter 22.

The *budget plan* gives the implementation plans a reality; they are required to live within the monetary constraints of the school district. At the same time, the other plans form an argument for the budget.

A STRATEGY FOR IMPLEMENTATION PLANNING

Implementation planning pivots on developing a teacher training plan because it governs the rate at which the curriculum can be utilized; the time at which curriculum materials need to be ready; the time frame for monitoring, evaluating, and revising the program; and represents the major portion of budget expenditures.

Often it is best to develop at least two implementation plans. The first would be the best-case scenario and the second would be the worst-case scenario. The latter represents the extreme viewpoint, beyond which you would predict almost certain program failure. Realizing this point can help determine whether time and energy should be expended. The following 12-step procedure facilitates implementation planning.

Identify Personnel Resources

Planning and implementing a SM program requires a core group of trained personnel. Help is needed primarily in three areas: curriculum construction, teacher training, and adaptation activities. Those involved, or the supervisor in each area, needs to have knowledge of the contents of this text. Identifying or training these people may be your first implementation task.

Initially, there will be a scarcity of teacher training personnel. Say, for example, there are two trainers who have established and carried out a SM program in their classrooms for one or two years. Because a trainer can train 15 or 16 people at one time, that means by the end of the year about 30 to 32 teachers can be trained. If 20 to 25 percent of these can be used as trainers the next year, you can have about eight more trainers, for a total of ten. At this point 150 to 160 teachers can be trained. That is 150 to 160 classrooms with trained teachers by the end of the second year. By releasing both initial trainers from classroom teaching responsibilities, training can be staggered, allowing for many more to be trained and observed. At the same time, they could start to work on the curriculum and adaptation plans with other professionals.

Decide on a Curriculum Sequence

Chapter 20 covered the development of curriculum sequences. Table 20.1 illustrated an example. Additionally, many will want to catch those students who were in the district at the start of the program but missed out on the skills because of the selected curriculum utilization sequence. Developing a middle- or high-school SM program, as indicated in Chapter 20, can accomplish this. The sequence in Table 20.1 is the model for this chapter.

Determine Who Needs to Be Trained

Three types of personnel need to be trained. The first group, strategy teachers, includes those who perform initial and expansion teaching of the SM strategies. The second group, support teachers, includes those who interact with students following strategy teaching. At the elementary level, this group includes the specialty teachers for such areas as art, music, and physical education. These teachers help expand and maintain strategy skills. At the middle- and high-school levels, support teachers are all the other teachers with whom the students interact. The third group includes administrators and any other personnel who have contact with the students in the program. Their relationship with the program is usually connected to the school's student management system.

Determine Which Skills Have to Be Taught

Each type of personnel has to be given different training. Table 21.1 outlines the skill areas (including an introduction to SM) and indicates who receives which training relative to the curriculum sequence selected. The numbers in parentheses on the left indicate the relevant chapters of this text. The letter or letters in the cells indicate the focus of that skill training. First, give basic skills training, marked with an "X" in Table 21.1, to all strategy and support teachers. From there on, which strategy skills are taught them depends on the teacher's place in the curriculum sequence (Table 20.1). The integration of strategies would include the verbal transfer procedures.

The emphasis given strategy skills also differs across teachers. Those who are going to initially teach (T), expand (E), integrate (I) and refine (R) a strategy or a management system need the extensive training in how to model, prompt, test, and correct students for each teaching procedure. This requires that they study and practice several early applications of the strategy presented in the curriculum materials.

Those who are going to refine or maintain (M) a skill area need knowledge of the steps of the strategy, its posting, a basic correction procedure, and where it fits within their teaching. Combined with a little practice and their basic skills training, they are sufficiently prepared for teaching.

The training of administrators and other staff begins with a general introduction to the program. From that point, their training is very specific to the part they play in the student school management system. They have to be guided to view their jobs in terms of activities, and to determine

Table 21.1
Teaching Skills

TEACHING SKILLS	STRATEGY TEACHERS							SUPPORT TEACHERS							AD
	K	1	2	3	4	5	6	K	1	2	3	4	5	6	I
Introduction to SM Strategies (1, 3)	X	X	X	X	X	X	X	X	X	X	X	X	X	X	X
Design a classroom organization (2, 4-5)	X	X	X	X	X	X	X	X	X	X	X	X	X		
Use basic teaching skills (6-12)	X	X	X	X	X	X	X	X	X	X	X	X	X	X	X*
Teach a classroom organization (13*)	X	X	X	X	X	X	X	X	X	X	X	X	X		
Teaching Organization (13)	TER	TER	R	M	M	M	M	R	R	R	M	M	M	M	
Teaching Helping/Sharing (14)	TER	TER	R	M	M	M	M	R	R	R	M	M	M	M	
Teaching Supervision (15)		TER	ER	R	M	M				ER	R	R	M	M	
Teaching Planning (16)		TER	ER	R	M	M				ER	R	R	M	M	
Teaching Intervening (18)		TE*	TER	IR	R	M					IR	R	M	M	
Teaching Learning (17)		TE*	TE*	TER	IR	IR	IR				R	R	R	R	
Teaching Integration of Strategies (19)			IER	ER	ER	ER					R	R	R	M	
Student Classroom Management (18*, 19)			ZER	ER	ER	ER	ER			ER	ER	ER	ER	ER	
Student School Management (18*, 19)				ZER	ER	ER						ER	R	R	ZER*

T = Initial Teaching   E = Expansion Teaching   I = Integration Teaching
M = Maintenance Teaching   R = Refinement Teaching   Z = Transfer Teaching
AD = Administrators   * = Restricted Teaching

which parts students could do, how students can help them plan and manage these tasks, and how to set the occasion for student performance and reward a job well done. Their training, in other words, is a very restricted subset of basic skills supplemented with the school management system training.

Determine How the Training Will Be Done

I advocate a three-part training program for teachers. The first part, basic skills training, covers the skills in Chapter 1 through 12 of this text. This training, usually done in a workshop format the year before the teachers participate in the program, requires little in the way of curriculum materials. The text and its planning activities constitute the primary training sources.

The second part, follow-up training, teaches the applicable strategy or management system skills. This training would take place just before the start of school, and two or three more times during the year. Use a workshop format and the required text and curriculum material sources. Each year some follow-up training will be needed to update and refine teaching skills. This update training usually requires less time.

The arrangement of these first two parts of training facilitates SM program planning in three ways. First, it provides time to design the SM curriculum and lesson materials. Second, it allows a chance to identify those who could be potential trainers and those requiring additional training. And third, it facilitates strategy management system training because basic skills will be firm. All increase the likelihood of success in the classroom.

The third part of training, monitoring, occurs throughout the school year. It is done by program teachers, trainers, and those concerned with program adaptation. Monitoring occurs in two parts: observation and feedback. First, monitors observe SM teaching. Next, they give the teacher feedback immediately after observation or in a debriefing at the end of the day. Those monitored should have complete knowledge of what is being observed and be given feedback on that observation. The goal is to improve teaching skills. Some portion of monitoring will relate to program adaptation. Chapter 22 expands on monitoring procedures and the instruments used.

Administrators and others involved in the student management systems would receive the same three-part training. The first part would introduce the program, help them analyze tasks, and cover basic statement and questioning skills. Follow-up training would complete and enhance the last two skill areas. Chapter 22 covers the monitoring and evaluation of these program participants.

Determine When, Where, and for How Long Training Will Occur

With knowledge of who has to be trained, what they need training in, the curriculum sequence, and the personnel to do the training, a determination can be made about when, where, and for how long training will occur. Basic skills training should take 40 to 48 hours of instruction spread over a time period of at least 12 weeks for maximum benefit. The second part of training, follow-up, should take an additional 12 to 24 hours broken into two or three parts as indicated. The exact time needed for follow-up training depends on the extent to which teachers have to work out specifics for their classrooms. The more they have to do, the longer the training time. On the other hand, designing their own activities often facilitates their commitment to the program.

Monitoring should occur from eight to ten times throughout the year. Every teacher needs to observe other teachers at least three to four times per year. The rest of the monitoring can be done by trainers and those involved in program adaptation activities. The instruments for both activities could be the same (see Chapter 22). The schools will need teacher monitoring schedules. Schedule monitoring so that a range of teaching skills is observed. The major portion of observation feedback can occur during a debriefing at the end of the day. Monitoring requires training in using the monitoring instruments and should only be performed by personnel who have received program training.

The location of training depends on district facilities. Overall, the specific place is less important than establishing the proper training atmosphere. This involves the openness and brightness of the location, and the positiveness of activities.

Draft a Training Plan

With the last step, all components of the training plan are known. The training plan projects these components several years into the future.

Table 21.2 illustrates a training plan that utilizes a start-up year to give kindergarten and first-grade teachers basic skills training (BS). Because kindergarten and first-grade teachers teach much of the content, except for the initial knowledge-type discriminations, the first year of the program is implemented in both grades. Just before the start of the first year of the program, follow-up (FU) training is started. As the first year begins, additional follow-up training occurs and basic skills training for the second-grade strategy and support teachers begins.

Table 21.2
Outline of Training Plan by Year of Program

PROGRAM YEAR	STRATEGY TEACHERS							SUPPORT TEACHERS							AD
	K	1	2	3	4	5	6	K	1	2	3	4	5	6	
Start-up	BS 40	BS 40						BS 40	BS 40						BS*
First	FU 24	FU 24	BS 40					FU 12	FU 12	BS 40					BS*
Second	UD 12	UD 12	FU 16	BS 40				UD 6	UD 6	FU 12	BS 40				BS*
Third		UD 12	FU 24	BS 40					UD 6	FU 12	BS 40				FU*
Fourth			UD 12	FU 24	BS 40					UD 6	FU 12	BS 40			FU*
Fifth				UD 12	FU 24	BS 40					UD 6	FU 12	BS 40		UD*
Sixth					UD 12	FU 24						UD 6	FU 12		
Seventh						UD 12							UD 6		

BS = Basic Skills Training UD = Up Date Training FU = Follow Up Training
AD = Administrators   * = Restricted Training   Numbers = Hours of Training

During the second year of the program, update training (UD) is given to kindergarten and first-grade teachers, follow-up training is given to the second-grade teachers, and the third-grade teachers are given basic skills training. Although not on the plan, update training would continue as necessary to inform of program changes and improve teaching. With each year, the next grade is included.

Table 21.2 makes sense if an entire grade level can be trained each year. If the trainers are not available or the budget does not allow it, training has to be staggered. This means implementing the program in only part of a grade level each year. Thus, the time frame for implementation lengthens. Another option is to implement the program at an accelerated rate in a few schools to demonstrate its workability. This helps provide trainers so that a training plan such as the one presented in Table 21.2 can be undertaken. The options are extensive but always limited by resources, and the primary resource is trained, enthusiastic teachers.

Write a Preliminary Training Manual for the Start-Up Year

To insure that instruction is consistent from trainer to trainer, prepare a training manual for each group of participants. The training manuals for the start-up year of training can be developed primarily from the contents of this text. The additional curriculum materials are minimal. Eventually, training manuals will be needed for all other training.

Outline a Curriculum Development Plan

The curriculum development plan indicates who constructs the SM curriculum sequence and materials, and when and where they do so. The individuals involved must have a good working knowledge of the SM curriculum or at least be supervised by someone who does. Select from those who have taught SM during the first year of implementation or implemented parts of the SM curriculum on their own.

The time devoted to building the curriculum materials, especially for the learning strategy, will be extensive. The training plan indicates the dates by which various materials should be completed. To determine a time to start development activities, project backward from the completion date. A rule of thumb is to double the preparation time you think will be needed. After the first year, include time for revision of materials. Better ways will be found to organize and teach. Revise the materials in light of this information for next year's training group (Chapter 22).

Outline a Curriculum Utilization Plan

The next step is to decide how to implement the program across schools. The utilization plan is bounded by the training plan. The ideal consistent with Table 21.2 would be to start in kindergarten and follow the students through the grades, each year catching the incoming students so that after six years all grade levels would be implementing their portion of the curriculum.

If implementation must be done in a subset of schools each year, select schools with logistics in mind. Do not use up time traveling for training or monitoring. The whole matter is simplified if enough trainers exist to cover a grade level each year. Update training still has to be given to those who have already received basic skills and initial follow-up training. Staggering training by giving more time for trainers to train and observe helps eliminate complex utilization planning. This is the recommended route even though it increases short-term costs.

Outline a Budget Plan

A large percent of the budget will be for personnel, and much of it is for teachers to attend training. By having a clear training plan, the number of personnel and hours involved in training are known. Add the time needed for developing the curriculum materials and monitoring, along with material reproduction costs, and you have a good working budget.

Use a Data Base to Plan Your Implementation

All of the preceding tables and plans can be produced by a computer data base manager/report generator. In setting up the data base, the fields of a record relate to teachers, their schools, grade level, dates of all types of training, and observations. This data base can help keep track of all aspects of implementation. It helps in the notification of training, monitoring training, planning and confirming training participation, budgeting for and allocating payment for training, and generating all implementation plan tables and reports.

SUPERVISING AN IMPLEMENTATION

A SM program requires at least three levels of interrelated supervision. The first level directs the development of the implementation plan. Thus far this chapter has provided assistance on that level. Chapters 20 and 22 provide additional support.

The second level is carrying out the implementation. To be successful, supervisors must deal with the working of the large organization of which the SM program is a part. The implementation plan tells you when, what, and who is needed for some task, and the time it should take to do the task. Determine how long it should take to bring all that together. Now double that estimate and start to make contacts with those involved at this earlier point in time. Do not be satisfied with a first or second contact. To insure that things occur on time, keep checking. These contacts set the occasion for, monitor, and reinforce progréss.

Within an organization, knowledge about procedures is not always consistent. When performing procedures for the first time (e.g., budget, purchasing, payroll), ask two sources about them, and if they agree, fine. If they do not, go to a third source. Finally, always have extras on hand. Materials get lost and personnel get sick or leave. Be prepared for these eventualities, and it will be possible to carry out the SM program successfully and calmly.

The third level of supervision is marketing. It occurs throughout the other two levels of supervision. The first part of selling the program is to establish positive adoption contingencies, to insure that all parties, from administrators to school staff, want the program to occur. Making this happen requires that each person know what his or her role will be, when it will be performed, how it will be learned, and the consequences for performing it. Although knowing what, when, and how are important for insuring that all parties want the program, consequences are the key. The following consequences are important.

1. The quality of student learning.
2. The type of student-instructor interaction.
3. The potential for motivating students.
4. The degree of management required.
5. The cost (total and parts such as teacher training).
6. The compatibility with existing procedures and felt needs.
7. The training can be accomplished.
8. The observability of the program.

Letting those involved know that student learning will improve or that the program will be manageable is important. The best way to establish a positive view is by implementing the program on a small basis first. This provides those who will be involved a chance to see the positive results of the program and to picture their part in it. Additionally, knowledge is gained about program components, local implementation problems are clarified, and a core of trainers becomes available.

The second part of marketing is to establish positive implementation contingencies. Now the parties involved move from their picture of the program to the reality of it. Positive implementation contingencies (1) set the occasion for, (2) build the necessary behaviors for, and (3) reinforce progress for implementing the SM program. In other words, they insure that everyone enjoys performing their parts in the program and believe it is of value. This can only happen with clear plans and the pointing out of consequences as they occur.

SUMMARY

The goal is to plan an implementation that has a high probability of success in the short and long run. The following planning outline summarizes this chapter from the supervisor's perspective.

1. Identify how positive adoption contingencies can be established.
   a. Point out the positive benefits to parents, teachers, and administrators.
   b. Market by illustrating how the program will:
      1. Improve the quality of student learning.
      2. Increase positive student-teacher (or parent-child) interaction.
      3. Motivate students to want to learn.
      4. Decrease teacher and school management requirements.
      5. Not require expensive equipment and materials.
      6. Require training that can be done at the district level.
      7. Foster student academic skills.
2. Identify how positive implementation contingencies can be established.
   a. Involve parents, teachers, and administrators in planning.
   b. Follow the strategy to outline the five implementation plans: development, utilization, training, adaptation, and budget.
      1. Identify personnel resources. Identify persons for:
         a. Curriculum construction (see Chapter 20).
         b. Skill training.
         c. Monitoring, evaluation, and revision (see Chapter 22).
      2. Determine who needs to be trained. Consider: strategy and support teachers, and administrators.
      3. Decide on the curriculum sequence (see Table 20.1).
      4. Determine which skills have to be taught (see Table 21.1).
      5. Determine how training will occur. Consider:
         a. A four-part training program including basic skills, follow-up, update, and monitoring.
         b. Training within the district, giving college or inservice course credit.
         c. Using a workshop format for training.
      6. Determine when and for how long training will occur. See Table 21.2 for estimates.
      7. Determine training locations.
      8. Draft training plan (see Table 21.2).
      9. Write a preliminary training manual for the start-up year.
         a. The curriculum sequence and the list of training skills are the primary guide.
         b. Most of the training material can come from this text.
      10. Using the training plan as a guide, draft an outline of the remaining plans:
         a. Curriculum development (see Chapter 20).
         b. Curriculum utilization.
         c. Program adaptation (see Chapter 22).
         d. Budget.

       11. Use a data base manager to help build the plans.
3. When supervising during implementation planning and implementation, consider:
    a. Doubling the lead time that is considered necessary.
    b. Contacting, recontacting, and recontacting those involved.
    c. Backing up knowledge and resources where necessary.
       1. Get confirmation on procedures and policies.
       2. Do not begin implementation start-up activities until:
          a. All implementation plans are outlined.
          b. Approval has been documented.
    d. Continually step back to assess successes and failures on all planning and implementation fronts.

22

ADAPTING THE
SELF-MANAGEMENT PROGRAM

The SM program emerged in response to social problems. To insure that these problems are solved, the SM program must adapt. By adapting, the need to implement new programs on a continual basis or to discard the SM curriculum for the latest fad ends. The resulting program continuity gives districts, schools, teachers, and students a stability that helps them move into the future. This chapter outlines a strategy to plan SM program adaptation activities.[1]

ANALYSIS OF PROGRAM ADAPTATION

Program adaptation is a cyclical, year-by-year problem-solving process that seeks answers to two questions: (1) How can the program be examined to learn about its operation? And (2) What is needed to change the program so it operates as desired? The process of obtaining answers has five phases.

1. Design monitoring (observational) instruments to determine how the program components are working.
2. Design the organization of all adaptation activities.
3. Design specific procedures to carry out adaptation activities.
4. Implement adaptation activities.
5. Revise adaptation activities, teacher training, and instructional procedures.

Monitoring instruments are designed to observe teacher training, teacher behavior, and student behavior. The major adaptation activities include monitoring, evaluating, designing solutions, and presenting program outcomes. Implementation includes monitoring, evaluating, and presenting program outcomes. With the knowledge gained from monitoring and evaluating, the needed revisions are made. With each succeeding year, these phases are carried out to insure that the SM program adapts to the changing needs and resources of the community.

The model that makes the adaptation process possible is the instructional program and its relationships with teacher training and student outcomes. Figure 22.1 depicts these relationships.

The instructional program sets the occasion for teacher behavior (instruction), which sets the occasion for student behavior (outcomes). The teachers' instructional behavior is represented in each lesson exercise and the student outcome behavior by the program-specified student responses, teacher-directed and independent exercises. By developing the instructional program as outlined in Chapter 20, you have the foundation for program adaptation. The instructional program specifies the content of teacher training (if not the training procedures), and the monitoring devices (if not the procedures to gather the data). Thus, it contains the standard for teacher and student behavior, teacher training, and monitoring measures. There is a *direct* relationship between each of these and the instructional program—one can go back to the instructional program and point to the place where it indicates the content of teacher and student behaviors, teacher training, and monitoring measures.

A STRATEGY FOR PROGRAM ADAPTATION PLANNING

The following strategy steps guide the planning and implementation of the program adaptation activities. The steps parallel the five phases of adaptation planning.

Design Monitoring Instruments

The three areas of monitoring are teacher training, teacher instruction, and student outcomes. For each a decision is needed about which measures to monitor and which instruments to use.

Teacher Training. The monitoring of teacher training involves three measures:

1. If the training took place as scheduled.
2. If the training covered the intended skills.
3. If the training covered the skills as planned.

All three are specified in the teacher training plan. The first question is one of date, time, and duration. This can be determined from attendance

Figure 22.1
Instructional Program Relationships and Monitoring Measures

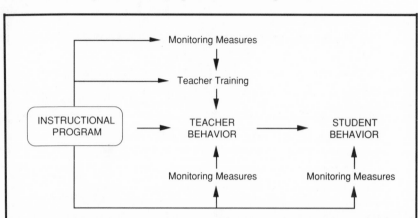

records. The second is a checklist of training skills. The third is a check for each skill against the procedures in the training manual. This latter measure requires sampling training with a training manual in hand.

Teacher Behavior. The instructional program indicates three inclusive classes of teacher behavior (measures). The first involves using the instructional skills (Chapters 4 through 11 and 13) to manage and organize the classroom. The second concerns following the daily SM lessons. And the third focuses on implementing individual and group activities that allow for the expansion of the SM strategies. A teacher instrument guides the observation of these measures.

Figure 22.2 presents an example of a potential instrument. The form begins with a section that facilitates data gathering and analysis by specifying teacher, date, grade, school, observer, and limited instructions for using the form. The first part covers the teacher's management and organizational practices. These relate to basic skills training. For each, the observer assesses a level of consistency in performance, and identifies one or more components of the skill or procedure that were observed. At times some of these are not observed because of the time of observation or because the students did not require it. The confirmation on the latter inference is the extent to which students are on task during activities and transitions. For example, if they were following instructions and activity task requirements, you would not see the intervention procedures used.

The second part of the form focuses on SM lesson teaching. It essentially asks if the observed teaching was consistent with the lesson slated for presentation. This part of the form is simply an overview. The daily lesson manual would be the observer's guide. If major instructional problems

Figure 22.2
Self-Management Program: Teacher Observation Form

SELF-MANAGEMENT PROGRAM: TEACHER OBSERVATION FORM

Teacher: _____   Grade: _____   Date: _____

School: _____   Observer: _____

1 = Consistent   2 = Inconsistent   3 = Absent   4 = Not Applicable

(1) Classroom Management/Organization

1 2 3 4   a. Organization Postings: goals   rules   procedure   intervention

1 2 3 4   b. Strategy Postings: SUP   PLN   INT   LRN   SYSTEM

1 2 3 4   c. Reviews Postings: student examples / fast paced / many participate

1 2 3 4   d. Statements: condition   reward   combination

1 2 3 4   e. Questions: prediction   evidence   confirmation

1 2 3 4   f. S/Q Presentation: positive   focus   clarity   short
                                   important   style   individual   group

1 2 3 4   g. Intervention Procedure Used

1 2 3 4   h. Students On Task: activities   transitions

(2) Self-Management Lesson   Lesson Day _____

1 2 3 4   a. Strategies Observed: ORG HLP SHR SUP PLN INT LRN

1 2 3 4   b. Teaching Procedures: T   E   I   R   M   C

1 2 3 4   c. Teaching Elements: M   P   T (Individual Group)   C

1 2 3 4   d. Students' Responses: _____

1 2 3 4   e. Student On Task: _____

(3) Classroom Activities

1 2 3 4   a. Activities Established Per Program

1 2 3 4   b. Strategy Statement and Question Focus:
           ORG   HLP   SHR   SUP   PLN   INT   LRN

1 2 3 4   c. Student Use of Strategies: Individual   Group
           ORG   HLP   SHR   SUP   PLN   INT   LRN

were discovered, notes about particular exercises would be taken.

The third part looks at the classroom activities to see if they are implemented according to the program. The observation focuses on students' use of strategies and the teacher's facilitation of them. At this point in the program, the teacher may deviate from the prescribed program to adjust to student requirements. If students remain engaged in instruction, use the SM skills, and are enthusiastic, we are witnessing adaptive teaching. No program can specify the needs for all students at all times. Nor should the observer be locked into looking for rigid adherence to lessons.

Student Behavior. Student monitoring measures fall into two categories: SM behavior and SM behavior consequences. SM behavior data can be grouped into four types.

1. Appropriate response to teacher instruction.
2. Use of strategies in the classroom.
3. Use of strategies in the school.
4. Use of strategies in the home, workplace, or community.

The first three are specified in the instructional program. The use of the strategies in the home, workplace, or community represents the transfer of SM behavior. As you move from the first to the last, the ease of monitoring decreases, but the degree of relevance, or significance, increases.

Figure 22.3 illustrates a potential checklist for student SM behaviors within the classroom or during school-level management. It begins by asking for background data for observing. Next, a place is provided to indicate which strategies were observed. For each strategy noted, the observer further indicates which steps of the strategy or subtype of strategy were observed, and if the use of the strategy was appropriate to the situation. The supervisor's or teacher's involvement and type of involvement is also requested for each strategy.

The second category of measures, the behaviors that are consequences of SM behavior, are the real reasons for carrying out a SM program. We teach SM not to have SM skills but to facilitate the rest of our behavior. These behaviors also fall into a number of categories including:

1. On-task behavior increases.
2. Academic behavior facilitation.
3. Classroom conflicts decrease.
4. School problems decrease.
5. Social problems outside the school change.

If students are self-managing, there should be an increase in percent of time devoted to work (on task). By the very definition of SM, students' academic work should increase and improve at the classroom level. With helping, sharing, and intervention skills, conflicts should decrease. This holds for both classroom and school locations. But SM skills should also change other behaviors at the school level; attendance should increase and school vandalism should decrease. If students have firm management skills by the end of school and transfer procedures have been used, there should

Figure 22.3
Self-Management Program: Student Behavior Checklist

STUDENT BEHAVIOR CHECKLIST

Supervisor: _____ Date: _____

Location: _____ Observer: _____

Activity   Type: Classroom ActivityClassroom ManagemenSchool Management
                         Individual   Group   Classroom

Strategies Observed: ORG   HLP   SHR   SUP   PLN   INT   LRN

Planning: Identify ___   Design ___   Select ___   Implement ___   Evaluate ___
                 Independent Activity: yes   no   Teacher: model   prompt

Supervision: Appropriate Need ___   Inform of Plan ___   Set Goals ___
                 Directed Flow ___   Look for Success ___   Consequences ___
                 Members Contribute ___   Group Members Enthusiastic ___
                 Supervision Adjusted to Group Members ___

Learning: Identify Need   Identify Sources   Unpack   Pack

Intervention: Arbitration   Mediation   Negotiation
                 Stop ___   Document ___   Settle ___   Practice Options ___
                 Document Settlement ___   Did settlement fit? ___
                 Did individuals appear satisfied with settlement? ___

Organizing: Locate ___   Transfer ___   Arrange ___

Helping: Identify the Need ___   Appropriate Helping ___

Sharing: Identify the Need ___   Appropriate Sharing ___

COMMENTS: _____
_____
_____
_____

be positive changes outside the school. Employers should register an increase in satisfaction with employees' performance and the community should experience a decrease in crime and violence. Because students have learned to cooperate and work in group settings to solve problems, there should be changes in a whole host of community behaviors toward solving problems.

The latter longitudinal measures will not be available for some time after the start of the program. Although there is not immediate reinforcement for gathering such data, it must be done. Fortunately, extensive data on school and community SM consequence behaviors is already being taken. Many other measures are possible and with a bit of thought can be monitored with very little time and effort. A strong SM program, in combination with a strong academic program, should radically alter social problems as we know them.[2]

For the SM consequence behaviors, it may be helpful to perform a detailed analysis of on-task behavior or classroom facilitation of academic work that may require new monitoring instruments. Such an analysis compares those who do not receive the program with those who do. After the first grade, differences should be observed.

The instruments for monitoring the other SM consequence behaviors are already being used to gather that data. The examples include standardized test data, the number of school repairs and the money spent on them, the visits to the office and the reasons for them, the parent conferences for inappropriate behavior, and the percent of students who drop out or participate in school or community crime. These and similar measures can tell you a lot about how your program impacts the community.

Design the Organization of Adaptation Activities

Once monitoring instruments are designed, five adaptation activities remain: monitoring, remediation, evaluation, program revision, and the writing and presentation of reports. For each of these, it is necessary to determine who will perform them along which time line. These are not easy determinations because of the interaction with the other implementation plans. For example, monitoring has to be coordinated carefully with the training and curriculum implementation plans.

Design Adaptation Procedures

Both the monitoring and remediation activities of adaptation require detailed procedures besides solving the problems of logistics.

Monitoring. Monitoring has two parts: observation and feedback. Both require procedures. The monitoring procedures concern how it is carried out in the classroom. The goal is to be as unobtrusive as possible while observing. The practice of greeting the teacher and the class should be done during times of transition or breaks in the classroom activities. Questions can be asked and statements made if necessary. The observer should be seen as a helper, not an intruder. "All athletes need a coach" is a useful perspective. When teachers act as observers, they see the program from both positions, and learn a lot about the range of appropriate teaching and student behavior.

The feedback portion of monitoring needs to be an educational as well as a rewarding activity. For many teachers, awareness can be enough to change inappropriate behavior. The observer should point out what was correct and what appeared inappropriate. Statements and questions described in Chapters 6, 7, and 8 are important tools. The critical question for inappropriate behavior would be, how would you change it? Let the observed teacher enter into the problem-solving process. If a teacher does something that is not in the program but seems to be working, ask about it. It just may be a good example of adaptive teaching that others should know about.

Remediation. Remediation concerns correcting teacher and student behavior. From the observation of instruction, you may identify teachers and students who for some reason are not performing to program standards. Remediation for teachers can occur during instruction, in review, or during small group retraining. In deciding on these procedures, careful assessment of resources needs to be considered. Often a proficient teacher can practice with one who has specific deficiencies.

Remediation for students proceeds in two directions. The first is when students are not performing SM behavior or strategies as expected. The procedure is to repeat lessons or insert more (new) expansion activities. If this does not work, program revision must be carried out. The second direction is used to bring incoming students to the point of other students as quickly as possible. The teacher may provide initial introduction of the strategies that have been learned and from that point a student who has demonstrated proficiency can be assigned as a teaching assistant to model and prompt the new student in the classroom procedures and the strategies.

Monitor Program Implementation

Once the program is under way, the three types of monitoring begin. Additionally, monitoring of program adaptation activities is necessary. This observation is usually informal. For example, if a monitoring instrument or procedure is difficult to use or not working, it is usually known shortly after its implementation.

Evaluate

To find program problems, you look in two places: within and outside it. The first is a prerequisite to the second and the second is the most relevant.

Examining Data from within the Program. If teacher and student behavior corresponds with program specifications, no problem exists. This is how we would like things to be; but usually you find that some discrepancies exist. Given the direct correspondence between the program and monitoring measures, the basic evaluation decisions can be reduced to three general statements.

1. If teacher behavior corresponds with the program but their students' outcomes do not, then the program needs revision.

It may happen that teachers follow a portion of the instructional program and their students do not exhibit the SM behaviors taught. If such is the case for a large percentage of teachers, a strong inference exists for revising the program.

2. If teachers' behavior does not correspond with the program and their students' outcomes also do not, then teacher training needs revision.

When both teachers and their students fail to learn, a strong inference exists for changing training. You cannot evaluate the program until teachers perform as specified. It could be that the program is unteachable, but this is unlikely given the procedures in Chapter 20.

3. If there is no correspondence between teacher behavior and student outcomes, then no strong inference about revision exists.

It may happen that at times teachers do not follow the program and their students learn, and at others that teachers follow the program and their students do not learn. If such is the case, no clear evaluation can be made. The program, the training, or the monitoring could all need revision.

Statistical procedures can be used to compare groups of teachers and their students. Yet these numbers do not indicate whether the program needs revision. They only tell if differences exist.

Curiously, the decision to remediate has more to do with economics and resources than exact knowledge about the deficiency of program parts. Revision is often less expensive in the long run than remediation. A training and instructional program that works consistently across the range of teachers and students saves work by getting things right the first time. This is very reinforcing.

Examining Data from Outside the Program. The preceding analysis focused on considering program data. The nonprogram or transfer data about SM consequence behavior needs as much consideration. Here knowledge of the variability, trend, and stability (Chapter 12) of several types of data help determine if the real goals of the program are being achieved. It will take a few years before the first of these data are in. It will take 10 to 15 years before large-scale social changes take place because program students must enter responsible positions in the community.

Let us say that the program works in the classroom. Students attend to instruction, there is an increase in academic performance, and there is an almost immediate decrease in school-level problems. Yet over the years, the SM consequence behavior does not show a change in the community. Does this mean the whole program needs to be revised or replaced? No. Only the transfer portion of the program. There needs to be an improvement in the use of the verbal, classroom, and school transfer procedures.

Design Revision Solutions

Revision will most likely be needed for parts of the teacher training and the instructional program. Evaluation has pointed out where but not how. As with all problem solving, the solution that changes as little as possible and still achieves the desired results is the one needed. Finding it is an inductive process based on your knowledge of instruction. Additionally, it is necessary to ask what else changes when revisions are made. The curriculum, training, instruction, and implementation plans are tied together and each has to be reviewed if one is changed. The following presents some of the major places to look in the process of building revision solutions.

Teacher Training. Teachers do not perform according to program specifications for one or more of three reasons. First, their performance is discrepant because they refuse to comply with the program. Often the terms *unmotivated* and *poor attitude* are applied. The data gathered from teacher training and monitoring clearly point out this problem. If such a problem is found, the positive consequences for teaching are not present. The solution is to change the teacher or change the consequences. If many teachers fit the category, the answer is obvious.

Second, teachers fail to perform as specified because of insufficient management skills. When management skills are in need of remediation, the monitoring data show that the teachers perform inconsistently across a range of exercises and tracks. They often fail to finish an exercise or lesson without student disruptions. There is no continuity to the instruction and, thus, students fail to learn. As a result, these teachers fall behind on lessons. They may perform very well in training, but they cannot perform in the classroom. The teachers' behaviors are telling you that more training is needed in the basic classroom management skills as outlined in Chapter 21 and the first half of this text.

Third, teachers do not perform specific track components according to specifications. The analysis task is to find out where they are different. Just which teaching procedures are they not performing as needed? This helps pinpoint the cause of the problem. At each point of difference, look carefully at the models, prompts, tests, and consequences being used.

All of the SM strategies require the extensive use of teacher-delivered prompts. Here many teachers have problems; the program cannot specify these in the detail needed for teachers new to the program. Three types of problems associated with prompts show themselves: failing to fade a prompt (never giving the students a history of performing independently), prompting too long (students come to expect help), and dropping prompts too fast (students will fail). Training time needs to be spent on giving teachers a picture of where the track is going and how independent (of prompts) the students need to be at key points.

Instructional Program. The pattern of student failures helps point out the problems with the instructional program. Problems usually become most evident when students begin to work individually and in groups with a greater degree of independence. The cause is often in the sequencing of that portion of the program. One solution is to insert more exercises with greater teacher support into the program. When this is done, other shifts may have to be made in the rest of the program sequence.

Teacher behavior can also exhibit patterns of failure that indicate problems with the instructional program. When they follow the program, pace themselves sufficiently, manage students adequately, but just cannot do all the exercises in a lesson in the time allotted, one solution is to "lean out" the lessons. Fewer exercises must be done within each lesson. This requires that the sequencing be stretched and new predictions be made about time in the program.

These few guidelines for solving training and instructional problems are by no means complete. They are just the more obvious places to look for particular kinds of problems. The best guideline is to select the solution that changes as little as possible but appears to solve the problem.

Summarize and Present Program Outcomes

From the first year, the program will begin to show positive changes. Kindergarteners and first-graders will cut through the regular instructional program, and teachers will express their amazement with the way their students are learning. Shortly, school problems will begin to decrease and parents will begin to express a change in their relationship with their children. If there is an accelerated SM program in the middle or high school, the SM consequence behaviors should show themselves fairly quickly. Advertise these changes; point out consequences as suggested in the supervising strategy.

National norms are not needed for indicating success. What is needed is the comparison between what the program population did and what it is now doing. Comparing students from a similar nonprogram population and the program population is another avenue. Moreover, the direction of improvement should be moving toward program goals at an adequate rate.

The problem of presenting data has two intersecting considerations. First, the presentation is an inductive argument. It needs to be strong enough to convince others that the SM program is making the changes in school and community as hypothesized. Additionally, the changes must be meaningful, easy to see, and lacking in excessive variability (Chapter 12). The SM program is an educational reform.

Second, teachers, administrators, parents, and community leaders see different data as important. This difference enters into decisions on data selection and presentation. Multiple measures combine for a strong argument, but the individual measures are selected with the different audiences in mind. Thus, careful data selection, in combination with multiple data presentation, form the foundation for continuing positive implementation contingencies in school, district, and community.

Usually an expert in educational research and evaluation will be given the task of finding relevant and consistent data measures, as well as finding ways to present them as strong arguments. When the decision for selection is at hand, you should be ready to ask the following questions:

1. Do the data measures cover the range of audiences?
2. Would the presentation convince the audiences that the program is successful?
3. Would the presentation convince the audiences that the program caused the changes?
4. Are the measures and presentations simple and straightforward?

The answers should be affirmative and indicate that the expert has sampled the audiences for their opinions about what they would like to see in measures and presentation.

SUMMARY

The following summarizes the major steps of program adaptation. With each year, the time devoted to adaptation activities decreases.

1. Design monitoring instruments. Consider:
   a. Teacher training. Get answers to:
      1. Did it occur as scheduled?
      2. Did it cover the intended skills?
      3. Did it follow the training manual procedures?
   b. Teacher behavior (see Figure 22.2). Consider:
      1. Using the program lessons as a guide.
      2. Using monitoring measures such as those in Figure 22.2.
   c. Student behavior. Consider:
      1. SM behavior monitoring measures such as those in Figure 22.3.
      2. SM consequence behavior such as:
         a. On-task behavior.
         b. Academic behavior facilitation: classroom or standardized test data.

      3. The SM consequence behavior data has more relevance to the long-term goals of the program.

2. Design the organization of adaptation activities. Consider:
    a. Monitoring, evaluating, designing solutions, presenting program outcomes.
    b. Ask by whom, when, and where (a) will be performed.

3. Design adaptation activity procedures. Consider:
    a. Monitoring.
       1. Observe as unobtrusively as possible, but greet teachers and students when convenient.
       2. Give feedback to teachers mainly at the end of the day.
       3. Teachers need to monitor each other.
       4. Monitoring should be viewed as a cooperative venture.
    b. Remediation.
       1. Students can be remediated by repeating exercises related to the skill deficiency.
       2. Incoming students can be coached by students who have mastered the SM skills.
       3. Teachers can be remediated during feedback or in small groups on the school site.

4. Gather data throughout the year with monitoring instruments and at specific points during the year for SM consequence measures.

5. Decide which problems exist (evaluate). Consider:
    a. The basic evaluation decisions.
       1. If teacher and student behavior correspond with the program, then no revision is needed.
       2. If teacher behavior corresponds with the program, and their students' behavior does not, then revise the program.
       3. If teacher behavior does not correspond with the program and student behaviors also do not, revise teacher training.
       4. If there is no correspondence between teacher behavior and student outcomes, then no strong inference can be made about revision.
    b. Base revision decisions on:
       1. Revision resources.
       2. If time alone would cure it.
       3. If revisions look extensive.
       4. If a little remediation would do it.

6. Design revision solutions. Consider:
    a. Teacher training.
       1. If teachers fail to finish lessons without student disruptions, retrain in basic management/organizational skills first.
       2. If teachers have problems using prompts, see if they are:
         a. Failing to fade prompts.
         b. Providing prompts too long.
         c. Fading prompts too fast.
    b. Instructional program. Consider:

   1. If a small percent of students with teachers who follow the program have problems, change the sequence so that students are given more practice.
   2. If students fail during later expansions on individual and group tasks, continue prompting for a longer time.
   3. If teachers cannot finish lessons when following exercise procedures, then shorten the lessons.
8. Summarize and present program outcomes. Consider:
   a. Selecting SM consequence behavior measures that satisfy the range of audiences.
   b. Select presentation methods that include strong inferences about program outcomes.
   c. Select presentation methods that would convince the audiences that the program caused the changes.
   d. Select measures and presentations that are simple and straightforward.
   e. Sample your audience in the early stages of the program to insure the measures will be effective.

NOTES

CHAPTER 1

1. Skinner's three-term contingency unit provides the theoretical foundation for self-management instruction (Skinner, 1938, 1968).

2. The condition-behavior match is related to the matching-to-sample paradigm. See Fester and Culbertson (1982).

3. Becker (1986) and Cooper, Heron, and Heward (1987) elaborate on the principles of behavior.

CHAPTER 2

1. Skinner (1935, 1938, 1953) fathered the analysis of behavior when he made the class-instance distinction. See Sidman (1986) for current expansions.

2. A class definition is also called a behavioral objective in an educational context. See the founding work of Mager (1975).

3. Mager (1975) provides a broad list of such terms.

4. Skinner (1968) notes the importance of making covert behavior overt during instruction. Becker (1986), Engelmann and Carnine (1982), and Meichenbaum (1979) present instructional applications.

5. Engelmann and Carnine (1982), Gagné and Briggs (1979), and Romiszowski (1984) represent a range of perspectives on the analysis of classes and subclasses of behavior in the design of instruction.

CHAPTER 3

1. As early as 1953, Skinner identified the need for a self-management curriculum:

It is of little help to tell a man to use his "will power" or his "self-control." . . .
An alternative analysis of the *behavior* of control should make it possible to
teach relevant techniques as easily as any other technical repertoire. It
should also improve the procedures through which society maintains self-
controlling behavior in strength. (1953, page 241, italics his)

By 1968 Skinner uses the term *self-management* in place of *self-control* (1968,
1971, 1974).

2. John Wellens (1974) emphasized the importance and place of planning in
successful task performance. Miel (1952) and Yvonne Waskins and Louise Parrish
(1967) pioneered the use of student-based classroom planning.

3. Brigham (1989), Braziano and Mooney (1984), Karoly and Kanfer (1982),
Martin (1984), McKinnon and Kiraly (1984), Rosen (1982), Shapiro (1981), Wang
(1979), Wielkiewicz (1986), and Workman (1982) provide a range of perspectives on
self-management theory and practice.

4. Hake and Olvera (1978), Rhoades and McCabe (1985), Schwartz and Howard
(1982), Sharan (1980, 1984), and Slavin (1983) illustrate the diversity of theory and
research on cooperation.

5. Reschly (1985) reviews educational perspectives on adaptive behavior.

CHAPTER 4

1. Bolvin (1982), Bossert (1979), and Doyle (1986) present research on and reviews of classroom organization.

2. Texts on cooperative learning procedures provide extensive examples of how
group activities can be structured (e.g., Cohen, 1986; Johnson, Johnson, Holubec,
and Roy, 1984; Slavin, 1983; Sharan, 1984). Mosston and Ashworth (1989) provide
another interesting perspective. None of these use the language of organizing used
here, but all provide interesting perspectives on the construction of activities.

3. Axelrod, Hall, and Tams (1979) and Weinstein (1979) review research on
classroom structure.

4. Texts on cooperative learning procedures (note 2 of this chapter) also illustrate many ways members of groups can function. None of these use the language
of self-management, but all provide interesting perspectives on how students can
work together.

5. The procedure presented relates to task analysis. See Dick and Lou (1985);
Jonassen, Hannum, and Tessmer (1989); Reigeluth and Merrill (1984); and Romiszowski (1981).

CHAPTER 5

1. The eight perspectives on consequences are consistent with the analysis of
contingencies presented in Chapter 1.

2. See, for example, Cangelosi (1988); Charles (1983); Evertson, Emmer, Clements, Sanford, and Worsham (1989); Lemlech (1988); and Paine, Radicchi, Rosellini,
Deutchman, and Darch (1983).

3. Linking can also be accomplished by using group contingency procedures.
See Medland and Vitale (1984).

4. See Becker (1986) and Good and Brophy (1986) for analyses of intrinsic reinforcement/motivation.

CHAPTER 6

1. Medland and Vitale (1984) originally analyzed the three types of statements.

2. Brophy (1981) and Brophy and Good (1986) have researched the content of teacher statements. Also see Cazden (1986).

CHAPTER 7

1. Skinner (1957, p. 39–40).

2. Skinner (1953, 1968, 1974).

3. This section is based on the work of Skyrms (1986) and Goodman (1983).

4. Bean (1985) and Wilen (1986) cover classroom questioning strategies. For a picture of research and practice on questioning, see Graesser and Black (1985).

CHAPTER 8

1. Paine et al. (1983) present a parallel set of guidelines for presenting statements.

2. The refinement procedure is a classroom formulation of scheduling reinforcement contingencies to shape the rate, duration, latency, and accuracy of behavior (see Skinner, 1968).

CHAPTER 9

1. The rules for sequencing, or juxtaposing, examples comes from a number of theorists and researchers. See Ali (1981), Engelmann and Carnine (1982), Klausmeier and Feldman (1975), Markle and Tiemann (1969), Merrill and Tennyson (1977), Park and Tennyson (1980), Tennyson (1980a, 1980b), and Tennyson and Cocchiarella (1986).

2. Engelmann and Carnine (1982) present the same set of rules.

3. Engelmann and Carnine (1982) define and give examples of the three types of expansion teaching.

CHAPTER 10

1. Fleming (1987) reviews research on what he terms displays. Additionally, see Mayer (1989) and Szlichcinsky (1979).

2. Engelmann and Carnine (1982) illustrate the use of displays to teach what they call fact systems.

CHAPTER 11

1. Engelmann and Carnine (1982) have given the most detailed presentation of this standard.

CHAPTER 12

1. Skinner (1966, 1984, 1985) has framed the analysis of behavior within evolutionary theory. Engelmann and Carnine (1982) illustrate initial, expansion, integration, and correction teaching procedures.

2. Becker (1986) extends this introductory presentation on prompts.

3. Skinner (1969).

4. Johnson and Pennypacker (1980) and Medland and Vitale (1984) provide a fuller treatment on the course of change. Sidman (1960) provides the clearest and most comprehensive treatment, although his subject is infrahuman learning.

CHAPTER 13

1. Doyle (1986) reviews the research on classroom management and organization. Cangelosi (1988), Charles (1983), Jones and Jones (1984), and Medland and Vitale (1984) are but a few that present classroom management procedures.

CHAPTER 14

1. Schwartz and Howard (1982) present a similar definition for helping.

CHAPTER 15

1. The founding model for building the supervision strategy comes from Meichenbaum (1979; Meichenbaum and Goodman, 1971). Pressley (1979) and Manning (1988) review and present research illustrating the positive outcomes that result from teaching students to supervise themselves.

2. Rudkin and Veal (1973) identified the functions of management as planning, organizing, supervising (directing), controlling (evaluating), and improving. Additionally, they defined supervising as the implementation of plans and organization. Many later texts, for example DuBrin (1987) and Lowery (1985), have identified the functions of supervising as planning, organizing, directing, and controlling. This text agrees with Rudkin and Veal's definition of supervising and sees its functions, for the most part, related to directing and controlling. Improving is seen as an attribute of planning. Japanese management practice strongly emphasizes improving and calls it *kizen*.

CHAPTER 16

1. Skinner (1968, 1969) illustrates how problem solving is part of a self-management repertoire.

2. Both Simon (1980) and Skinner (1968) advocate the direct teaching of problem solving.

3. For the present model, Skinner (1969) provided the theoretical foundation and Goodman's process of worldmaking (1978) expanded the vision.

4. Miel (1952), Romiszowski (1981), and Sharan and Sharan (1975) point out other advantages to group work.

5. VanGundy (1981) illustrates the basic problem-solving process and the range of procedures to implement it.

CHAPTER 17

1. Skinner (1968) placed learning skills within the self-management repertoire and advocated their direct instruction.

2. Skinner (1968) placed problem-solving and learning skills within the self-management repertoire. I have simply expanded on their relationship.

3. Learning strategies come in many forms. See Campoine and Armbruster (1985), Dansereau (1985), Derry and Murphy (1986), Weinstein and Mayer (1986), and Weinstein and Underwood (1985).

4. There is little argument that prior knowledge is important to learning. Specifically, the argument rallies around what kind of knowledge is required. See Glaser (1984), Keil (1984), Shuell (1986), Siegler (1983), and Sternberg (1984) for views and reviews.

5. Engelmann and Associates (1978) illustrate build up procedures in the decoding track of their *Corrective Reading Program*.

6. Jones, Amiran, and Katims (1985) express the view that learning skills can be taught within the language arts program.

CHAPTER 18

1. Burger (1977).

2. The perspective of this chapter influenced by Li (1978), Moore (1986), and Woodall (1979).

3. The United States Supreme Court has ruled that students have many of the same inalienable rights as other citizens. For example, see Supreme Court cases *Goss v. Lopez*, 1975; *Ingraham v. Wright*, 1977; *Tinker v. Des Moines Independent School District*, 1979; *Wood v. Strickland*, 1975.

4. Christopher Moore (1986) presents a very clear account of the intervention process and advocates teaching it to students.

CHAPTER 19

1. Compared to traditional analyses of transfer, the definition appears restricted (see Ellis, 1965). In this text, the traditional categories of transfer can be reformulated in terms of problems of emerging behavior (see Chapter 12 and note 4 for this chapter).

2. Marholin and Siegal (1978) and Stokes and Baer (1977) present arguments for programming transfer.

3. Marholin and Siegal (1978) and Stokes and Baer (1977) categorize the procedures to promote transfer.

4. Sidman has pioneered the work on stimulus equivalence and its relationship to transfer. Transfer in this context is a problem of expanding a class of behavior. See Sidman and associates (1973, 1974, 1982, 1985).

CHAPTER 20

1. Patten, Chao, and Reigeluth (1986) review research on sequencing instruction.

2. The Rand Corporation's pioneering research on program implementation

points out the importance of a school district's participation in the development of the curriculum and instructional materials (Berman and McLaughlin, 1976, 1977, 1978).

CHAPTER 21

1. This chapter is based on the recommendations that came out of the Rand Corporation's research on program implementation and continuation (Berman and McLaughlin, 1976, 1977, 1978). Burkman (1987) and Fullan (1986) describe recent research on implementing educational programs.

CHAPTER 22

1. The Rand Corporation's research on educational implementation illustrates the importance of the adaptation of an innovation. See Berman and McLaughlin (1976, 1977, and 1978).

2. Campbell (1969) saw social reforms as experiments requiring strong evaluation for long-term adaptation. Baer (1987) looks at what is needed for successful social reform.

REFERENCES

Ali, A. M. (1981). The use of positive and negative examples during instruction. *Journal of Instructional Development, 5,* 2–7.

Axelrod, S., Hall, R. V., & Tams, A. (1979). Comparison of two common classroom seating arrangements. *Academic Therapy, 15,* 29–36.

Baer, D. (1987). Weak contingencies, strong contingencies, and many behaviors to change. *Journal of Applied Behavior Analysis, 20,* 335–37.

Bean, T. W. (1985). Classroom strategies: Directions for applied research. In A. C. Grasser & J. B. Black (Eds.), *The Psychology of Questions.* Hillsdale, NJ: Lawrence Erlbaum.

Becker, W. C. (1986). *Applied Psychology for Teachers: A Behavioral Cognitive Approach.* Chicago: Science Research Associates.

Berman, P., & McLaughlin, M. W. (1976). Implementations of educational innovation. *Educational Forum, 40,* 347–70.

———. (1977). *Factors Affecting Implementation and Continuation.* Vol. 7 of Federal Programs Supporting Educational Change. Santa Monica, CA: Rand. (ERIC document: ED 140–432.)

———. (1978). *Implementing and Sustaining Innovations.* Vol. 8 of Federal Programs Supporting Educational Change. Santa Monica, CA: Rand. (ERIC document: ED 159–289).

Bolvin, J. O. (1982). Classroom organization. In Harold E. Mitzel (Ed.) *Encyclopedia of Educational Research,* Vol. 1. New York: Macmillan.

Bossert, S. (1979). *Tasks and Social Relationships in Classrooms.* New York: Cambridge University Press.

Brigham, T. A. (1989). *Self-Management for Adolescents: A Skills Training Manual.* New York: Guilford Press.

Brophy, J. (1981). Teacher praise: A functional analysis. *Review of Educational Research, 51,* 5–32.

Brophy, J., & Good, T. L. (1986). Teacher behavior and student achievement. In M. C. Wittrock (Ed.) *Handbook of Research on Teaching,* 3rd ed. New York: Macmillan, 392–431.

Burger, W. (1977). Our vicious legal spiral. *Judges Journal, 16,* 22–24.

Burkman, E. (1987). Factors affecting utilization. In R. M. Gagné (Ed.) *Instructional Technology: Foundations.* Englewood Cliffs, NJ: Lawrence Erlbaum.

Campbell, D. (1969). Reforms as experiment. *American Psychologist, 24,* 409–29.

Campione, J. C., & Armbruster, B. B. (1985). Acquiring information from texts: An analysis of four approaches. In J. W. Segal, S. F. Chipman, and R. Glaser (Eds.) *Thinking and Learning Skills (Volume 1): Relating Instruction to Research.* Hillsdale, NJ: Lawrence Erlbaum.

Cangelosi, J. S. (1988). *Classroom Management Strategies.* White Plains, NY: Longman.

Cazden, C. B. (1986). Classroom discourse. In M. C. Wittrock (Ed.) *Handbook of Research on Teaching,* 3rd ed. New York: Macmillan, 432–63.

Charles, C. M. (1983). *Elementary Classroom Management.* White Plains, NY: Longman.

Cohen, E. G. (1986). *Designing Groupwork: Strategies for the Heterogeneous Classroom.* New York: Teachers College Press.

Cooper, J. O., Heron, T. E., Heward, W. L. (1987). *Applied Behavior Analysis.* Columbus, OH: Merrill.

Dansereau, D. F. (1985). Learning strategy research. In J. W. Segal, S. F. Chipman, & R. Glaser (Eds.) *Thinking and Learning Skills (Volume 1): Relating Instruction to Research.* Hillsdale, NJ: Lawrence Erlbaum.

Derry S. J., & Murphy, D. A. (1986). Designing systems that train learning ability: from theory to practice. *Review of Educational Research, 56,* 1–39.

Dick, W., & Lou, C. (1985). *The Systematic Design of Instruction,* 2d ed. Glenview, IL: Scott, Foresman.

Doyle, W. (1986). Classroom organization and management. In M. C. Wittrock (Ed.) *Handbook of Research on Teaching,* 3rd ed. New York: Macmillan, 392–431.

DuBrin, A. J. (1987). *The Practice of Supervision: Achieving Results Through People,* 2d ed. Plano, TX: Business Publications.

Ellis, H. C. (1965). *The Transfer of Training.* New York: Macmillan.

Engelmann, S., & Associates (1978). *Corrective Reading Program.* Chicago: Science Research Associates.

Engelmann, S., & Carnine, D. (1982). *Theory of Instruction: Principles and Applications.* New York: Irvington.

Evertson, C. M., Emmer, E. T., Clements, B. S., Sandford, J. P., and Worsham, M. E. (1989). *Classroom Management for Elementary Teachers,* 2d ed. Englewood Cliffs, NJ: Prentice-Hall.

Fester, C. B., & Culbertson, S. (1982). *Behavior Principles,* 3d ed. Englewood Cliffs, NJ: Prentice-Hall.

Fleming, M. L. (1986). Displays and communication. In R. M. Gagne, (Ed.) *Instructional Technology: Foundations.* Englewood Cliffs, NJ: Lawrence Erlbaum, 233–60.

Fullan, M. G. (1986). The management of change. In E. Hoyle & A. McMahon (Eds.) *World Yearbook of Education 1986: The Management of Schools.* New York: Nichols.

Gagné, R. M., & Briggs, L. J. (1979). *Principles of Instructional Design,* 2d ed. New York: Holt, Rinehart and Winston.

Glaser, R. (1984). Education and thinking: The role of knowledge. *American Psychologist, 39,* 93–104.

Good, T. L., & Brophy, J. E. (1986). *Educational Psychology*, 3d ed. White Plains, NY: Longman.

Goodman, N. (1978). *The Ways of Worldmaking*. Indianapolis, IN: Hackett Publishing.

Goodman, N. (1983). *Fact, Fiction, and Forecast*, 4th ed. New Haven, CT: Yale University Press.

Goss v. Lopez, 419, U.S. 565 (1975).

Graesser, A. C., & Black, J. B. (Eds.) (1985). *The Psychology of Questions*. Hillsdale, NJ: Lawrence Erlbaum.

Graziano, A. M., & Mooney, K. C. (1984). *Children and Behavior Therapy*. Hawthorne, NY: Aldine de Gruyter.

Hake, D. F., & Olvera, D. (1978). Cooperation, competition, and related social phenomena. In A. C. Catania & T. A. Brigham (Eds.) *Handbook of Applied Behavior Analysis: Social and Instructional Processes*. New York: Irvington.

Humkins, F. P. (1976). *Involving Students in Questioning*. Boston: Allyn and Bacon.

Ingraham v. Wright, 430 U.S. 308 (1977).

Johnson, D. W., Johnson, R. J., Holubec, E. J. (1986). *Circles of Learning: Cooperation in the Classroom*, revised ed. Edina, MN: Interaction Book Co.

Johnson, J. M., & Pennypacker, H. S. (1980). *Strategies and Tactics of Human Behavioral Research*. Hillsdale, NJ: Lawrence Erlbaum.

Jonassen, D. H., Hannum, W. H., and Tessmer, M. (1989). *Handbook of Task Analysis Procedures*. New York: Praeger.

Jones, B. F., Amiran, M., & Katims, M. (1985). Teaching cognitive strategies and structures within language arts programs. In J. W. Segal, S. F. Chipman, & R. Glaser (Eds.) *Thinking and Learning Skills (Volume 1): Relating Instruction to Research*. Hillsdale, NJ: Lawrence Erlbaum.

Jones, V. F., & Jones, L. S. (1984). *Comprehensive Classroom Management*. Boston: Allyn and Bacon.

Karoly, P., & Kanfer, F. H. (Eds.) (1982). *Self-Management and Behavior Change: From Theory to Practice*. New York: Pergamon Press.

Keil, F. C. (1984). Mechanisms of cognitive development and the structure of knowledge. In R. J. Sternberg (Ed.) *Mechanisms of Cognitive Development*. New York: Freeman, 81–99.

Klausmier, H. J., & Feldman, K. V. (1975). Effects of a definition and a varying number of examples and nonexamples on concept attainment. *Journal of Educational Psychology*, 67, 174–78.

Lemlech, J. K. (1988). *Classroom Management: Methods and Techniques for Elementary Teachers*, 2d ed. White Plains, NY: Longman.

Li, V. (1978). *Law without Lawyers: A Comparative View of Law in China and the United States*. Boulder, CO: Westview.

Lincoln, W. F. (1976). *Mediation: A Transferable Process for the Prevention and Resolution of Racial Conflict in Public Secondary School*. New York: American Arbitration Association.

Lowery, R. C. (1985). *Supervisory Management: Guidelines For Application*. Englewood Cliffs, NJ: Prentice-Hall.

Mager, R. F. (1975). *Preparing Instructional Objectives*, 2d ed. Belmont, CA: Fearon.

Manning, B. H. (1988). Application of cognitive behavior modification: First and third graders' self-management of classroom behaviors. *American Educational Research Journal*, 25, 193–212.

Marholin, D., & Siegal, L. J. (1978). Beyond the law of effect: programming for the maintenance of behavior change. In D. Marholin, II (Ed.) *Child Behavior Therapy.* New York: Gardner.

Markle, S. M., & Tiemann, P. W. (1969). *Really Understanding Concepts.* Chicago: Tiemann.

Martin, J. (1984). Toward a cognitive schemata theory of self-instruction. *Instructional Science, 13,* 159–80.

Mayer, R. E. (1989). Systematic thinking fostered by illustration in science text. *Journal of Educational Psychology, 81,* 240–246.

McKinnon, A. J., & Kiraly, J. (1984), *Pupil Behavior, Self-Control and Social Skills in the Classroom.* Springfield, IL: Thomas.

Medland, M. B., & Vitale, M. R. (1984). *Management of Classrooms.* New York: Holt, Rinehart & Winston.

Meichenbaum, D. (1979). Teaching children self-control. In B. Lahey & A. Kazdin (Eds.) *Advances in Child Psychology,* Vol. 2. New York: Plenum.

Meichenbaum, D., & Goodman, J. (1971). Training impulsive children to talk to themselves: A means of developing self-control. *Journal of Consulting and Clinical Psychology, 40,* 148–154.

Merrill, M. D. & Tennyson, R. D. (1977). *Teaching Concepts: An Instructional Design Guide.* Englewood Cliffs, New Jersey: Educational Technology Publications.

Miel, A (1952). *Cooperative Procedures in Learning.* New York: Columbia University. (Reprinted by Greenwood, 1972).

Moore, C. W. (1986). *The Mediation Process: Practical Strategies for Resolving Conflict.* San Francisco: Jossey-Bass.

Mosston, M., & Ashworth, S. (1989). *The Spectrum of Teaching Styles: From Command to Discovery.* White Plains, New York: Longman.

Paine, S., Radicchi, J., Rosellini, L., Deutchman, L., & Darch, C. (1983). *Structuring Your Classroom for Academic Success.* Champaign, IL: Research Press.

Park, O., & Tennyson, R. D. (1980). Adaptive design strategies for selecting number and presentation order of examples in coordinate concept acquisition. *Journal of Educational Psychology, 72,* 362–70.

Patten, J. V., Chao, C., and Reigeluth, C. M. (1986). A review of strategies for sequencing and synthesizing instruction. *Review of Educational Research, 56,* 437–71.

Pressley, M. (1979). Increasing children's self-control through cognitive interventions. *Review of Educational Research, 49,* 319–370.

Reigeluth, C. M., & Merrill, M. D. (1984). *Extended Task Analysis Procedure (ETAP): User's Manual.* Lanham, MD: University Press of America.

Reschly, D. J. (1985). Best practices: adaptive behavior. In A. Thomas & J. Grimes (Eds.) *Best Practices in School Psychology.* Kent, OH: The National Association of School Psychologists.

Rhoades, J., & McCabe, M. E. (1985). *Simple Cooperation in the Classroom.* Willits, CA: ITA Publications.

Romiszowski, A. J. (1981). *Designing Instructional Systems: Decision Making in Course Planning and Curriculum Design.* New York: Nichols.

————. (1984). *Producing Instructional Systems: Lesson Planning for Individual and Group Learning Activities.* New York: Nichols.

Rosen, J. M. (1982). Self-help approaches to self-management. In K. R. Blankstein & J. Polivy (Eds.) *Self-Control and Self-Modification of Emotional Behavior.* New York: Plenum.

Rothen, W., & Tennyson, R. D. (1978). Application of Bayes' theory in designing computer-based adaptive instructional strategies. *Educational Psychology,* *12*, 317–23.

Rudkin, D. A., & Veal, F. D. Jr. (1973). *Principles of Supervision.* Philadelphia, PA: Auerback.

Schwartz, S. H., & Howard, J. A. (1982). Helping and cooperation: a self-based motivational model. In V. J. Derlega & J. Grzelak (Eds.) *Cooperation and Helping Behavior.* New York: Academic Press.

Shapiro, L. E. (1981). *Games to Grow on: Activities to Help Children Learn Self-Control.* Englewood Cliffs, NJ: Prentice-Hall.

Sharan, S., & Sharan, Y. (1975). *Small-Group Teaching.* Englewood Cliffs, NJ: Educational Technology.

Sharan, S. (1980). Cooperative learning in small groups: Recent methods and effects on achievement, attitudes, and ethnic relations. *Review of Educational Research, 50,* 241–71.

Sharan, S. (1984). *Cooperative Learning in the Classroom: Research in Desegregated Schools.* Hillsdale, NJ: Lawrence Erlbaum.

Shuell, T. J. (1986). Cognitive conceptions of learning. *Review of Educational Research, 56,* 411–36.

Sidman, M. (1960). *Tactics of Scientific Research: Evaluating Experimental Data in Psychology.* New York: Basic Books.

_____. (1986) Functional analysis of emergent verbal classes. In T. Thompson & M. D. Zeiler (Eds.) *Analysis and Integration of Behavioral Units.* Hillsdale, NJ: Lawrence Erlbaum.

Sidman, M., & Cresson, O. (1973). Reading and crossmodal transfer of stimulus equivalences in severe retardation. *American Journal of Mental Deficiency, 77,* 515–23.

Sidman, M., & Kirk, B. (1974). Letter reversals in naming, writing, and matching to sample. *Child Development, 45,* 616–25.

Sidman, M., Kirk, B., & Wilson-Morris, M. (1985). Six-member stimulus classes generated by conditional-discrimination procedures. *Journal of the Experimental Analysis of Behavior, 43,* 21–42.

Sidman, M., Rauzin, R., Lazar, R., Cunningham, S., Tailby, W., & Carrigan, P. (1982). A search for symmetry in the conditional discriminations of rhesus monkeys, baboons, and children. *Journal of the Experimental Analysis of Behavior, 37,* 23–44.

Siegler, R. S. (1983). Five generalizations about cognitive development. *American Psychologist, 38,* 263–77.

Simon, H. (1980). Problem solving in education. In D. T. Tuma & R. Reif (Eds.) *Problem Solving and Education: Issues in Teaching and Research.* Hillsdale, NJ: Lawrence Erlbaum.

Skinner, B. F. (1935). The generic nature of the concepts of stimulus and response. *Journal of General Psychology, 12,* 40–65. (Reprinted in *Cumulative Record: A Selection of Papers,* 3d ed. New York: Appleton-Century-Crofts, 1972).

_____. (1938). *The Behavior of Organisms.* New York: Appleton-Century-Crofts.

_____. (1953). *Science and Human Behavior.* New York: Macmillan.

_____. (1957). *Verbal Behavior.* New York: Appleton-Century-Crofts.

_____. (1966). The phylogeny and ontogeny of behavior. *Science, 153,* 1205–13. (Reprinted in Skinner, 1969.)

_____. (1968). *The Technology of Teaching.* New York: Appleton-Century-Crofts.

_____. (1969). *Contingencies of Reinforcement: A Theoretical Analysis*. New York: Appleton-Century-Crofts.

_____. (1971). *Beyond Freedom and Dignity*. New York: Knopf.

_____. (1974). *About Behaviorism*. New York: Knopf.

_____. (1984). The evolution of behavior. *Journal of the Experimental Analysis of Behavior, 41*, 217–21.

_____. (1985). The evolution of verbal behavior. *Journal of the Experimental Analysis of Behavior, 45*, 115–22.

Skyrms, B. (1986). *Choice and Chance: An Introduction to Inductive Logic*, 3d ed. Belmont, CA: Wadsworth.

Slavin, R. E. (1983). *Cooperative Learning*. New York: Longman.

Sternberg, R. J. (1984). Mechanisms of cognitive development: A componential approach. In R. J. Sternberg (Ed.) *Mechanisms of Cognitive Development*. New York: Freeman, 163–86.

Stokes, T. F., & Baer, D. M. (1977). An implicit technology of generalization. *Journal of Applied Behavior Analysis, 10*, 349–67.

Szlichcinski, K. P. (1979). Diagrams and illustrations as aids to problem solving. *Instructional Science, 8*, 253–74.

Tennyson, R. D. (1975). Adaptive instructional models for concept acquisition. *Educational Psychology, 15*, 7–15.

_____. (1980a). Instructional control strategies and content structure as design variables in concept acquisition using computer-based instruction. *Journal of Educational Psychology, 72*, 525–32.

_____. (1980b). The teaching of concepts: A review of instructional design research. *Review of Educational Research 50*, 55–70.

Tennyson, R. D., & Cocchiarella, M. J. (1986). An empirically based instructional design theory for teaching concepts. *Review of Educational Research, 56*, 40–71.

Tennyson, R. D., Steve, M. W., & Boutwell, R. C. (1975). Instance sequence and analysis of instance attribute representation in concept acquisition. *Journal of Educational Psychology, 67*, 821–27.

Tinker v. Des Moines Independent Community School District, 393 U.S. 503 (1979).

VanGundy, A. B. (1981). *Techniques of Structured Problem Solving*. New York: Van Nostrand Reinhold.

Wang, M. (1979). The development of student self-management skills: implications for effective use of instruction and learning time. *Educational Horizons, 57*, 169–74.

Waskin, Y., & Parrish, L. (1967). *Teacher-Pupil Planning for Better Classroom Learning*. New York: Pitman Publishing.

Weinstein, C. E., & Myer, R. E. (1986). The teaching of learning strategies. In M. C. Wittrock (Ed.) *Handbook of Research on Teaching*, 3rd ed. New York: Macmillan, 315–27.

Weinstein, C. E., & Underwood, V. L. (1985). Learning strategies: The *how* of learning. In J. Segal, S. Chapman, & R. Glaser (Eds.) *Thinking and Learning Skills*, Vol. 1. Hillsdale, NJ: Erlbaum, 241–58.

Wellens, J. (1974). *Training in Physical Skills*. London: Business Books.

Wielkiewicz, R. M. (1986). *Behavior Management in the Schools*. New York: Pergamon Press.

Wilen, W. W. (1986). *Questioning Skills, for Teachers,* 2d ed. Washington, DC: National Educational Association.

Wood v. Strickland, 420 U.S. 308 (1975).

Woodall, M. V. (1979). *Manual for Improving Student Discipline.* Milford, DE: The Longfield Institute.

Workman, E. A. (1982). *Teaching Behavioral Self-Control to Students.* Austin, TX: PRO-ED.

INDEX

accuracy, 84, 131, 153, 171, 222

activities, as classroom procedure, 36, 107; designed to promote helping and sharing, 155; functioning of, 36–37; organization of, 36; regular and special, 35–36

activity procedure, 108; interactive, example of, 109

activity setup, 137

activity SM behaviors, analyzing classroom, 35–40; defined, 23–24; relative to inclusive SM classes, 44–46

adaptation plan, 250; analysis of, 261–62

adaptation, relative to SM, defined, 31–33; planning as a component of, 175

arbitration, 208–10, 218; posting, 209

argument analysis, 193

assumptions, of the SM curriculum, 5

behavior-consequence relationship, 6

behaviors, classroom, 5; referencing instances and classes of, 11–13; stability of, 131; trend of, 131; types of, 17–20; variability of, 131

budget plan, 250, 256

challenges, open and modeled, 65–66

classes of behavior, 12–17; inclusive and exclusive, 14–15; names and definitions of, 13–14; performance dependent, 16; procedurally dependent, 16–17; types of relationships, 14–17

classroom procedures, 107

combination statements, 59

commonality and flexibility, in activity design, 42–44

condition-behavior: match, 5–6; non-match, 6

condition statements, 59

conditions, classroom, 5

conflict, defined, 208; example set, 94; posting, 211

consequences, analysis of, 47–50; classroom, 5; compatibility of, 49; describing as part of statements, 63–64; determining, 50–53; direction of, 49; as element of teaching, 129; evolution of, 49–50; placement of, 50; for posted behaviors, 112; range of, 48; reciprocity of, 49; reinforcing in example sets, 101; relativity of, 47–48; schedule of, 50; in strategy system integration teaching, 226; supplementing, 53–54. See also correction procedures; principles of behavior and technology

context opportunities, 242, 246–47

contingencies, classroom, 5, 9–10, 18;

replanning, 175
retest, as a correction procedure, 116
revision, program, 270–71
reward statements, 59; as a correction
   procedure, 116
rules of interaction, 155

schedule of instruction: defined, 132;
   helping and sharing strategy,
   148–50; intervention strategy, 211;
   learning strategy, 194–95; planning
   strategy, 178; relationship to the
   procedures of teaching, 132–34;
   relationship to sequencing, 240;
   supervising strategy, 160. *See also*
   curriculum sequences and sequencing, analysis of
selection, elements of, 129–30
self-management (SM), defined, 1, 23;
   importance of language to, 3–4, 11;
   reasons for teaching, 2
sequencing: analysis of, 239–42; relationship to schedule of instruction,
   240; self-management (SM) strategies, 244–45. *See also* curriculum
   sequences and schedule of instruction, defined
setting, classroom, 4
settlement (intervention), 209, 215–17
setup, defined, 91
sharing strategy: analysis of, 147–48;
   defined, 30; example set, 93; initial,
   expansion, and refinement teaching
   of, 150–54
SM. *See* self-management
stability of behavior, 131–32
statements: combination, 59, 67–68;
   complete descriptive, 66–68; components of, 60–66; condition, 59,
   66–67; delivery of, 81; evaluating,
   86–87; partial descriptive, 68–69;
   reward, 59, 67; timing of, 82–83,
   85
student management plans, implementation of, 233–34, 251–52

supervising strategy: analysis of,
   157–59; defined, 27; initial, expansion, integration, and refinement
   teaching of, 160–72; posting example, 162
system of strategies, SM: definitions
   of individual strategies: helping, 29;
   intervening, 29; learning, 28; organizing, 26; planning, 25; relative to
   activity SM behaviors, 24; sharing,
   30; supervising, 27

task, task environment, task behavior,
   defined, 23
taxonomy of knowledge (knowledge
   types), 192–93
teacher training plan, 249, 252–55;
   evaluation of, 262–63; outline of,
   254; revision of, 270–71
teaching procedures: elements of,
   129–30; relationship to principles of
   behavior and technology, 6–8; types
   of, 126–29; used in self-management system strategies, chapters
   13–19
teaching, process of, 132–33. *See also*
   teaching procedures
test examples, defined, 89–90
testing, 73, 76–77; corrections, 116; as
   element of teaching, 129; with
   postings, 111; in strategy system
   integration teaching, 226
transfer of behavior, 127
transfer teaching of SM strategies,
   226–33; across behaviors, 228;
   across locations, 227–28; activity
   consequences, 228; equivalences,
   228–29, 230–32; matrix chart in,
   232–34; student management in,
   229–30
trends of behavior, 131–32

variability of behavior, 131–32
variation, elements of, 129–30

ABOUT THE AUTHOR

Over the past two decades Michael B. Medland has taught elementary school and university students and has researched public schools. Presently he resides in Minneapolis where he devotes his time to both writing and consulting.